on the new adviser, Wolsey. The lay members of the Council had been against a war policy managed by a priest from the beginning, and had intrigued to get rid of him. But Henry VIII and the Pope never wavered. The Pope, who had been besieged by a French force in Italy, had grown a beard, a thing never before seen on a Pope, swearing he would not shave until he was revenged on the King of France. He had excommunicated the entire French army, and Henry, not to be outdone, also grew a beard, contrary to the English custom. It was auburn, like his hair. He arranged to hire the Holy Roman Emperor, Maximilian of Austria, with the Imperial artillery and the greater part of the Austrian army, to serve under the Royal Standard of England. The Emperor, we are told, was requested to spread his standard but refused to do so, saying he would be the servant, for the campaign, of the King and St George.

These arrangements, though costly, were in the long run brilliantly successful. The English, with Austrian assistance, routed the French at the Battle of the Spurs, capturing Bayard, the most famous knight in Europe, together with Louis of Orleans, a Duke of the Blood, and a host of French notables. Tournay, the richest city of all North-east France, surrendered at the mere sight of the Imperial artillery, and was occupied by an English garrison. To crown all, Catherine, who had been left behind as Regent of England, sent news that a crushing victory had been inflicted on the Scots at Flodden, James IV, King of Scots, had been slain.

206262

CHURCHILL AS HISTORIAN

MAURICE ASHLEY

CHURCHILL
AS HISTORIAN

SECKER & WARBURG   LONDON

First published in England 1968 by
Martin Secker & Warburg Limited
14 Carlisle Street, London w.1

Copyright © 1968 by Maurice Ashley

SBN 436 02150 1

Printed in Great Britain
by Ebenezer Baylis and Son, Limited
The Trinity Press, Worcester,
and London

Contents

The endpapers show a corrected galley proof from 'A History of the
English-speaking Peoples': the corrections in red are Churchill's own;
the notes in pencil are by G. M. Young.

The quotations from Winston Churchill's historical works on pages 41, 49, 62, 70, 71, and 74 are by permission of the Hamlyn Publishing Group Ltd, London, and that on page 175 by permission of Cassell & Co. Ltd, London.

Foreword

I AM grateful to Dr A. L. Rowse and to Fredric Warburg for suggesting that I should write this book. I wish I could have written it when I was younger, but that would have been impossible. I have to thank F. W. Deakin, Sir Keith Feiling, Alan Hodge, D. H. Pennington and others for sharing with me their recollections of Churchill as a historian. I myself was lucky to work with him when he was both in his prime and at his most fertile during some years in the political wilderness. He was among those from whom I learned what I know of the art of writing history. My book is a commentary and a critique, not a work of research, but I am glad to have the opportunity to pay this tiny tribute to his memory.

April 1968   Maurice Ashley

1

Introduction

IN 1929 I had just taken my final examinations in modern history at Oxford and believed, or at least hoped, that I was due for a first-class degree. Earlier I had won a university essay prize and a university open scholarship, so I was feeling pretty pleased with myself. On the other hand, I badly wanted a job so as to become completely independent of my parents who had made sacrifices to see me through the university; and agreeable jobs for university graduates were not so easily acquired then as they have come to be since. True, I had been virtually promised research grants to open the gateway to a scholastic career, but I needed something more to buy comfort and security and had started shopping around. That June, at the time in a young man's life when summers are always bright and life promises to be eternal—although at twenty-one I was rather perplexed—I received a message from Keith Feiling, then a senior history Fellow (or, precisely, Student) at Christ Church ('the House'), that Winston Churchill was looking for someone to assist him in writing a definitive life of his ancestor, the first Duke of Marlborough, that he would pay £300 a year on a half-time basis, and would I be interested?

I had met Feiling through a school friend of mine, Clere Parsons, who was a Scholar of Christ Church. Already it looked certain that Clere would become a poet of originality and distinction—perhaps a poet of genius such as Stephen Spender and W. H. Auden were to be in that same generation of ours. Clere was to die within two years of a combination of diabetes and influenza in his 'digs' in Oxford, while I happened to be

A*

away for the week-end. We were close friends. (Some of his poems were broadcast by the British Broadcasting Corporation and republished a year or two ago and I was glad to be involved in that belated tribute to his memory.) Feiling, who admired Clere, was such a polite and attractive man, a scintillating writer on English history, though handicapped as a lecturer by a slight stutter. I suppose I ought to have rejoiced at this generous offer from such a man who had met me only at lunch. Not at all. For I was a young radical and socialist, chairman of the undergraduate Labour Club, exponent of 'Red Oxford'. I felt, as do most young men who are highly educated, intellectual, and relatively poor, that I must march forward on the Left. To me Winston Churchill was the politician who, only three years before, had helped to crush the General Strike. My sympathies were entirely with the coal-miners who were earning eight shillings a shift when they were in work and were lucky to obtain four shifts a week: I had seen them and their families making the best of things, singing their humourless songs in their crowded houses in the Rhondda valley. To me Churchill was not merely a Conservative, a turncoat from the milder Liberals, but a reactionary of the deepest dye. I told Feiling that I did not wish to work for Winston Churchill.

But that week-end, contemplating the future in my large and agreeable room in the front quadrangle at New College, I wondered if I had been a fool. After all, a job was a job. Churchill might be a reactionary, but unquestionably he was a famous man who had played many parts and dwelt in a world to which I as a middle-class boy not from Eton or Harrow or Winchester (how those Wykehamists at New College used to snub me) did not have access. I hastily wrote an apologetic note to Feiling to say that if the post were still open, I should like to be considered for it. I received a courteous reply saying that Churchill himself was coming to Oxford during the next week and would I come to lunch to meet him in Professor Lindemann's rooms in Christ Church?

I recall some of that meeting as if it were but yesterday.

Lindemann's rooms were in the Meadow Buildings facing out
upon Christ Church meadow which leads down to the river Isis
where the college barges, now nothing but historic relics, were
moored, where one walked with one's friends and talked im-
provingly if naïvely about the future of mankind. In a biggish
room where a table was laid my seniors awaited me. Lindemann
(later Lord Cherwell, head of Churchill's personal statistical
staff during the war) was a strange man, with scrupulous manners,
utterly charming when he wished to be, yet by nature withdrawn,
and lit, above all, by an overwhelming ambition to be welcomed
everywhere at the highest levels of English society. Born in
Germany, with a German father who was naturalized, which
embarrassed him somewhat, he was not, as was often alleged, a
Jew. No task was too menial, no service too petty for him to
perform in order to gratify the wishes of the titled or important
in his adopted country. Since he was in fact a rich man, he could
afford to feed his ambition. He was not much loved in Oxford
university where it was thought at first that they had acquired a
young Rutherford and where they did not admire, or maybe
envied, his devotion to his extra-mural activities. His indulgences
were an expensive motor-car and chauffeur (not then, before the
television days, the usual perquisites of Oxford dons) but he
neither ate meat nor drank alcohol, nor smoked nor married. He
once told the mother of a colleague at Christ Church that 'he
did not like putting animal matter into his body, since there
might be little creatures that would in turn attack him.' He lived
on whites of egg, stewed apple, rice croquettes, and Port Salut
cheese, which was a little tiresome to the society hostesses whose
houses he frequented. But though austere himself, he was a
generous and considerate host. Soon after I arrived he asked
Churchill if he would like champagne with his meal. That
impressed me. But Churchill said that he always drank beer for
his lunch. (Beef and beer, once the British breakfast, were long
his staples in the middle of the day.)

There were just the four of us at lunch: Lindemann, Churchill,
Feiling, and myself. Before we started eating, the Great Man sat

[3]

down beside me on a sofa and putting his hand on my shoulder said: 'I hear you are going to work for me?' There was no interview, no examination. I suspected that Feiling had told him about the nature of my political views, and I believe Churchill thought it was not improper for young Oxford intellectuals to be socialists. I mumbled something, overwhelmed by the magnetism of his personality, and then settled down to listen to my elders and betters talking. It was arranged that Churchill would introduce me to his cousin, the ninth Duke of Marlborough, and that I should afterwards regularly drive over to Blenheim Palace (nine miles from Oxford) to work on the archives and should from time to time report to Churchill and help him with the reading and preparations for his biography. He estimated that it would take him two years to complete a two-volume book, which suited me finely. In fact I worked for him for four years and the book in four volumes was not finished for nine years. This gave me the opportunity to see Churchill at work as a historian at a time when my heart was young, my mind malleable, and my memory good.

The introductions at Blenheim Palace duly took place. The ninth Duke of Marlborough struck me then as an inspissated little man. I have since read that, much to his credit, this Duke (always called 'Sunny' by Churchill and his intimates, not because he had a sunny disposition but because of his other family title, that of Sunderland) devoted much of his life to intelligently and self-sacrificingly restoring the glories of his ancestral home which had been stripped of many of its treasures because of the extravagances of his predecessors, notably the fifth, sixth, and eighth Dukes. The eighth Duke, for instance, made an almost complete sweep of the paintings and porcelain, having an enormous clearance sale of Rembrandts and Rubenses, Van Dycks and Dobsons, which are now scattered all over the civilized world. The seventh Duke, himself a solid Victorian churchman, had set the example by disposing of the Sunderland library, a collection of rare books which had adorned the famous Long Gallery. The ninth Duke had purchased a new library and the books were kept carefully under lock and key in their cases lest they should be stolen by his servants. The Duke had a complex—possibly based on some realities—that everyone was out to rob him and he certainly did not much care for the lower classes. This was the eve of the Great Depression. I remember standing with Churchill and the Duke in one of the courtyards where they were discussing the rising unemployment figures. The Duke said disagreeably that he hoped they would reach two million. Churchill saw me visibly blench and hastened to assure me soothingly afterwards, when the Duke had gone, that his cousin had not really meant what he said.

It was arranged that I should work in the muniment room on the Marlborough correspondence. Winston had informed me I could work there all day if I wanted to and that lunch would be provided for me. However, I was soon given to understand that I must carry out my researches under the supervision of one of the estate clerks so that it was quite certain that I did not steal any of the manuscripts, which were of course of considerable value. I fancy that the Duke suspected a previous visitor—Hilaire Belloc, I believe it was—of helping himself to one of the first Duke's letters. At any rate he insisted that a close eye should be kept upon my activities. In fact the clerk knocked off for his own lunch and locked up the muniment room at one o'clock and, as no food was offered to me in the Palace, for a time I went and bought myself a lonely meal at the Bear hotel in Woodstock village. But I soon tired of solitary beef and rice pudding and preferred to drive back to Oxford and not return.

The ninth Duke had promised Winston Churchill that he should be the first historian to have the complete run of the archives in order to write the biography of his ancestor. Even George Trevelyan, who had already embarked on his three-volume book on the reign of Queen Anne, was refused permission to examine this material. One or two historians previously had full access to the archives, including Archdeacon William Coxe, a notable historian who wrote in the second decade of the nineteenth century, and Dr Stuart Reid, who had put the manuscripts

[5]

in order and produced a catalogue of them for the ninth Duke before the 1914–1918 war. So it was not entirely virgin territory. With a copy of Coxe's *Memoirs* of the first Duke by my side I laboured for two or three years in the stuffy muniment room, solemnly copying out letters in my own hand. I suppose that photostating was not invented then or that I did not know about it or maybe was told the Duke would not have liked it. I shall discuss in the course of this book how Churchill made use of the material collected.

It was to me a very strange world. Each morning I drove my second-hand Morris Cowley slowly up the long drive to the Palace. Somewhere along the drive there was a concealed hump so that if any unsuspecting motorist exceeded the speed limit that the Duke had laid down he got the springs of his car rattled. Once I was invited to stay at the Palace for a week-end when Churchill was a guest. After dinner the guests wandered out on to the lawns and I was overwhelmed by the beauty of the terraces and trees beneath a summer moon. But Vanbrugh's buildings and Capability Brown's gardens were constructed for a more exclusive and more spacious age; they say they are a little tattered now. They are open to trippers and hired out to television companies. But in the nineteen-thirties the aristocracy was still putting up a sturdy fight against the advancing waves of taxation. One could not help but admire the battle fought by the ninth Duke on behalf of his heritage amid the onslaughts of socialist democracy. Churchill himself loved it all. After all, he had been born in this very house and his father had represented the defunct constituency of Woodstock. In his historical writing Winston paid tribute to the glories of 'an Italian palace in an English park' with its 'green lawns and shining water, banks of laurel and fern, groves of oak and cedar, fountains and islands . . . conjoined in artful disarray to offer on every side a promise of rest and shade'. But he knew far too much about life to imagine it represented anything other than a disappearing world, an aristocratic oasis, an eighteenth-century relic, grand but no longer real.

The ninth Duke had by then been divorced from his first wife, the wealthy and much loved and admired Consuelo Vanderbilt. His second wife, also an American, was not without taste. She persuaded her husband to have his bust sculpted by Epstein who was at the height of his fame and fashion. The bust then stood in the entrance hall at Blenheim; the Duke disliked it intensely, just as Winston Churchill was to dislike the portrait of himself by Graham Sutherland. Because of his divorce the Church of England—so I was told—had refused the Duke Communion and he had subsequently and consequently joined the Roman Catholic Church. It was odd that the descendant of John Churchill, the first Duke, should have become a convert since his celebrated ancestor had been prepared to show the 'resolution of a martyr' rather than be untrue to his Anglican religion. I once had a tête-à-tête with Sunny's second Duchess at a small table in the centre of the Long Gallery. All I can remember now is being over-awed both by her and by the statue of Queen Anne and swallowing the smallest sandwiches I have ever seen.

So it was that for four years, on and off, I worked for Winston Churchill and watched him pretty closely in operation both as a writer and a family man at his home of Chartwell. He was then in Opposition and even broke with his own party over India. Robert Rhodes James is writing about him in those years and I don't suppose there can be much new left to say about his character and habits after all that has been put out by his son and daughter, his former secretaries, doctors, generals, and detectives. But of course I have often been asked what it was like to work for him in those far-off days of the Great Depression.

To me Winston Churchill was always the soul of consideration, courtesy, and charm. He expected one to work hard but not a quarter as hard as he worked himself. I retain several distinct impressions of Churchill from those days of my youth.* In the first place, he was a man of splendid humour with a capacity for living every hour of the day. I am aware that some people who

* I have adapted one or two passages from an article I wrote for *The Listener* immediately after his death.

[7]

knew him much better than I did have asserted that he possessed wit but not humour. But if humour consists of the ability to see a joke against oneself—even if belatedly—then certainly he possessed it. He was as generous as he was brave. I recall one summer's afternoon at Chartwell when we were sitting in the garden and he was talking with his usual animation about history: after a while he started to look pale and distraught. A doctor was called for and it turned out that for some time he had been bleeding internally, the aftermath of a street accident in New York. As he left Chartwell on a stretcher, he perceived my anxiety and said: 'Don't worry, Ashley, I'm not going to die.'

He was always expansive, at any rate among those he liked or trusted. He delighted to develop his thoughts and ideas in private before a small audience. He did not conceal his tastes or opinions and did not expect others to betray his confidences. He was very angry, we are told, when Frank Owen, once the editor of the *Evening Standard,* wrote for Beaverbrook's benefit an elaborate account of a private conversation at Chartwell. I remember a similar instance. One day Tom Clarke, then the editor of the *News Chronicle,* which was going to serialize his book, *My Early Life,* came to lunch at Chartwell, bringing his son uninvited. After lunch the four of us talked—Tom Clarke egging on Churchill. Next morning Churchill was furious to read an account of this 'interview' splashed across the front page of the newspaper. The incident made a permanent impression on me. I decided, and kept to the decision, never to write anything about him until he was dead.

Secondly, Churchill had an enormous respect for intellect and for expert professionalism at all levels. He often expressed regret that he had not been to a university. It has since been revealed that he seriously considered doing so after he left the army, but was abashed by the need to do Latin prose again. He was sorry that his son appeared to be wasting his time at Oxford. I do not agree with what Roy Harrod has written about Churchill and Oxford. I honestly believe that he felt when he visited there that he was moving in a superior kind of world.

[8]

I am not sure that I should have cared to be Winston Churchill's chauffeur, valet, or even secretary (though his secretaries, often kept going till very late at night, usually adored him) but he treated me with the utmost kindness—almost as an equal—never criticizing me for mistakes or omissions of which I was perfectly capable. On one occasion he was so excited by the queries of a printer's reader on his proofs that he asked the publishers to send the man down to Chartwell to meet him. (The publishers skilfully evaded this request.) During the war young officers in Operations or Intelligence at the War Office, where I served, were sometimes surprised to hear that the Prime Minister was on the line to them in the middle of the night. On the other hand, I noticed that when the worthies from his constituency came to see him at Chartwell he was quickly bored and pushed off as soon as he decently could, leaving them to Mrs Churchill. He did not suffer fools gladly.

What a contrast it was between the Palace of Blenheim and Chartwell Manor; the first was a show-place, the second a home. At Chartwell a welcome was written on the mat. It is a matter of sadness to me that this house, which has no architectural distinction, is no longer a home but a crowded museum. Thirty-five years ago it was all very comfortable there: sherry in the morning, whisky for tea, champagne for dinner. In those days Churchill, in spite of his American connections, disapproved of those new-fangled cocktails. He also disliked the smell of Virginian cigarettes and pipe-smoking. Little unappetizing boxes of Turkish cigarettes lay about the place and one could always help oneself to cigars (not that one did without being invited). 'Never relight a cigar,' he used to say, but I felt guilty when I let a large Corona Corona go out. Occasionally distinguished visitors came to Chartwell and Churchill had silently to suffer them smoking their pipes. I recall on one occasion sitting alone at breakfast when a rather brash and seemingly young man in Air Force uniform entered the room and asked, 'Where's Winston?' It turned out to be T. E. Lawrence. But even for less important figures Chartwell was Liberty Hall.

When I was at Chartwell we would invariably do an hour's work before lunch, an hour or two after tea. Dinner was for me the supreme occasion of the day when Churchill would usually seat me by his side and any other guest next to him and after the ladies had departed and the port and brandy were circulating would expand on any subject that took his fancy. He was the wittiest man I have ever met and had an extraordinary gift for irony, which can be discovered in his writings. He had a prodigious memory. His main interest lay in politics or history; he rarely talked about the arts and did not waste his time listening to the wireless, but he would quote with relish vast chunks of poetry he had memorized in his younger days. His conversation was never dull or boring and was never in the least egotistical. It is true that I was once present at the table when one of Franklin D. Roosevelt's sons was a guest and that Churchill insisted on expounding the functioning of the United States constitution for his benefit; but that was not showmanship; he was just absorbed in the subject.

After dinner Churchill would usually play a game of back-gammon with his wife. Then about eleven p.m. the day's work would really begin. He liked particularly to try out ideas or arguments to see if he could make them work. At about two Churchill would express well-feigned surprise at the time and his secretary would be sent home in a hired car. An hour or so later he would reluctantly allow me to go to bed. Then he himself retired to do some serious reading, going to sleep around four. Next morning he would be reading his newspapers and correspondence in bed about eight. Like Napoleon, he was able to manage with four hours' sleep. He rarely appeared to be in a hurry. When he signed a contract he always delivered the goods on time, though he sometimes left his newspaper articles until the very last moment. Much of the day he spent out of doors, building wall after wall, occasionally painting, feeding the swans on his lake, walking round and round his estate, ceaselessly talking.

So I see him across the years exuberant, witty, generous both in his private life and his outlook on public affairs. In a later chapter I shall discuss his method of writing history, based not merely on my own recollections but also on conversations with others who worked for him. I shall examine in an impartial spirit his attitude to history and his contribution to knowledge. Henceforward I shall not intrude myself too much. Perhaps I have overdone it already. But no recollections of a great man can be entirely without value.

2

Churchill's interest in history

HISTORY,' it used to be said, not without some justification, 'is past politics.' It is no longer fashionable to accept that point of view. But unquestionably one of Winston Churchill's first loves was politics, and it was politics that attracted him to the study of history. When he was over eighty Lord Moran found him one day reading Moneypenny and Buckle's *Life of Disraeli* and said to him: 'It must be heavy-going old politics?' 'I like old politics,' answered Winston.

Most of Churchill's ancestors had been politicians of one kind or another. The first Duke of Marlborough, though, like Winston himself, beginning his career as a professional soldier, engaged in elaborate political intrigues during the reigns of King James II and King William III and became a leading member of the Cabinet in the reign of Queen Anne. Marlborough's father, Sir Winston Churchill the first, had been an active Member of Parliament in the reign of King Charles II—as well as the first historian in the family. Churchill's grandfather, the seventh Duke, had been a friend of Benjamin Disraeli, a member of his Cabinet, and first Lord President of the Council and then later Lord Lieutenant of Ireland. Winston's father, Lord Randolph Churchill, was Chancellor of the Exchequer in Lord Salisbury's Government and a leading member of the Cabinet until he suddenly resigned; before that he had made his name as an exceptionally effective spokesman of the Opposition when Gladstone's last Ministry was in power. Thus Winston Churchill had been born into the ruling class and politics tingled in his blood. Political history was to him an absorbing interest if only because it was in part the story of his own family.

For in Churchill family loyalty was deeply engrained: he was always a family man par excellence. It has been pointed out that in his novel *Savrola* the hero is based on his father, the heroine on his mother, while the whole tale is one of political events in a Ruritanian setting which nevertheless could still be England. To him the writing of history was to be first and foremost an act of piety towards his ancestors, towards his parents, even towards himself. Churchill took after his father in many ways and loved his mother devotedly: he kept her photograph by him until the very end of his life. It was said that his father was 'always at his best in a small and congenial company'; so was Winston. Lord Randolph did not suffer fools gladly; neither did Winston. Randolph was not a highly educated man in the accepted sense of the term: he slacked his way through Eton and when he was an undergraduate at Oxford spent much of his time hunting around Woodstock. Winston too did not take the fullest advantage of the education with which he was provided, being both obstinate and individualist, though the idea that he was a dunce at school has been grossly exaggerated, chiefly by himself. Lord Randolph had a superb gift for telling phrases—'an old man in a hurry,' 'those damned dots,' 'Ulster will fight and Ulster will be right': Randolph's bon mots, like Winston's, reverberated through London society. Even in small things there were similarities between father and son. If Randolph smoked 'the eternal cigarette,' Winston had his eternal cigar.

Churchill's first full-scale historical book was his life of his father. What many consider to be his next best book, his *Life and Times of Marlborough,* was also a long-meditated tribute to an ancestor; while others of his historical books, such as *The River War, The World Crisis,* and *The Second World War,* were written round his own personal experiences. Thus to him the writing of history was essentially a personal and a family affair. His loyalty to his family and its habits was intense. For example, James Bain in Charing Cross was the family book-shop. He ordered his books from there when he was at Sandhurst and continued to do so until the outbreak of the second world war.

I do not mean by this to suggest that the fascination of politics and the historical background of his family were the only sources of his interest in history, but they were compelling ones. He was also of course absorbed all his life in the history of war. One day his father saw him playing with toy soldiers and decided—a trifle hastily it appears—that he had best go into the army; once Churchill was at Sandhurst he had to study military history and it was natural that he should respond to it. For the fact is that military history is a challenging intellectual pursuit. Some of the finest British historians in the nineteenth and twentieth centuries have found it to be a rewarding exercise: in the earlier period one may recall the names of Sir Charles Firth and Sir Charles Oman; in our own times scholars like Michael Roberts and Michael Howard. Few serious students today are contemptuous of the study of military history, even if modern history in general was once widely thought—by those who disliked it—to consist of boring accounts of battles and peace treaties.

The history of politics and of war, then, offers a worthy claim upon an active and inquiring mind. Churchill from his earliest youth and right into his seventies always had the insistent urge to find out. As Baroness Asquith wrote in the first chapter of her book, *Winston Churchill as I Knew Him*:

> To Winston Churchill everything under the sun was new— seen and appraised as on the first day of creation. His approach to life was full of ardour and surprise. Even the eternal verities appeared to him to be an exciting personal discovery. (He often seemed annoyed to find that some of them had occurred to other people long ago.)

I think this was the fundamental reason why he always regretted that he had not been to a university. It was not that he wished that he had acquired the academic discipline of mind or the power of logic that is necessary to the philosopher or exact scholar. But he believed that he would have found out about a host of things that he had in fact to teach himself from books and from searching conversations with other men. And his respect for scholars and scientists was always profound because he honestly believed that they possessed the secrets of subjects that he wanted to know more about. What he did not always recognize, I fancy, was the inhibiting character of the purely academic approach which is generally a disadvantage in a politician.

In a brief couple of paragraphs in his book *Winston Churchill, the Struggle for Survival* in which he discussed Churchill as a historian, Lord Moran wrote: 'One wonders whether, if the personal slant had been wanting, Winston would have troubled to write history.' It was of course an important factor, but even more important, I am sure, was the itch to find out, a genuine desire to explore the causes and the nature of political events and to describe how things happened. Churchill might at times have accepted the cynical epigram: 'He who can, does; he who can't, writes.' He once said, for example, 'after all, a man's life must be nailed to the cross of thought or action.' In his youth he was intensely ambitious and perceived that one way in which he might make his name was through writing. He took immense pains to master the art and thus his first books at once rose above the level of skilful or slick journalism. Rapidly discovering that the writing of books, once he had established his name with the reading public, was quite profitable, more especially if he could sell the serialization rights to newspapers or magazines, he did so to earn a living and support a family. Politics was not a paying profession then and he had no wish to stay in the army. In fact he very largely earned his income by writing until 1919 when he received an inheritance. Before the war of 1939–1945 this source of income enabled him to live in modest luxury when he was out of office; but he did not make a fortune out of his books until after he became Prime Minister and a world figure.

I hope I am not being unduly cynical if I say that the writing of historical books—if one has come sort of a gift for presenting material in a lively manner—is a facile means of earning money.

[15]

Anybody who has sufficient application can become a journalist or a historian of a sort: it is not necessary to have enjoyed a university education. Moreover few of the people whom one meets in life are unwilling to impart instructions on these arts: they are much less prepared to offer advice when it comes to the sciences. Though Churchill had an extremely powerful and daring imagination, it did not lend itself either to fiction or to play-writing. While he was gratified by the financial results yielded by his unique novel, it was clear to him that it had grave weaknesses of style and structure; therefore during his early life historical writing was to a large extent a means to an end, that of earning a living and keeping his name before the public. In his autobiography of those days he admits frankly that the reason why he left the army was that he thought that, living at home, he could do as well by writing as by remaining a serving soldier, kicking his heels in barracks. In 1897 he quoted Dr Johnson: 'No man but a blockhead ever wrote a book except for money.'

Much of his writing both then and later was sheer journalism. He did, however, draw a sharp distinction between journalism and history or at least between newspaper articles and books. Nothing, he said, was as dead as yesterday's newspaper. On the other hand, most of his journalism—such as the articles that he wrote for *Strand* magazine—was of a historical character. After all, most journalists are historians *manqués*—and not all that *manqués* either. He enjoyed mulling over political or military events that interested him, even if he had not taken part in them. For not only was he concerned to find out precisely how politics worked in the past but also how wars were won and lost. Yet he did not on paper draw lessons from history, but rather the contrary; he used his own knowledge of modern politics and warfare to illumine what had happened in the past.

Another thing that attracted him to history was the light it threw on the characters of great, successful, or important men. In so far as he hoped one day to become a great man himself, he was eager to find out all he could about them. Lord Moran has said, a little unkindly, that he had 'a decided preference for a certain type of character, the pattern of men he found congenial in his own life—Max Beaverbrook, F. E. Smith, Lloyd George—on the whole an immoral lot in their outlook.' It may be that this was so, though he himself was not immoral or even amoral. But what happened, I think, was that he came to recognize as he went through life that most men of distinction have their individual quirks, tricks of character or behaviour that set them apart from other men. He would not have pretended to be an amateur psychologist, but these odd characteristics were a source of perpetual entertainment or amusement to him: the Emperor Francis Joseph of Austria who used to get up at four in the morning, walk out of his palace and take breakfast with his respectable mistress, Frau Schratt, have his evening meal between three and four in the afternoon, and then retire early to bed; the 'inveterate drunkenness' of Robert Harley, Earl of Oxford, in the reign of Queen Anne, who was never too sodden to outwit his political opponents; Arthur Balfour, with his contrasts between the speculations of a philosopher and the habits of a statesman; Joseph Chamberlain, so charming towards his friends, so bitter towards his enemies; the aggressive Ludendorff, who yet lacked the full military understanding of an Alexander or a Hannibal. For years Churchill was fascinated by Napoleon I and had an impressive collection of magnificently-bound books about him. He contemplated undertaking Napoleon's biography: that indeed must be reckoned one of the great unwritten books of our time.

It used commonly to be asserted that Churchill's interest in history was not first aroused until he was a subaltern in India and devoured the works of Gibbon, Macaulay, and Lecky. But the facts revealed by his official biography show that he enjoyed history ever since he was a schoolboy. At his first school, St George's, he was bullied and unhappy, but even there his reports said that he was 'fair' at history and geography, though slow and poor at other subjects. After he was taken away from St George's and put under the care of two elderly ladies in Hove, he found that he 'was allowed to learn things which interested him,' among which he included history. At Harrow his house-master wrote in one of his very earliest reports that he was extremely pleased with 'some history work' that Winston had done for him. In the following term (when Churchill was four-teen) he received a prize for history and two years later he did pretty well in an examination when he had the chance of choosing the American civil war as an essay subject. Though he failed twice in the entrance exam to Sandhurst before he was finally admitted, each time he secured excellent marks in his English history paper: the first time he came eighteenth out of 415 candidates with 987 marks out of 2,000; the second time he received 1,273 marks out of 2,000; and the third time 1,278 out of 2,000: that was in fact the highest mark received by any successful candidate who took the subject. Apparently one of the masters at Sandhurst increased his interest in history, a fact that he recalled with gratitude in his later years.

Did Churchill have a philosophy of history? He certainly did not possess a philosophic habit of mind. After all, he was a politician. He was quite capable of arguing a case one way at one time and then later taking the diametrically opposite side, if only for the fun of it. He was fully proficient in making the worse appear the better cause, of acting as a prosecuting counsel, a defending attorney, as well as occasionally a judge. I remember clearly across the long span of years his once saying to me: 'Give me the facts, Ashley, and I will twist them the way I want to suit my argument.' I was a little shocked at the time, but he did not often do this. Nevertheless in much of his historical writing he was engaged in presenting a case, argued with persuasiveness and incomparable oratory. Yet I would be prepared to say that he did have a philosophy of history of a kind. The notion that there was a materialist or economic interpretation of history or a determinist history of any sort was anathema to him; he was convinced that man was the master of his fate and that great men had their roles to play and their duties to fulfil. He did not believe in an after-life—that is plain not only from his novel but also from the letters he wrote when a young man—but he thought that men were on earth to serve a purpose. Thus they could be judged.

As he grew old he became increasingly convinced of the value and significance of the judgments of history. This fact has been noted by all those who have studied his speeches, especially his speeches during the second German war. He followed Lord Acton in thinking that there was a standard of right and wrong by which the actions of individuals can be measured. Thus if Hitler was a tyrant, then Oliver Cromwell was also a tyrant, and therefore both of them—however patriotic they might have been—were 'wicked men' whom history condemned. Again, Churchill believed in the sanctity of family life. Thus historical figures were expected to be true to their wives. They might sow their wild oats if they wished, but after that they were required to be respectable. The first Duke of Marlborough was entitled to accept the 'favours' of Barbara, Countess of Castlemaine, when he was a young unmarried officer—even allowed to be the 'rival' of his King. (Although Churchill himself was intensely loyal to the monarchy, he had reason to recall his father's brush with the future Edward VII.) Afterwards, however, Marlborough's life is pictured as a prolonged love story. Married women were occasionally permitted to look elsewhere, as Barbara Castlemaine did—rather frequently—and the high-minded Lucile in Churchill's novel *Savrola,* but men were different: for them love was a thing apart, though it was woman's whole existence. Hence Bernard Shaw was roundly castigated for preaching free love, even if he were praised for living in a state of connubial rectitude.

Winston Churchill would therefore, on the whole, have accepted Lord Acton's view that we must have moral standards and liberal principles and should not condone conduct in one age that we would condemn in another. He would have rejected the opinion of Professor Herbert Butterfield and others of his school that the historian has no right to make any moral judgments at all but should leave them to the Almighty who knows all the circumstances and can search the hearts of men. Churchill believed passionately that in the end the truth about events would emerge with the accumulation and analysis of evidence not available to contemporaries. Thus while he would put the case for a course of action as strongly as he possibly could, he seldom thought that a final verdict could be reached which might not have to be modified in the light of later knowledge. I once told him how much I had enjoyed reading his life of his father. 'Ah!' he said, 'if I had known then what I know now I should have written it very differently.' So in all the events in which he himself took part he was conscious that history was watching him and would one day judge him. She was an arbiter as well as a Muse.

In his book on *Churchill and Beaverbrook* Kenneth Young describes how in 1928 Beaverbrook sent proofs of his *Politicians and the War* for Churchill to read. In acknowledging them, Churchill wrote to Beaverbrook:

> Candour and faithful keeping of confidences are not easy to combine. But you have succeeded. And in addition you have produced a vital—the limited—too limited—contribution to the slowly emerging truth. 'What happened & Why!' After all that is history or what history ought to be.
>
> But what a tale! Think of all these people—decent, educated, the story of the past laid out before them—What to avoid—what to do etc patriotic, loyal and clean—trying their utmost—What a ghastly muddle they made of it!
>
> *Unteachable from infancy to tomb*—There is the first & main characteristic of mankind.

If we may judge firmly from that (though I incline to think it represented merely the sentiment of the moment) Churchill did not believe that mankind learned anything from history. But he himself learned a good deal from it. His biographers will say surely that much of his conduct as Prime Minister and Minister of Defence in the war of 1939–1945 was powerfully influenced by what he had learned not only in taking part in the previous world war but also in writing about it.

From his study of history he could discern some sort of pattern in politics and in the waging of war, which is the continuation of politics by other and more violent means. History is, if you like, a two-way affair: it has its own innate dualism. We can understand what happened in the past because our own experience of living enables us to interpret and clarify the historical facts that we collect. Both I myself and F. W. Deakin, who at different times worked as his historical assistants, were impressed by the sure manner in which he was able to throw light on historical occurrences because he knew—few men better—how politicians behave and the kind of pressures to which they are always subjected. We thought we knew all about it because we had assiduously amassed and sorted out the known facts. But we didn't and couldn't. At the same time I am sure that he would have admitted that history can teach lessons, if we are capable of being taught. The trouble was (as he told Beaverbrook) that we are not capable. But he himself, as I have said, perceived a pattern to politics throughout the ages. And history was indeed to Churchill largely past politics.

———

Since this book went to press, I came across the following sentences in a letter written by Churchill to his uncle by marriage, Moreton Frewen, on August 31, 1896:

> The only great prose writer I have so far read is Gibbon who cannot certainly be accused of crispness. It has appeared to me so far as I have gone that composition is essentially an artificial science. To make a short sentence or succession of short sentences tell—they should be sandwiched in between lengthy and sonorous periods. The contrast is effective.

—Allen Andrews, *The Splendid Pauper* (1968), p. 191, quoted by permission of George G. Harrap and Co. Ltd.

3

Churchill's method of writing history

CHURCHILL'S method of writing history, if not unique, was unusual to an extreme. It evolved gradually and the way in which he wrote his last historical book was very different from that in which he wrote his first ones. *The River War* and his life of his father were written in his own hand and he himself collected and sifted the material for them. When it came to his last book, *A History of the English-speaking Peoples*, he hired a whole team of qualified historians to help him, some of whom he never even met; and he employed a kind of editorial staff which checked and re-checked his facts and his fancies.

Yet in the early books one may detect the general pattern of the method. First he decides his subject and his broad theme. He envisages the grandeur of the story, the qualities and weaknesses of the men whom he characterizes; he sets the scene; he develops his account chapter by chapter—each chapter being of a more or less equal length; he embodies the documentation at appropriate points in the narrative; he reaches valid conclusions, marshalling the arguments on both sides. But he does not attempt to draw an elaborate moral because he profoundly believes that history speaks for itself.

Like other historians, Churchill does not necessarily make up his mind how he will treat any particular episode until he comes to it, but he ensures that it fits into the broad framework of his narrative or the general purport of his argument. The collection

[22]

of the material goes on simultaneously with the actual writing. The text therefore may have to be modified or even radically altered afterwards. I shall show, for instance, how in writing *The River War* he was reluctant to sacrifice what he had written about General Gordon, even when Lord Cromer had later persuaded him that Gordon's character was less heroic than Churchill had at first imagined it. Nor did he find the time to revise his books in great detail, though naturally he liked to correct errors of fact.

Churchill always preferred to get something down on paper and to fill in gaps later. I always remember my astonishment to find myself listening to him dictating an introductory chapter about Marlborough before, as far as I could make out, he knew anything at all about him beyond the skeleton of his career as it was familiar to every schoolboy. (In fact the chapter never saw the light.) Brought up, as I had been, in the most rigorous atmosphere of Oxford historical research—in the world of venerable scholars like Sir Charles Firth and Reginald Lane Poole—I found it difficult to envisage how anyone could start writing an important work of history without previously mastering all possible sources, comparing them and sorting out the wheat from the chaff. But of course, I was not being altogether fair, as I now can see. For Churchill had an incredible memory and once he had read a book or committed to mind a quotation or absorbed an historical episode he stored it up for future use and rarely got it wrong. He knew Macaulay almost by heart and during the years he spent in Blenheim Palace he had imbibed and absorbed a mass of facts and opinions about his ancestor. Moreover he possessed an imagination and a grasp of the essential qualities of a historical story far more powerful and penetrating than those of most dons. Thus he was capable of illuminating the bare facts as he dictated them; and in any case his first drafts were usually largely scrapped.

Moreover he took the view that history could be made exciting —and war and politics, in particular, could be made attractive— if the writer constantly bore in mind that events must be placed in a realistic setting and be so clarified that even the most ignorant reader could understand them (though his readers were expected to be familiar with the bare facts about politics and war). Thus—and I think this can be established from a meticulous examination of his work—he tended to begin his chapters with generalizations about the position or backgrounds of events before launching upon a detailed narrative.

The early books were entertaining because they were written by a keen young professional officer who was examining the whole problem of the war or the campaign which he was describing in the light of the resources available to the commander and the overriding necessities and atmosphere of the moment. In the later books Churchill never forgot to consider the general strategy, whether it was of war or of politics, as it related to any one chain of events: to concentrate exclusively on manuscript sources is a trap into which purely academic historians, and especially young authors of Ph.D. theses, are liable to tumble. I remember an American professor once telling me with simple pleasure that he had unearthed an unusual and sensational fact about the early life of John Churchill, first Duke of Marlborough. He did not perceive at the time that it was the wrong John Churchill disclosed by his manuscript reference or that he ought to have guessed this.

Churchill therefore loved to get something down on paper and to fill in gaps afterwards. He would walk up and down the room (when I worked for him it was usually his bedroom) puffing at a cigar while a secretary patiently took it all down as best she could in Pitman. Occasionally he would pause to say 'scrub that and start again.' At times he would stop while he contemplated the next point he wanted to make; at others he would be entirely swept on by the stimulus of his imagination; he had perceived how like what had happened was to something else he had read about or even experienced himself. The problems of Marlborough might be similar to those of Napoleon or Marshal Foch. The struggles inside Queen Anne's Cabinets would remind him of what had happened under Lloyd George or Stanley Baldwin.

[24]

The invasion of William the Conqueror conjured up memories of the battle of Normandy.

Dictation certainly offers a rapid means of compiling books. Edgar Wallace, once the most famous of British thriller writers, was capable, it may be remembered, of dictating a whole novel in one week-end. Churchill enjoyed counting the number of words that he had produced in any given space of time. In the early hours of the morning, after an exhausting session which he had begun not long before midnight, he would observe with deep satisfaction: 'Well, we must have done three thousand words.' 'We'—that is to say the tired secretary and anyone else who had been watching the performance and trying to avoid falling asleep—might not have experienced the same sense of pleasurable achievement. Furthermore one knew that those three thousand words might be torn to shreds or even destroyed the next day; should that not happen, they would have to be re-examined in detail, all the statements carefully verified, and the argument analysed in the light of facts not known to the master.

Churchill's early books were circulated in the form of draft chapters for the advice and criticism of his friends and knowledgeable acquaintances. His first book was passed for press by an uncle; his second was edited for him by a fellow soldier and journalist. Once the story had been written or 'got off his chest' then he relied on others to do the checking and tidying up. He learned at an early stage how necessary that was and how important it was to find experts to assist him at every stage of the writing and book production. This was, of course, not unusual. The busy and successful man who elects to write a book—notably a book of memoirs—always employs assistants; though not ghosts, for unless he is in desperate need of money there is little joy in projecting a book and then hiring others to put it together. Thus at every stage in his historical writing Churchill did the bulk of the work himself; it was his own mind, his own method of presenting the facts, his own rhetorical prose style that shaped all his books. Nothing irritated those who worked for him more than to be introduced as one who wrote Churchill's books for him. In fact, he used people to do his research for him, much in the same way as an established professor does. The only difference was that whereas Churchill paid his helpers generously, professors have occasionally been known to induce research students or scholars to aid them for nothing other than the promise of future patronage.

The duties of Churchill's research assistants were threefold: in the first place, they were required to feed him with material. This meant not only the collection and marshalling of historical documents but the provision of all the books that he needed in order to write a given chapter. If possible, the books were bought for him and added to his library; otherwise they had to be borrowed. And not only were the books he needed selected for him and put at his disposal but the actual pages he was required to read were marked. (Keith Feiling was shocked once when Churchill told him to cut out of a book the pages that Feiling thought he ought to read.) The research assistant was thus expected to have the whole bibliography of any given subject at his finger tips and to know where to find the answers to any awkward questions he might be asked. When exactly Churchill found the time to read all the material that was collected for him I am not completely sure; some of it was certainly absorbed during the small hours of the night when lesser men were fast asleep. But once a marked passage or a transcribed letter had been read, it took its place in the capacious pockets of his memory. And woe betide the assistant who forgot a fact which he himself had unearthed! Thus none of his paid helpers could afford to be indolent. The expert was expected to know his stuff, but he was not necessarily required to be an ideas-man, though if he was lucky his ideas would be courteously listened to. F. W. Deakin, who worked longer for Churchill as a historical adviser than anyone else, relates an amusing story about the murder of the young princes in the Tower of London. The evidence that this murder was done at the orders of King Richard III (as is the tradition enshrined in Shakespeare) comes largely from Tudor sources and some historians have felt that it is not complete.

Several historical writers, ranging from Horace Walpole to Philip Lindsay, have expressed doubts and C. R. Markham argued that the murder was committed after Richard III's own death at the orders of his successor, King Henry VII. Churchill himself was not convinced that Richard III was the murderer and he could not be persuaded to change his mind even after Deakin had made him read a book by James Gairdner refuting Markham. For Churchill had earlier read a detective novel entitled *The Daughter of Time* by Josephine Tey upon this very subject, embodying Markham's thesis. He exploded to Deakin, muttering something about 'you goddam dons,' and even wrote him a letter (Churchill wrote very few letters about his historical work) in which he assured Deakin that he found Gairdner's arguments 'not at all convincing or well argued.' [See page 237 below.]

The second main duty of Churchill's research assistants was to make sympathetic and co-operative noises while Churchill dictated. They were required to sit by and if possible to fill in the gaps in his knowledge; but they were not expected immediately to criticize his line of argument or form of presentation. Churchill might discuss a matter with them before he committed himself to paper, but once he had decided how he was going to tell the story, he liked to go full steam ahead. Sometimes, inevitably, the argument might run completely off the rails not so often because he had the facts wrong (though there might indeed be facts missing from his knowledge—but then of course the research assistant ought to have provided him with them to start with) but because his imagination was so tumultuous that he would be carried away by the exuberance of his own rhetoric.

When this happened it was very unwise to protest. For Churchill could grow angry. Usually it was late at night and the assistant's brain was tired while Churchill's mind was at its sharpest. One can read in the Alanbrooke memoirs the same kind of experience framed in the graver duties of war-time government. The Minister of Defence could be carried away by some strategic scheme or tactical device which he thought at the time to be irresistibly convincing: useless then to state that the resources were not available, for surely they could be found. But next morning it would all be different. Those like Alanbrooke who stood up for themselves and for their point of view usually found that the truth would prevail. So too it was with Churchill in his writing of history: an untenable line of argument, which was sustained by no recognized authority, would be speedily and completely abandoned the morning after it had been adumbrated. If Churchill recognized that an idea could not be made to work that was the end of it, though he rarely apologized or admitted that he had been in the wrong.

The third duty of Churchill's research assistants was to ferret out facts and get points checked. The advantage of having a competent academic historian always at his elbow was that Churchill was unlikely to make a howler. I remember how once a former British diplomatist thought he would try his hand at writing a book on eighteenth-century English history. In his book, which was duly published, he argued that Frederick, Prince of Wales—'Poor Fred', the son of King George II—was an enthusiastic democrat because he once wrote that they must always defer to the needs of the electorate. But the trouble was that the electorate to which Frederick was in fact referring, was the Electorate of Hanover, which was his native patrimony and should have been spelt with a capital E. Churchill took precautions never to fall into such a bog as that.

Churchill not only liked to get something down on paper as soon as he possibly could, but he demanded to see at once how what he had dictated looked like in type. He was unenthusiastic about reading even original letters and documents in manuscript. Thus, as soon as a chapter had been finished—and sometimes even before the facts in it had been fully checked— it would be sent off to a printer. The printer's reader would then make the obvious marks on the galley proofs and they would be sent back to Churchill ready for the next treatment. In his later years it was seldom that a galley proof was not revised and substantially rewritten five or six times. Of course, this was an exceptionally expensive method of producing a book, even in days when printers' wages were not as high as they are now. A publisher had to be confident that he had a best-seller on his hands before he was willing to meet Churchill's far-reaching demands. I don't know what the precise financial arrangements were, but Churchill himself was wont to say airily about his expenses in writing history books that he got half of them back from the Inland Revenue.

It is true, however, that Harrap in England and Scribners in the United States who obtained the contract for Churchill's life of Marlborough feared at one time that they had bitten off more than they could chew. In the first place, it took much longer to write than he had said it would and, in the second place, the book turned out to be at least twice as large as had been estimated. One reason for this was that in the course of this period when Churchill was acting almost as a lone voice in the House of Commons first in opposition to Baldwin's India policy and then to Neville Chamberlain's foreign policy, he not only completed the *Marlborough* but wrote two other books (*My Early Life* and *The Unknown War*) and began planning a third. The third book which he projected, his *History of the English-speaking Peoples*, had a little difficulty in finding a publisher on the terms he wanted; for it was common knowledge in the publishing world how Harrap had burned their fingers over the *Marlborough* contract. Anyhow, Cassell took the risk and won a huge reward. And in the long run, after the war, neither Harrap nor Scribners regretted the *Marlborough* contract.

While the *Marlborough* was being written Harrap sent off the book chapter by chapter to their printers and provided Churchill with the number of revises he needed. No doubt they breathed a sigh of relief when at last a chapter arrived marked 'final revise.' But that wasn't really final, for page proofs had now to be sent. But Churchill was pretty good over page proofs and did not make the huge alterations in them that appeared everywhere in his galleys.

As the cost of printing increased Churchill found it necessary in order to pursue his usual method of writing to employ his own printer. A firm at Chiswick was found, which set his last two

[29]

books for him in long narrow galleys. These galleys again would go through five or six revises before the whole book was dispatched to the publisher. That did not preclude the publishers from having to furnish revised galleys several times. I estimate that the chapters of the *English-speaking Peoples,* which Churchill started before the war and went back to well after the war, may have gone through as many as twelve revises.

In the case of the last books, Cassell were required to send out seventy sets of galleys to different persons or concerns who were involved in the marketing or translation of the book. But before that, Churchill himself would have dispatched many copies of his printer's galleys for comment and criticism by experts and friends. A drill would be evolved. Churchill made many revisions in his own hand, usually in red; his chief research assistant might use green, and so on. Sometimes substantial additions were made in typescript and pinned on to the middle of the galleys. Then the next revise would come and the process of titivating the text start all over again. This method not only gave Churchill himself the opportunity to polish up his periods, but enabled his assistants to re-check any point of fact that might earlier have been overlooked.

Churchill displayed great interest in detail. He admired any vigilant proof-reader who caught him out in an inconsistency. Dr Desmond Flower of Cassell remembers an embarrassing incident. When the first volume of Churchill's *The Second World War* was due to appear, the firm found that it did not possess enough paper even to meet the original subscriptions for the book. That was in the days when post-war paper rationing still prevailed in Great Britain and although the publishers' paper pool placed at Cassell's disposal the maximum amount that could be spared, this was not enough to meet their obligations. It was therefore decided that the only thing to be done was to set the book in twelve-point Bembo instead of the thirteen-point that had been intended. Churchill was not at all pleased about this. His old friends told him that they would be unable to read his book without the aid of a magnifying glass. The publishers stuck to their guns, but soothed him by promising that when the volume was reprinted it should all be reset in thirteen-point.

As Churchill became more famous and more prosperous as an author, the staff he employed was expanded. On the *Marlborough* he had not only a principal research assistant but a military adviser and a naval adviser. His military adviser was Colonel Pakenham-Walsh who was to serve with distinction in the last war and retired a general. His naval adviser was Commander J. H. Owen who afterwards produced an excellent book on the navy in the reign of Queen Anne. Churchill also sent all his proofs to Keith Feiling, as a senior expert on modern British history, who was paid for his trouble. When it came to the last two books his staff grew larger. F. W. Deakin, who had helped Churchill with the later volumes of the *Marlborough* and the first pre-war draft of the *English-speaking Peoples*, was given leave of absence by his Oxford college to help with the war memoirs. General Sir Henry Pownall and Commodore G. R. G. Allen were his military and naval advisers and later Denis Kelly was involved in the work of checking. Kelly continued to work for Churchill on his last book as well as Alan Hodge, who had been recommended to Churchill by his friend, Brendan Bracken. From time to time Kelly and Hodge would be summoned to the south of France or wherever Churchill happened to be to receive their instructions.

Churchill in the end not only employed his own printer, but also his own proof-reader, Mr C. C. Wood. He had been on the staff of Harrap and Churchill had first come across him when he was writing his *Marlborough*. Wood was a proof-reader *in excelsis*, extremely meticulous and precise both in his work and in his manner. Undoubtedly, he did a lot of useful work on Churchill's proofs by inserting punctuation and so on. But I fancy that Cassell found him a bit of a nuisance; after all, they had their own editorial staff and their printers had their own readers. Moreover, in the end Churchill himself found the conscientious Mr Wood a little tiresome and begged that he should be kept away from him.

[31]

Apart from technical advisers, there was the inevitable 'Eddie' Marsh, who became Churchill's friend even before 'the Beaver' and 'the Prof.' He had been appointed his private secretary at the Colonial Office in 1905 and subsequently was to follow him from Ministry to Ministry over many years. In addition to his official duties, he constituted himself Churchill's adviser on prose style. He read all the proofs of Churchill's books, though his proposed emendations were not always accepted. But Churchill respected his judgment and taste, especially on the important matter of punctuation. He continued to help polish Churchill's proofs until he died in 1953 at the age of eighty. So long as he remained at his prime, the service of a Mr Wood was unnecessary.

Churchill was a lover of maps and of battlefields. When he set out to write a book in which military history played a part—and really there were none of his books in which it did not—he liked personally to examine the battlefields under expert guidance; or, in his younger days, himself to be present at the battle as they occurred. It was no wonder that he wanted to accompany the invasion fleet to Normandy on D-day in 1944. In the first world war he did fight. In order to master and digest the details of a campaign he would have special maps drawn for him and on occasions have them hung on the walls of his bedroom. Then his military adviser would be summoned and invited to demonstrate on the map what he thought had happened. Not that Churchill always accepted his adviser's interpretation of events any more than he did Eddie Marsh's punctuation.

A map, he insisted, must be absolutely clear and not distorted or confused by a lot of superfluous details. Anyone who reads Churchill's history books will note the excellence of the illustrative maps. Other such books might take them for models; too many historical works either contain no maps at all or contain bad maps, measured by Churchill's standards.

Until Churchill wrote his last book, he did not really require his research assistants or advisers to provide him with drafts but only raw material and information. When I was working for him on the *Marlborough* I offered voluntarily one or two jejune essays about which he was polite and indeed said that he had read. I believe that my successor, F. W. Deakin, did once or twice offer a contribution of his own, notably on the general election of 1710, which interested him. But Churchill, who understood as much as any man how elections were fought, tore Deakin's contribution to pieces, arguing not from books but from experience. When it came to his last book, the *English-speaking Peoples,* however, a number of drafts were prepared for him by university scholars recommended to him. But Churchill took these drafts merely as a basis on which to work. Even when he was eighty he dictated his book himself; it is, very apparently, still written in his own rhetorical style; and he did not always accept the interpretations or modifications of his advisers. His history books were to him at once a hobby, a convenient means of earning money, and a solace whenever politics grew troublesome or tiresome. During his ten years in opposition before the last war, he wrote four books; and a draft of the *English-speaking Peoples,* amounting to some half a million words, was in being when the war came. It was not completely forgotten, even during the war. At the time of the battle of Narvik, Churchill invited Deakin to Admiralty House and discussed with him into the early hours of the morning William the Conqueror's invasion of England.

When, after the war, Churchill returned to this book—much to the delight of his publishers—the drafts which were then prepared were transmuted by the Churchill touch. I can vouch for this myself, for I was once invited to write a draft chapter about Oliver Cromwell, for which I was handsomely paid. Years afterwards, when Churchill's second volume appeared, I turned idly to it to find out what he had, in fact, written about Cromwell and the Interregnum. I was astonished to find some of my facts and phrases embedded in it, but the whole draft had been stood completely on its head. For Churchill was convinced that Cromwell was a dictator of the stamp of Adolf

Hitler; and though a few things might be said in favour of the Lord Protector (he was, after all, a patriot) he was none the less, Churchill thought, a bad man.

What were the advantages and disadvantages of this curious method of writing history? One advantage, as has already been indicated, was that every word that Churchill wrote was elaborately checked and counter-checked. Thus his books avoid the errors that so often mar the work of those who are regarded in the universities as amateurs. Not that Churchill slavishly followed the advice of his counsellors; every question, whether it were of historical fact or controversy, of spelling or punctuation, had to be argued out before the author was himself convinced. Moreover, the combination of dictation and careful rewriting on proof meant that the final product had been chiselled, like a Henry Moore sculpture, according to the author's own style and so the imprint of his personality was demonstrated in the book as it finally appeared. Sometimes his research assistants and advisers tried their hands at revising, rewriting, or adding to his proofs; but it was only rarely that their emendations were accepted unaltered: he liked everything to be written in his own personal style.

The method worked out on the whole according to a set pattern. Chapters frequently began with generalizations and then moved into narrative. Enclosed within the narrative in all the later history books were letters or official documents, printed more or less verbatim, though occasionally in the form of extracts. Churchill did not much believe in summarizing documents. Occasionally, if he was attracted or amused by the writings of a particular memorialist or diarist, he would relate from memory what had been said. He uses, for example, General Gordon's journals or the eighteenth-century book known as the *Memoirs of an Old Campaigner* in this way. Moreover, in several books, notably in the war memoirs, Churchill intertwines descriptive passages about events in which he did not himself take a part with his own personal reminiscences or reactions at the time. In the introductions to two of his books, he says that this part of his method was influenced by Daniel Defoe's *Memoirs of a Cavalier,* also known as *Memoirs of the Honourable Colonel Andrew Newport, a Shropshire Gentleman.* Some Defoe scholars profess to believe that this book was based on the genuine memoirs of an actual royalist officer, but not Newport by name. No doubt Newport bore the same relationship to him as Robinson Crusoe did to Alexander Selkirk. But frankly, I doubt if anyone who takes the trouble to read these *Memoirs* carefully, will find much affinity between them and the historical writings of Sir Winston Churchill. I cannot help feeling that this is a self-perpetuated myth.

Churchill's method of dictating his narrative and then embodying the documentation in it has the defect that it does not make for easy reading, although it has the advantage that the documentation can be skipped. Churchill himself admitted that the first Duke of Marlborough was anything but a lively correspondent; nevertheless he felt it was his duty to include in his text a large selection from Marlborough's unpublished letters, which might perhaps have been better left to the meticulous editing of some dedicated scholar. The method also meant that most of the research on which Churchill's books were based was not personal. Research assistants or advisers would not only dig up the documents for him, but would make a selection from them at a preliminary stage in the work. Except when there was any doubt about a question or Churchill felt that he must at all costs justify a point of view (it might be connected either with himself or with his own hero of the moment) he did not himself indulge in that minute and conscientious collation of the evidence and all possible sources which is necessary in true historical research. That is not to say that there were never times when his combination of imaginative grasp of a historical situation and his own personal political or military experience might not confound the experts and leave them aghast at their own stupidity.

Nor should it be thought Churchill was unconcerned about accuracy in narrative. His prime consideration might have been always 'to give his readers a good ride' but he aimed to make his books as perfect as they could be. Dr Flower, the present chairman of Cassell, relates an episode that bears upon that. When *The Second World War* was being published, Dr Flower was embarrassed to find that the American publishers were able on more than one occasion to get a volume out ahead of Cassell. Indeed, one volume appeared in the United States about a year in advance of the British edition. The reason was, that Churchill insisted on every possible revision, including what Cassell called 'overtakes' (that is to say, last-moment corrections sent down to the printers after the book had been completely set up) should be included before any given volume was published in England. When Cassell protested that this was highly embarrassing for them and even bad for business, Churchill expressed his complete indifference over what the Americans did. It was the British edition that was to be the definitive one, and it had to be as perfect as it could be.

Another disadvantage of the method was that in spite of the constant revisions and the amount of advice that Churchill sought and obtained, his books were all written at a frantic speed. Between 1929 and 1939, for example, he dictated hundreds of thousands of words. His first two books had to be written quickly, because he was afraid lest some other war correspondent would get in first and spoil the market. Thus, it became a habit with him to write quickly and even to jump the gun; that is to say, his propensity for starting to dictate a chapter before he had fully mastered the detail meant that he was pretty well committed to a particular way of presenting his story, even before he knew how the story would develop; it was not all that easy to modify a chapter afterwards, although there were a few occasions when a chapter would be entirely scrapped.

Another reason for his speed in writing—at least up to 1939—was that he always wanted the money for the book and was under an obligation to fulfil a contract. He prided himself that he did keep his promises; that was why he had hastily compiled some 500,000 words or more of the *English-speaking Peoples* by the time that the war broke out. Cassell understandably put the wordage into cold storage and most of the book was, in fact, re-written long afterwards. Churchill was a generous man who lived in a pretty lavish way, and from his youth upwards he had earned his living by writing. Much of it came from day-to-day journalism, but he expected his history books to pay their way adequately. Thus he enjoyed counting the words he had written and calculating how much he had earned. When he could knock off an article in three-quarters of an hour and earn £200 or sometimes, through serialization, a great deal more for it, he was frankly delighted. But these articles were to him ephemera. On the other hand, he reckoned that his historical books and memoirs would live.

But the money nexus was something of a handicap to him. The writing of books did not have the same excitement or meaning for him as did his political career. He would much rather be making a speech, conversing with friends, or out in the open air, even if he were only painting or building a wall in his garden, than he would be getting down to the hard grind of dictating history. I am told that he regarded both his *Marlborough* and his later books as chores before he reached the end of them. He tended to lose interest and to tire (which was human enough).

Finally, one is inclined to believe that his method of writing, embodying not only the massive sweep of his thoughts, ideas and rhetoric, but also elaborate documentation, made his books far too long. Subsequently, publishers would seek his permission to reduce their size by judicious cutting and the books became more readable in consequence. He had, it is true, been brought up in the days of the Victorian two-decker or three-decker biography, the days of Moneypenny and Buckle's *Disraeli* and Morley's *Gladstone*. It was a very different world from our own, a world in which the middle classes subscribed to private lending libraries to obtain their weekly reading and eagerly awaited the latest instalments of Charles Dickens and others. Good books do not necessarily need to be long books. But books are almost bound to be long if they are dictated by an orator.

[37]

4

Early works

BEFORE he reached his twenty-sixth birthday Winston Churchill had written no fewer than five books, a remarkable achievement for a young man mainly occupied on military service. Admittedly four out of the five books derived from information which he had collected when acting as a war correspondent. The fifth was his unique novel, *Savrola*, which, he claimed, took him only two months to write, although he had in fact obviously pondered upon the plot and the ideas expressed by his hero over a longer period of time. The last two of the books, *London to Ladysmith* and *Ian Hamilton's March*, both published in 1900, were a collection of dispatches that he had written for the now defunct London newspaper, the *Morning Post*, and are not of much significance to the student of Churchill as a historian. But the first two, *The Story of the Malakand Field Force* (published in March 1898) and *The River War* (published in October 1899) are important. *The Story of the Malakand Field Force* was Churchill's initiation as an author: *The River War*, in its original version, contained a number of chapters which were purely historical, since they set out the whole political and military background and told the story of Kitchener's war against the Dervishes before Churchill himself joined the army in the dual capacity of a subaltern attached to the 21st Lancers and a war correspondent of the *Morning Post*. Afterwards the War Office wisely decided that the combination of these two functions should be prohibited. But it must be realized that Churchill was not then exceptional. For example, when he wrote his first book both Lord Fincastle, V.C., the correspondent of

The Times, and Lieutenant Greaves, the acting war correspondent of *The Times of India,* were also serving officers. Greaves indeed was killed in action.

Churchill received special permission from his regiment, the Fourth Hussars, stationed at Bangalore, to join the expedition led by General Bindon Blood to suppress the rebellious tribes in the Malakand valley, who had been aroused against the British by the Mad Mullah or Mad Fakir. Churchill represented both the *Pioneer,* an Indian newspaper, and the *Daily Telegraph.* After he returned to his regiment at Bangalore, he decided to write a book about the campaign (as did Lord Fincastle). The book may be said to be an examplar of several of Churchill's later historical writings. It begins by sketching in the outlines of the picture, depicting the country on the north-west frontier of India and the background of the campaign. Afterwards it relates events which he witnessed or learned about at first hand when he himself was serving with the expedition. Then he concludes with some reflections—incredibly mature for so young a man—upon the significance of what he himself called 'an episode of frontier war' and sets out the military and political lessons that might be obtained from it for the future.

Already he was fully aware that he was engaged in writing history. 'Hitherto,' he observed after some early chapters, 'the course of events has been recorded in the impersonal style of history. But henceforward I am able to rely on my own memory as well as other people's evidence.' He remarked half-humorously in 1930 that he had written 'a standard history of the subject' which was 'unfortunately out of print.' The book betrays certain stylistic faults, not, I would hasten to add, ones that would be regarded as fundamental in terms of modern prose, but which he himself would certainly have deplored—and in fact did deplore—afterwards. He had a propensity for using what has been called the hanging participle: 'Crossing a shallow stream . . . the second stage is reached. Stopping only to change ponies, the journey is resumed.' 'Crossing this and climbing the opposite bank, the great dimensions of the valley are displayed.'

'Standing on some lofty peak or commanding point in Dir, Swat or Bajaur, range after range is seen as the long surges of an Atlantic swell . . .' The use of commas was at times distinctly odd and he was not above a split infinitive, which, again, would not be regarded as of much moment today, but which he himself would have disliked had he realized at the time that it was considered incorrect. Indeed he eliminated the split infinitives in his early books when they went into second editions. Sometimes the punctuation went awry. *The Athaeneum,* a weekly magazine, in reviewing the book, as his son has reminded us, wrote of *The Story of the Malakand Field Force* that 'as it stands, it suggests in style a volume by Disraeli revised by a mad printer's reader.'

But though Churchill himself, when he received in India copies of his first book sent from England, was terribly upset by the number of errors it contained (he had entrusted its correction to an uncle whose chief claim to literary fame was as the author of a book on bimetallism) in fact these errors of punctuation, grammar, and slips of transcription were of little account. For the book showed high qualities. He had managed to make this 'episode in frontier war' intensely readable. He had mastered the way of expounding to his readers the detail of a military campaign without either confusing or boring them. His awareness of his readers was revealed throughout the whole of the book from the foreword onwards. He writes, for example: 'The attention of the reader is directed to the bravery of this officer' or 'The reader must now accompany me to the camp of the 3rd Brigade'; and in the foreword: 'I have always thought that if an author cannot make friends with the reader and explain his objects in two or three hundred pages, he is not likely to do so in fifty lines.' He also realized the value of the occasional aside or apothegm. 'A little plain food, and a philosophic temperament are the only necessities of life.' (I doubt if he would have altogether subscribed to that view in his later years.) 'They [frontier wars] are but the surf that marks the edge and advance of the wars of civilization.' (This was a quotation from a speech by Lord Salisbury.) 'A single glass of champagne imparts a feeling of exhilaration. The nerves are braced, the imagination is agreeably stirred, the wits become more nimble. A bottle produces a contrary effect. Excess causes a comatose insensibility. So it is with war, and the quality of both is best discovered by sipping.' 'It is better to be making the news than talking it: to be an actor rather than a critic.'

The Malakand Field Force discloses a romantic attitude to life. It also embodies the approach of a young officer who has savoured his first experience of war. Speaking of the relief of Chakdara in August 1897, Churchill wrote: 'In that moment the general, who watched the triumphant issue of the plans, must have experienced as fine an emotion as is given to man on earth.' 'She [the moon] was gazing on a different scene eleven miles away, in the valley we had met.' (This was one of the eccentric commas.) 'Few obstacles can stop brave men and good horses.' But at the same time he did not glory in war, as he was often accused of doing in later years. No serving officer does that. Speaking of the pursuit of the Pathans, Churchill wrote:

> The spectator who may gaze unmoved on the bloodshed of the battle must avert his eyes from the horrors of the pursuit unless indeed, joining in it himself, he flings all scruples to the winds and indulges to the full those deep-seated instincts of savagery over which civilization has but cast a veil of doubtful thickness.

In this ably planned, excellently arranged book, Churchill did what he always aimed to do in the writing of history: he combined his own experience of events and of men with a realistic description and understanding of what he believed had occurred. By that means he was able to make history live. He employed his imaginative gifts to persuade his readers of the way that men felt or the manner in which they confronted the problems that they had to face at a crisis in their lives. He never concealed the horrors of war; nor did he deny its excitements. And he never exalted war for its own sake.

In the last chapter of this book he discussed 'The Riddle of the

Frontier.' He began by explaining how the British Government had abandoned its previous policy of holding the line of the mountains in favour of a forward policy intended to counter the influence of Russia and of the Amir of Afghanistan. Such a policy, he believed, 'precluded the possibility of peace.' Whether the 'forward policy' was the right policy he was not prepared to say: 'the historian of the future, with impartial pen and a more complete knowledge, must pronounce on the wisdom of the act.' Logically such a policy could be most effectually carried out by going 'full steam ahead.' The frontier valleys might then be made 'as safe and civilized as Hyde Park.' But this was not practical, for the troops could not be provided to carry it out. Therefore a piecemeal advance was inevitable; and he believed that 'a system of subsidies' to the tribes would pay off; 'by increasing their wealth' one might 'lessen their barbarism.' That was at least a more promising way of keeping the peace than the older one, called in derision that of 'butcher and bolt.'

Thus, though Churchill reluctantly accepted the case for the forward policy, he searched for means to avoid perpetual war. This was a highly judicious chapter, revealing careful thought by a young officer. But he had specifically disavowed the intention of writing a 'party pamphlet on a great Imperial question.' His object was to record 'the facts as they occurred without attempting to make a case against any person or any party.' That is the 'impersonality' of his history. But he believed in himself and in his country: the year 1897, he thought, 'was marked by a declaration to the whole world of our faith in the high destinies of our race.'

In this, his first book, then, we see not merely how Churchill was quickly mastering the art of writing; one notes that his journalistic experience bestowed on him that gift which so many historians have lacked, of being able to convey to his readers the essence of a complicated story without skimping the detail or over-simplifying the argument. Also it revealed him to be a discerning writer, seeking to avoid the mere making of debating points which is part of the necessary equipment of the party politician. A clear line was drawn between ephemeral political arguments and the impartial view of history, a line to which, on the whole, he was to adhere throughout his career as an author. As we have argued in an earlier chapter, he deeply respected the judgments of history: he believed that truth will always arrive in time for history; and that the judgments of history are just.

The success of his first book—it sold 8,500 copies—inspired in Churchill a desire to do more. 'I may live to write something, that will take its place in permanent literature,' he told his mother, 'for the faults need not be repeated—and the power of writing will remain.' Soon after this he was approached by publishers to write a life both of the great Duke of Marlborough and of his own father: two books that he was in fact to complete at later dates. Among other books he also contemplated 'a short and dramatic history of the American civil war.' This was a subject that fascinated him all his days; he was ultimately to embody 'a short and dramatic history' of that war in his *History of the English-speaking Peoples*. Some good judges believe that this is the very best part of that book.

But his next book in fact was to be *The River War,* which was published in the autumn of 1899, and was written, like all his books, at enormous speed and at vast length. It was partly written in Bangalore before he finally resigned his commission in the British army in the spring of that year and partly in England after he returned home. Churchill himself served as an officer in Kitchener's campaign against the Dervishes, who were led by the Khalifa Abdullah, once the lieutenant of the Mahdi, the original inspirer of the revolt against the Egyptians. But the campaign lasted only six months and Churchill was on active service only for about six weeks. He was there in the dual capacity of a lieutenant of cavalry attached to the 21st Lancers and the war correspondent of the *Morning Post,* but he took his military duties very seriously. His book was published in two volumes and it was not until he reached the first chapter of the second volume that Churchill introduced himself upon the stage.

[43]

Thus the whole of his first volume is history and good history at that. Churchill took immense pains over collecting his material. He wrote to various officers who had served in the campaign asking them for information. He read all the relevant sources then available, such as the Blue Books, which he listed, General Gordon's *Journals,* and the memoirs of Slatin Pasha, an Austrian officer, and of Father Ohrwalder, a Roman Catholic priest, both of whom had been prisoners of the Mahdi and escaped from his camps. Sir Herbert, later Lord Kitchener, the Sirdar or commander-in-chief of the Egyptian army, would not allow him to obtain information from his aide-de-camp, Major Watson, because Kitchener had resented the way in which, by pulling strings, Churchill had been foisted on to his army as an officer. However, Lord Cromer (formerly Sir Evelyn Baring), the British High Commissioner in Egypt, freely gave him valuable advice: in consequence of his consultations with Cromer Churchill modified his chapter about Gordon. He was also helped by General Sir Reginald Wingate, who had long been in charge of the military intelligence of the Egyptian army and had written a book about Mahdism and the Sudan in 1891; and through Wingate's courtesy Churchill was able to interview the notorious Zubair Pasha, once a slave trader, whom Gordon had vainly pressed should be brought into the Sudan to rule it after the expected overthrow of the Mahdi. Finally, Churchill's book which in its first editions was described as 'an historical account of the Reconquest of the Sudan' (the word 'historical' was omitted in the later editions) was edited for him by Colonel Frank Rhodes, the military correspondent of *The Times*, who had been present during the campaign and was wounded at the battle of Omdurman. Thus nothing that could reasonably and immediately have been procured by means of research and inquiry, consultation or expert advice was omitted in the attempt to make the book complete. That was to be the pattern of nearly all Churchill's future historical work. But the writing was all his own.

Churchill begins his book with five chapters in which he sets the scene and describes the historical background to Kitchener's expedition to the Sudan. He argued that the main cause of the revolt in 1881 of the Sudanese tribes against the Egyptians under the leadership of the Mahdi was nationalistic and not religious. (Incidentally, he wrongly calls the Mahdi 'the son of a humble priest': the father was a boat-builder.) 'Fanaticism,' he observed, 'is not a cause of war. It is the means which enables savage peoples to fight.' No one, he thought, could have a better cause for rebellion than the Sudanese, whose country had been ruined, property plundered, and women ravaged by the Egyptians. The Egyptians had ruled the Sudan from 1819 to 1883 but their rule was 'neither kindly, wise nor profitable: it was a reign of rapacity, corruption and oppression.' 'The Arab tribes obeyed and the black population cowered.' But the Egyptian dominion was only 'a house of cards.' And though they possessed a garrison of 40,000 men, it was a poor one.

The British Government's advice to Egypt was to abandon the Sudan. The Egyptians acquiesced with reluctance. General Charles Gordon, 'Chinese Gordon,' was then sent out by the British Government in 1884 entirely by himself in order to arrange, if he could, for the evacuation of the Egyptian garrisons from the Sudan. In his book Churchill does not deal in any detail with the precise nature of Gordon's instructions which have since become a matter of virulent historical controversy. Gladstone, then the Prime Minister, was long convinced that Gordon had been sent out only to report, without commitment, on the possibility of evacuation and the means by which it might be done. Bernard Allen in his book *Gordon and the Sudan* (1931) contended that the nature of Gordon's instructions was decided or rather changed while he was en route to Khartoum, while Anthony Nutting in his more recent and forthright book *Gordon: Misfit and Martyr* (1966) argued that from the first Gordon was determined in his heart to overthrow the Mahdi or himself perish in the attempt. Mr Nutting claims that at any time between March, when Gordon established control in Khartoum, and the end of May, when the Sudanese occupied Berber down the Nile from Khartoum, Gordon could, had he wished, have got most of the garrison and the inhabitants away from the city back to Egypt. Moreover he asserts that right up until the end—a year after Gordon arrived—he himself could at any time have escaped from Khartoum had he wished to do so. But though he was besieged by the Dervishes, he never intended to make such an attempt. This appears to be unquestionable. On the other hand, it is equally clear from Gordon's own journals that almost to the end he believed that the arrival of even a small British force at or near Khartoum would have so undermined the authority of the Mahdi that he could have saved the Egyptian garrisons in the Sudan from annihilation.

Churchill did not attempt in 1899 to solve this historical puzzle nor did he do so in the subsequent editions of *The River War* published in 1902 and 1933. A historian rarely works in a void or in an ivory tower. Churchill certainly didn't. His father had attacked Gladstone violently in the House of Commons over the Sudan and the 'betrayal' of Gordon. On the other hand, Lord Cromer felt bitterly about Gordon's conduct: indeed Churchill, under Cromer's influence, described Gordon as an unbalanced, capricious neurotic who incessantly smoked cigarettes. In a private letter to his mother, written after he had seen Cromer in March 1899, he also added that 'his temper was abominable' and he was 'frequently drunk.' Lytton Strachey has been attacked by Gordon's admirers for saying in a celebrated essay in his *Eminent Victorians* that Gordon drank secretly, but it is striking that Churchill had heard this story, evidently from Cromer himself, twenty years before Strachey wrote.

Churchill, however, was reluctant to rewrite his chapter on Gordon. 'I feel it will be impossible for me to sacrifice all the fine phrases and pleasing paragraphs I have written about Gordon,' he told his mother. But he did, in fact, tone down or omit a good deal of what he had written originally about Kitchener. Kitchener, as we have said, was resentful over Churchill being in the army at all. (Incidentally Churchill seems skilfully to have overcome Kitchener's ban on Major Watson supplying him with information by talking to him in Cairo.) Churchill felt very strongly after

the battle of Omdurman and the subsequent capture of the town
that Kitchener behaved ignobly in desecrating the Mahdi's
tomb, circulating his head for medical inspection, and throwing
the rest of his remains into the Nile. He also blamed Kitchener
for the slaughter of wounded Dervishes after the battle had been
won. He pictured Kitchener as a stern and ruthless martinet, and
in private Churchill said that Kitchener was 'never a gentleman,'
that he was 'a vulgar, common man.'

Unquestionably Kitchener was as ambitious as Churchill was
himself. What Churchill did not criticize Kitchener for—which
presumably he did not know about, though Cromer knew—was
his strange vacillation before the battle of the Atbara earlier in
the campaign. When Churchill republished his book, he omitted
most of his criticisms of Kitchener as a commander. By that time
he had become an M.P. Thus although, in analysing the character
of Kitchener in his first edition, he wrote: 'the meanest historian
owes something to truth'—a typically ironical sentence—he was
evidently concerned at having hurt the feelings of so distinguished
an officer of the Empire.

The conquest of Omdurman, the Mahdi's capital, was preceded by a famous episode, a charge by the 21st Lancers with
which Churchill himself was serving as a second lieutenant. The
battle itself was the subject of the first of Churchill's famous
historical set-pieces and was given authenticity and vivacity by
the fact that he fought in it himself. As a first-hand account it is
unequalled. The battle, he explained, was fought in two parts;
the first consisted of the uncoordinated attacks by the Dervishes
which were repulsed by artillery and infantry fire; then followed
the swift occupation of the Mahdi's capital on Kitchener's
orders and the flight of the Khalifa. Although the Dervishes outnumbered the British and Egyptian troops by approximately
three to one, the superiority of the weapons at the disposal of
Kitchener was decisive. 'We had got the Maxim guns and they
had not.' Indeed it was hardly conceivable that the Anglo-
Egyptian army could have been beaten. But what was feared was
that the Khalifa might be able to sustain a frontal assault,

inflict heavy losses on his opponents, and then withdraw far into the desert. But the Dervishes never contemplated a defensive strategy: that was not their way of fighting. Nor did they believe in probing or guerrilla attacks, a fact which explained their earlier defeat at Atbara. The British camp on the banks of the Nile was protected by a zeriba or stockade and was supported by gunboats on the river. Nevertheless the Dervishes boldly advanced upon it, while keeping large forces concealed behind the Surgham and Kerreri hills in case their front line were driven back. If that happened, they hoped that their victorious enemy, moving into a counter-attack, would be overwhelmed from both flanks.

The four squadrons of the 21st Lancers in which Churchill himself was an officer had not yet been blooded in battle and were anxious to take their part in the fight. They had been stationed on the extreme left of the Anglo–Egyptian line to the south of Surgham hill. When the initial assault by the Dervishes in the centre had been successfully repulsed, the Colonel in command of the Lancers could not resist ordering a cavalry charge against a party of Dervishes who were spotted to the south-west of Surgham hill: his idea was to cut off the enemy's line of retreat westward to Omdurman. What was not realized was that a huge force of Dervishes (estimated at 17,000) commanded by the Khalifa himself lay concealed behind the hill. Thus the British cavalry charge against the infantry was both dangerous and foolhardy. After two charges the Dervishes in fact withdrew, but of the Lancers 'in 120 seconds five officers, 65 men, and 119 horses out of less than 400 had been killed or wounded.' At the end of the second charge the Dervishes retired 'in good order, towards the ridge of Surgham hill, where the Khalifa's Black Flag still waved, and the 21st Lancers remained in possession of the ground—and of their dead.'

In assessing the battle at the conclusion of his account Churchill wrote simply that 'the charge of the 21st Lancers had been costly, but was not ineffective.' This is a good example of his *pianissimo* style in the writing of history. But others took a very contrary view. G. W. Steevens, for example, who reported the campaign for the *Daily Mail* wrote: 'the charge was a gross blunder, a tactical crime; it suffered a heavier loss than it inflicted and by its loss in horses contributed to the escape of the Khalifa.' Thus does loyalty modify the views of the historian. In the first edition of *The River War* Churchill severely criticized Kitchener for the failure of the pursuit after the battle, saying it was 'the fault of the Sirdar alone'; in fact the Colonel of the 21st Lancers made his contribution to that failure. And Churchill wisely left the criticism out of the later editions of the book.

Churchill's account of the battle and of the campaign as a whole was fair and his generalizations were sound. The broad, sympathetic, and humane attitude which always characterized his writing on war was exemplified when he wrote about the enemy. The battle, in which he said 9,000 Dervishes were killed and 5,000 taken prisoner (that appears to have been an under-estimate) was 'the most signal triumph ever gained by the arms of science over barbarians,' but the Dervishes were 'as brave men as ever walked the earth.' And reflecting on the battle he observed:

I hope that if evil days should come upon our country, and the last army which a collapsing Empire could interpose between London and the invader was dissolving in rout and ruin, that there would be some—even in these modern days—who would not care to accustom themselves to the new order of things and tamely survive the disaster.

There prophetically spoke the Prime Minister of England and the leader of a disintegrating British Empire in the autumn of 1940.

Where, however, Churchill's humanitarian approach did not apply was in examining the causes of the war and one of its consequences. He assigned various reasons for the launching of Kitchener's offensive by the Conservative Government. 'The diplomatist said "It is to please the Triple Alliance." The politician said "It is to triumph over the Radicals." The polite person said "It is to restore the Khedive's rule over the Sudan."

The man in the street—and there are many men in many streets
—said "It is to avenge General Gordon." ' The campaign was
aimed first of all at relieving the pressure on the Italians who in
1896 suffered their humiliating defeat by the Abyssinians at the
battle of Adowa. 'The war in the Sudan,' Sir Philip Magnus has
justly written, 'was started deliberately by England as an act
of policy, a cold-blooded business enterprise to help the Italians
at Kassala.' Churchill realized that the Khalifa (again in the
words of Sir Philip Magnus) 'symbolized effectively the nationalist aspirations of the peoples over whom he ruled.' Churchill
fully understood that the Dervishes were brave and patriotic
soldiers who fought superbly for their cause; what he did not see
was the brutal character of European imperialism in Africa.

Once the campaign was started there can be little doubt that
it was Kitchener's intention and the hope of the British officers
who fought under him that they should avenge Gordon. Hence
the desecration of the Mahdi's tomb following the final victory
and the scattering of his remains. After the battle of Omdurman
the Khalifa himself escaped and managed to establish a camp in
Kordofan, 250 miles south-east of Omdurman, where he was
joined by the Dervish garrisons which had taken no part in the
battle. In December 1899 a small mixed force was dispatched by
Kitchener on what Churchill—in a chapter which he added to
the second edition of his book—called 'the honourable enterprise' of capturing Abdullah. As it happened, this small force
found itself vastly outnumbered and had to beat a hasty retreat
across the desert. A year later a very much larger expedition
under the command of General Sir Reginald Wingate and armed
with the latest weapons of war was dispatched to round up the
Khalifa and his Emirs. In November 1900 this last fighting
group of Dervishes was overwhelmed; the Khalifa himself
refused to retreat and 'pierced by many balls' was found 'stretched
dead on his sheepskin.' So the object of the war was achieved: to
reunite a militarily subdued Sudan with Egypt, an Egypt under
British imperial tutelage. Thus the Khalifa Abdullah was, in the
words of Philip Magnus, 'deliberately hunted down.' Today the

British Empire is no more; and the Sudan is an independent nation.

Obviously it would be wrong to overestimate the importance of these early works in Churchill's career as a historian. As a contribution to his own biography his novel *Savrola,* which was published a few months after *The River War,* in February 1900, is far more significant: for it throws a piercing light on his political beliefs (democratic, but anti-socialist), his attitude to women (romantic, but condescending), and his religion (sceptical, nurtured on Winwood's *Martyrdom of Man*). But there are three points that may fairly be made about these early works. The first is that they were all written with extraordinary speed in hot blood and with a full consciousness of the need for absolute clarity. His account of the building of the desert railway, for example, which was the backbone of the success of Kitchener's campaign, is absorbing and entertaining. Churchill realized that he possessed the gift of writing history for a wide readership. Secondly, Churchill was thorough and conscientious in collecting all the material that was available at the time on his subject; he had the itch to find out which is characteristic of the true historian. Finally, while he understood the need to place his stories of the Malakand and Omdurman campaigns in a geographical and historical setting, he appreciated that it was too early to reach a final judgment—for example with regard to the British policy on the north-west frontier or the exact relationship between Gladstone's Government and General Gordon.

If we compare other books written on these campaigns with those by Churchill, we can see that his had more weight; for he employed a historical setting and he was not afraid of drawing conclusions about the political and military significance of events when he was convinced that he had sufficient knowledge to do so. For this reason neither the book by Viscount Fincastle, V.C., and Lieutenant P. C. Eliott-Lockhart on the Malakand campaign nor that by G. W. Steevens on the Sudan campaign was of such permanent value as Churchill's two books. Steevens's *With Kitchener to Khartoum* went into no fewer than twenty-two editions and was hailed as being both 'bright and readable.' Presumably it sold more copies than *The River War*—at any rate during the reign of Queen Victoria. But Churchill's account endures.

Yet Churchill's work also had the defect of its merits. One does not write solid history in a hurry. I think perhaps he was too easily swayed by what Cromer told him. For example, he ascribes to Cromer, then Sir Evelyn Baring, the plan for sending a small camel-mounted force to Berber, which appears to have been one of Gordon's own plans. He does not seem to have got his facts about the Mahdi quite right, though presumably he could have discovered them from Wingate. The careful and detailed comparison of sources and authorities which is the stock-in-trade of the professional historian, was hardly his habit. It would be ridiculous to say that he was influenced by the last man he talked to, but it is likely that if he received what he regarded as a plausible description of events he was inclined to accept it, provided it did not conflict with his own instincts about what might reasonably have happened. At the same time he fully understood that the final judgments of history must be long-term ones. He was not confident that he had got all the facts exactly right and was not so foolish as to deliver a verdict when he knew that the evidence was still incomplete. To other historians it must seem a pity that while he made excisions, for example, with regard to the conduct of Lord Kitchener, he could not at the same time bring himself to revise his account in the light of the later information that became available. But of course, as I have said, the writing of history was not his main occupation in life.

5

Lord Randolph Churchill

WINSTON'S father, Lord Randolph Churchill, died of generalized and incurable paralysis at the age of forty-six while his son was still at Sandhurst. The relations between father and son had never been close and Winston was only a young schoolboy when his father's meteoric career came to a sudden end in 1886 with his resignation from the office of Chancellor of the Exchequer in Lord Salisbury's Conservative Government. 'One could not,' wrote Winston in his autobiography, 'grow up in my father's house, and still less among his mother and sisters, without understanding that there had been a great political disaster.' But that was all. Great political disasters mean little to a schoolboy. Moreover Winston Churchill spent much of his youth away from home at boarding schools. His mother, if we may judge from her memoirs and letters, was rather a silly woman absorbed by the demands of 'society,' who thought herself not well dressed unless she possessed forty pairs of shoes. Winston evidently learned little enough from her about his father's affairs. Indeed it is doubtful if Lord Randolph confided much in his wife. He certainly did not consult her about the fatal letter he wrote to Lord Salisbury. Father and son—even though the latter was nearly twenty-one at the time of Randolph's tragic death—had only one or two intimate conversations. But once in the autumn of 1892 the father said to him: 'Do remember things do not always go right with me. My every action is misjudged, and every word distorted . . . so make some allowances.'

Winston loved his parents devotedly and treasured their

memories, paradoxically so perhaps in view of the way in which they had neglected him. Thus from an early stage he decided that he would write his father's biography and justify his career. As we have seen, a suggestion to that effect was made to him by a publisher after the success of his first books. But before he could embark on this enterprise he had first to launch his own career as a politician. When he resigned from the army in 1899 he at once sought for a constituency. His father's friends were active on his behalf, but his own exciting adventures in South Africa, as recorded in newspaper articles and his books, had spread his reputation as a man of individuality and courage. Thus he obtained the opportunity to fight a by-election at Oldham in 1899 and, though he was then defeated, he narrowly won a seat there at the so-called Khaki general election of 1900. Before delivering his maiden speech in the House of Commons on the subject of the South African war, which he had witnessed at first hand, he accumulated money by giving lectures both in England and the United States of America about his adventures and thus gained a financial independence that helped him on his way. His father had left little money, though his mother was of wealthy American parentage and was adequately provided for according to her own exacting standards. Moreover she married for the second time in 1900. Thus it was not until the summer recess of 1902 that, at the request of his father's literary trustees, he started to work on the biography.

For a son (or daughter) successfully to write a serious historical book about a father is rare. It can be either too eulogistic or too grudging. Certain advantages of course accrue: there is access to all personal papers, the memories of friends, the inherited traditions of the family. But readers are liable to discount an apologia which might be entirely credible from a more impartial pen. In the preface to the first edition of his book Winston made all the proper remarks: 'I have been fortunate in the abundance of the material supplied me . . . such omissions as have been necessary are made for others' sakes and not his own,' etc. But what he does not mention is the fundamental handicap of the parental relationship. He was writing, he maintained, simply 'the biography of an English statesman' and the difficulties he encountered were the difficulties common to all political biographers. It may, however, be fairly contended that the comparative neglect that Winston Churchill suffered at the hands of his parents made his biography more objective than it might otherwise have been. Lord Rosebery was of the opinion that it was both fair and tactful.

But there were other obstacles to the display of the impartiality of the historian, or shades round that 'calm flame' which Winston himself often spoke of as being the candle of truth held aloft by the historian. The first obstacle was the propinquity of time. Few historical biographies or histories of events have yet been satisfactorily written while the controversies innate in them were still burning. It is true that contemporary history is much more fashionable now than it once used to be; and Churchill's life of his father was not published until over ten years after the subject's death. Nevertheless many persons who had been involved in Lord Randolph's career were still alive and active while Winston was at work on the biography. Arthur Balfour, for example, who had succeeded his uncle Lord Salisbury as Prime Minister (Salisbury died in August 1903), was still Prime Minister when Winston was writing. It was therefore impossible for Winston Churchill to say exactly what he thought of the way in which Balfour had treated his father—and it seems to me that he treated him pretty badly. That such men and women who figured importantly in his father's life, as well of course as Winston's mother, were not only still living when Winston was writing but belonged to the society in which he moved, unquestionably restricted what he felt he could permissibly say. For Winston Churchill, though a man of infinite courage and never one to hold himself back in the give-and-take of political controversy, was both considerate and generous in his private life. He never wanted unnecessarily to hurt the feelings of others. We have seen how he modified his strictures on Lord Kitchener when he came to reprint *The River War*. So the full story of his father's life could not yet be told. Finally, during the period when he was writing, Winston himself left the Conservative party over the issue of Protection versus Free Trade and about eighteen months before the book appeared joined the Liberals, a step which his father had never contemplated taking, though it was perhaps within the logic of his political outlook. It is remarkable in the light of these considerable, if natural handicaps, that Churchill's biography of his father was to be a historical masterpiece which can be read with understanding and enjoyment by anyone really interested in history today, more than sixty years after its original publication.

At the beginning of the book Winston explained what he conceived to be the difficulties in writing a political biography. The style and the ideas of the writer have to be subordinated to the necessity of embracing in the text the documentary proofs on which the story depends. Wherever practicable, he says, he aims to employ Lord Randolph's own words. On the other hand, Lord Randolph's private letters, he thinks, 'do not lend themselves to publication as readily as those of some other eminent persons. They are spontaneous and scrappy. They deal with the little ordinary commonplaces of the writer's life . . . they are full of personal allusions. . . .' Nevertheless he considered that he had omitted scarcely anything of material consequence and that there was 'nothing more to tell.'

This was obviously not strictly accurate, as Churchill himself afterwards freely admitted. For instance, it would not have been proper at that time to have related in detail the reasons for Lord Randolph's quarrel with the Prince of Wales (who had become King of England as Edward VII by the time the book appeared). Randolph's elder brother, the Marquis of Blandford, already a married man, had an affair with a lady, the Countess of Aylesford, while her husband was in India shooting with the Prince of Wales. She eloped with her lover, and the affair became public. The Countess herself had at one time been the recipient of indiscreet letters from the Prince of Wales. So when the Prince advised Lord Aylesford that he had better divorce his wife and Lord

Blandford that he ought to obtain a divorce and marry the generous Countess, Randolph intervened vigorously on his brother's behalf, spoke to Princess Alexandra, the wife of the Prince of Wales, and even threatened to publish the correspondence between the Prince and Lady Aylesford (which Blandford had acquired from the Countess and given him) unless the Prince withdrew his pressure. The Randolph Churchills had been on intimate terms with the Prince of Wales who had given them a wedding present and dined with them at their London home. After the blackmail threat the Prince made it known that he wanted the Randolph Churchills ostracized from London society and announced that he himself would refuse to enter any house in which they were entertained. Nor did Lord Randolph's gratuitous efforts on his brother's behalf (for which Blandford was not in the least grateful) endear him to the Queen who insisted that if the Prince said that his correspondence with Lady Aylesford was innocent, that was good enough for her. It was partly in consequence of this ostracism that Lord Randolph Churchill, although he was already the Member of Parliament for Woodstock, spent three years as his father's unpaid private secretary in Dublin, where the Duke of Marlborough had been appointed Viceroy of Ireland. All that Winston Churchill wrote about this extraordinary episode is this: 'Engaging in his brother's quarrels with fierce and reckless partisanship, Lord Randolph incurred the deep displeasure of a great personage.'

But Churchill deliberately planned the book so that the space given to his father's earlier and later life was kept to a minimum. About five-eighths of the book is devoted to the years 1880–1886 when Lord Randolph was at the peak of his political career. His climb to power is succinctly related up to the time when he formed the so-called 'Fourth Party' and began to harass Gladstone, who was then Prime Minister, in the House of Commons, more effectively than the official leaders of the Conservative Opposition. And although more than 200 pages are given to Randolph's last years after he resigned from the Cabinet in 1886 until his death in January 1895, most of it concerns his activities

C

immediately following his resignation. Winston did not dwell upon his father's tragic last years when paralysis undermined his powers, as Lord Moran dwelt on Winston's own declining years in his unfortunate book.

Nevertheless the early part of the life of Lord Randolph is beautifully written. Churchill reflects upon Lord Randolph's youthful correspondence with his own father and remarks on the comparatively small influence that parents have: the child, he says, asserts his own personality; the schoolboy makes up his own mind, and nothing will change him much. So he pictured his father at Eton 'gaining neither distinction in games nor profit from his studies' and spending his time at Oxford 'living practically at home' in Blenheim Palace. He comments on the influence of the Bible, Gibbon, and 'Jorrocks' on his father's style in speech and writing. He relates how he fell in love for the first and last time, with Jennie Jerome, the American girl he met in Cowes. It is sometimes said nowadays that early nineteenth-century biographers went astray because they stuck too closely to the facts and were unaware of those psychological factors which were being unearthed by Austrian doctors. But this is not altogether fair. Churchill certainly drew attention to the moods of depression and excitement to which his father was subject from his youth onwards, and wrote that his whole life was 'a struggle against ill health.' He relates how his father told his mother before they married that the reading of Gibbon 'soothed him' and he remarks upon his smoking of countless cigarettes. He sketches his father's evolution from a sportsman and a dandy into an ambitious and serious-minded politician who spoke with fire and fury in the House of Commons. At first politics was only one among his several occupations or amusements. But the three years he spent in Dublin attracted him more to politics; though he never favoured Home Rule, he was aware, after visiting every part of Ireland, of the importance of raising both the economic and educational standards in a country where the contrasts between rich and poor were only too clearly visible.

An Irish crisis disrupted Gladstone's Government in 1880,

although it had won a substantial victory over the Conservatives in the general election of that year. Lord Randolph used the knowledge that he had acquired on the spot to attack Gladstone's Irish policy. He consistently opposed coercion. But this was not the only question on which Lord Randolph and his three friends, Sir Henry Wolff, John Gorst, and Arthur Balfour, who made up his 'Fourth Party' of intellectual frondeurs, harassed the Government. They were equally concerned with foreign and domestic affairs—with Egypt and the Sudan, with the antics of Charles Bradlaugh, the atheist M.P., with the Reform Bill of 1884. Randolph showed his sympathy with nationalist leaders like the Egyptian Arabi Pasha and the leader of the Irish party, Charles Parnell—just as his son was to admire the Mahdi and Michael Collins, the Irish patriot. And after the death in 1883 of the veteran Tory leader, Benjamin Disraeli, Earl of Beaconsfield, who had become an admirer of the Fourth Party, Lord Randolph proceeded to outline for the first time 'the conception of Tory Democracy which had now possessed his mind.' He condemned the Whigs as the party with prejudices and maintained that the Tories 'are of the people.' Both by his energetic work in the House of Commons and by the fight that he waged against the establishment group within the organization of the Tory party, he made his mark on political society; and when in 1885 Lord Salisbury formed a 'caretaker government' after Gladstone had been defeated in the House of Commons, he was obliged to recognize the growing influence of Lord Randolph by inviting him to take charge of the India Office. Thus Lord Randolph became a Cabinet Minister at the early age of thirty-six.

The meteor shot up and was soon to fall from the sky. Gladstone won the general election of 1885, but in the following year went to the country again upon the question of Home Rule for Ireland and was beaten. A large number of Liberals differed from Gladstone over Home Rule, including Lord Hartington and another brilliant politician, Joseph Chamberlain, and though Salisbury was unable to induce them to join with his Tories in a coalition, he himself now had a sufficient majority to form a stable government in which Lord Randolph Churchill became not only Chancellor of the Exchequer but also the Leader of the House of Commons. He took up office in July 1886. His son relates how a Liberal friend asked him how long his leadership would last and he answered 'six months.' 'And after that?' 'Westminster Abbey.'

In describing his father's moment of triumph Winston Churchill wrote: 'To the Tory Democracy no news could be so good as his success. The English like to be governed by men they know. . . .' But the very drive, enthusiasm, invective, inventiveness, and independence that had fashioned Lord Randolph into such an exciting leader of opposition to Gladstone now proved to be fatal inside the Cabinet. For not only did he differ from his colleagues on some domestic matters but he also took a strongly individual line over foreign affairs, violently criticizing the policy of the Foreign Secretary, Lord Iddesleigh. (In Lord Randolph's younger days, Iddesleigh, then Sir Stafford Northcote, had been the official leader of the Opposition in the Commons. Lord Randolph thought so poorly of him that he nicknamed him 'the Goat': hence the formation of the 'Fourth Party.') The final clash in the Cabinet was expected to come over Lord Randolph's demand that there should be a reduction in the War Office estimates to be included in his first Budget. After discussions with the Service Ministers on the eve of Christmas Lord Randolph wrote to Lord Salisbury from Windsor Castle, where he was dining with Queen Victoria, to say that he was sure he himself would receive no support in the Cabinet for large reductions in expenditure but he felt so strongly about their necessity that without them he could not continue to be responsible for the national finances. Salisbury replied in a carefully worded letter in which he implicitly accepted the resignation of the Chancellor of the Exchequer. On 22 December 1886 Lord Randolph replied from the Carlton Club in a letter in which he also complained of the contemplated domestic legislation and the foreign policy of Lord Salisbury's Government; after dispatching it he burnt his boats by personally going to inform the editor of *The Times* of his resignation. The differences between him and Salisbury, his son argued, were 'fundamental' —differences of 'belief, of character, of aspiration.' But Lord Randolph's resignation was an entirely disinterested action: 'I had to do it,' he said, 'I could no longer be useful to them.'

There was, wrote Winston Churchill, no simple explanation for his father's resignation such as historical writers like to find. But 'the gulf that separated the fiery leader of Tory Democracy' from 'the old-fashioned conservative statesman,' Lord Salisbury, could never have been permanently bridged. Lord Randolph, however, resigned at a bad time and on a bad pretext. And because he did not want to endanger the Government, he 'delivered himself, unarmed, unattended, fettered even, to his enemies.' Nevertheless Winston made it clear (and this is confirmed by other later evidence) that Lord Randolph had not really believed that his resignation would be accepted. His friend, Joseph Chamberlain, assured him that he was indispensable. But he had ruined his career. His behaviour in the Cabinet had been sharp and overbearing. Winston omits a phrase that he used in a letter to the Secretary of State for War that fateful December, reprimanding him for 'his frightful extravagance.' Such things are neither forgiven nor forgotten. Salisbury was determined never to have Churchill back in the Cabinet, while he had also offended the Queen by writing his letter of resignation on Windsor Castle notepaper. Salisbury induced one of the Unionist Liberals, G. J. Goschen, to take Churchill's place as Chancellor; and it was ironical that Goschen succeeded in a large measure in effecting economies for which Randolph had striven in his Budget plans. But, as Winston observed, that was not the crux of the quarrel.

After his speech of resignation in the Commons in which Lord Randolph made no reference to his differences from his Cabinet colleagues over foreign and domestic policy—and thus forfeited public sympathy—he went on a long holiday abroad. On his return to England he delivered a number of public speeches demanding a liberal and progressive policy from the Salisbury

Government and continued to wage his war on extravagance in public expenditure. His son describes him as 'a lone wolf' with only one or two allies, but never contemplating joining the Liberals or creating a political 'cave.' Nevertheless in a series of speeches during the years 1887-1890 he took a highly independent line: for example, he attacked the brewers, then pillars of the Tory party, and the Irish landlords. He sided with the Opposition on the question of the Sudan. He annoyed Joseph Chamberlain by proposing to stand for a Birmingham constituency—the area that Chamberlain regarded as his own backyard—and he quarrelled with one of his political supporters, Louis Jennings, who died, in Winston's words, having 'suffered the vexations and disappointments which must always harass those who fight for lost causes and falling men.' A complicated quarrel over what was known as the Parnell Commission was, Winston observed, 'not yet illumined by the calm lamp of the historian.'

In his last years Randolph Churchill had 'collectivist tendencies' but was never seduced by the arguments for 'Fair Trade' i.e. Protection (the question over which Winston himself broke with the Tories in 1904). Lord Randolph amused himself by owning and backing horses and by constant restless travel. 'There was neither need nor place for a leader of Tory Democracy.' From 1891 he was a dying man. He found increasing difficulty in making speeches. Winston concluded his biography by saying that his father's name 'will not be recalled upon the bead-roll of either party'—the Conservatives whom he supported or the Liberals some of whose finest principles he notably sustained:

There is an England which stretches far beyond the well-drilled masses who are assembled by party machinery to salute with appropriate acclamation the utterances of their recognized fuglemen; an England of wise men who gaze without self-deception at the failings and follies of both political parties; of brave and earnest men who find in neither faction fair scope for the effort that is in them; of 'poor men' who increasingly doubt the sincerity of party philanthropy. It was to that England that Lord Randolph appealed; it was that England he so nearly won; it is by that England he will be justly judged.

There are three questions Winston Churchill considers at length in his father's biography. The first is Lord Randolph's behaviour over Ireland. This is a highly complicated question which then divided both the two principal parties. Whereas Gladstone lost some of his colleagues, including Chamberlain, because they were unionists, Lord Carnarvon, the Tory Viceroy in 1885–1886 and an old school friend of the Prime Minister, urged that the Salisbury Caretaker Government should introduce Home Rule, while Gladstone as leader of the Opposition offered to make it a non-party issue. But Randolph 'was a rock.' He was not, however, a rock over the question of coercing the Irish nationalists, about which he now changed his mind. Winston Churchill wrote that 'the controversy of 1886 can never be resolved. Whatever may happen in the future, neither party can be brought to the bar of history and proved by actual experience to be right or wrong.' 'That Lord Randolph was consistent and sincere in his opposition to Home Rule was at the time much questioned on both sides,' he added, 'and some shadow of suspicion had remained.' Nevertheless 'no unionist politician has a clearer record.' R. R. James, Lord Randolph's modern biographer, does not concur. 'Scarcely a single major political reputation,' he writes, 'emerges untarnished from the first Home Rule controversy' and 'personal conviction played little part in Churchill's action on these matters.' Certainly—Winston Churchill admitted this—his father realized that to fight the election on the Home Rule question was the surest way of dishing the Liberals under Gladstone. Even if it was true, as Winston wrote, that his father was 'never what is nowadays called an Imperialist,' he certainly profited from 'the slumbering genius of Imperialism' that Gladstone had awakened.

The second question to which Winston devoted much attention

[63]

in his biography was his father's policy as Chancellor of the Exchequer and his passion for economy, though he also suggests that his plans were of a revolutionary character aimed to assist the 'small householder,' the 'petty tradesman,' and 'the struggling professional man'—that is to say the 'lower middle classes.' The proposed Budget of 1887 (like Winston's own Budgets of the late nineteen-twenties) showed considerable ingenuity including a proposed raid on the Sinking Fund. The Cabinet does not appear to have been opposed to Lord Randolph's general proposals. The quarrel which led to his resignation took place over a mere matter of £300,000 in the army estimates. In his letter from Windsor he seemed obsessed by a death wish since he admitted that he knew he would find no supporter in the Cabinet for reducing the Service estimates. Salisbury's point of view was perfectly understandable. Great Britain in those days was an imperial power with military responsibilities stretching from southern to northern Africa and from India to Burma. Whatever criticisms might be made about British foreign policy—and Lord Randolph favoured ceasing to oppose Russia and acting in co-operation with Germany and Austria (he was later to be attracted by the aged Bismarck)—these were inexorable facts which no government could possibly ignore. In order to justify his father's conduct Winston is obliged to argue that 'this insignificant reduction of a military vote' was merely 'the peg upon which the tremendous issue of a peaceful domestic legislation as against an ambitious foreign policy supported by growing armaments depended.' 'But,' he adds, 'what a bad peg to have chosen!' There speaks the historian who himself is a skilled politician. Yet it is also a Liberal M.P. speaking who himself stands for peace, retrenchment, and reform. The innate dualism of the biographer is revealed.

Lastly, as I have already shown, Winston Churchill painted his father if not as the founder, at any rate as the 'fugleman' of Tory Democracy. In 1886 he is pictured as the isolated representative of Tory Democracy in the Cabinet who expressed his pleasure when Lord Salisbury's nephew, Arthur Balfour, his friend from the 'Fourth Party,' was invited to join the Cabinet because Churchill fancied that he had acquired an ally. So delighted was he that he prematurely sent the news of Balfour's appointment to *The Times*. In fact Balfour was no ally at all. He advised his uncle to ensure that Randolph Churchill resigned over a point on which he did not carry the sympathy of the party and observed 'we cannot turn Radical even to preserve the Tory party!'

Winston Churchill's defence of his father ultimately rests on the assumption that he bravely tried to carry forward the standard of Tory Democracy in face of the resistance of reactionary elements in the Conservative party and the Tadpoles and Tapers of Disraeli's political novels. 'Lord Randolph Churchill,' writes his son, in discussing his father's resignation, 'did not think of himself as a man, but rather as the responsible trustee of the Tory Democracy.' A speech which Lord Randolph had delivered at Dartford on 2 October 1886, fewer than three months before his resignation from the Cabinet ('probably the most important speech of his life,' his son called it) set forth 'the Tory Democratic programme.' That programme, like Lord Randolph's Budget proposals, was nominally accepted by Lord Salisbury and the other members of the Cabinet. In fact, however, Lord Randolph's whole political philosophy, so Winston Churchill contended, ran contrary to the wishes of old-fashioned Conservative statesmen who were content merely to belong to a continually governing class. So Lord Randolph fell, in Lord Rosebery's words, 'like the son of the morning ... not to rise again.'

A criticism that has been put forward of this point of view is simply that there was in fact no such thing as Tory Democracy: at most it was, in Lord Randolph's own phrase, just 'a democracy which supports the Tory party.' It is hard to derive any harmonious or integrated political outlook from Lord Randolph's speeches. The famous Dartford speech was a rag-bag of half-considered ideas for domestic legislation and foreign policy. Emphasis was laid on the need for economies and for tinkering

C*   [65]

with such matters as land purchase and tithe. Lord Randolph undoubtedly toyed from time to time with radical and even socialist notions. For he was half an aristocrat and half a radical; he was not an imperialist, yet he was the implacable foe of Home Rule for Ireland; he had a schoolboy's sense of humour, but he did not suffer fools gladly; he boasted of his Cabinet loyalty, yet he revealed the secrets of his Budget to Joseph Chamberlain, who was not a member of the Government; he liked to think of himself as a Bohemian, but he had been brought up in the purple and never shook off the extravagances of the English nobility.

Soon after Winston Churchill's biography appeared, Lord Rosebery, who was a Liberal but a close friend of Lord Randolph Churchill, with whom he was at Oxford, expressed his doubts about the whole concept of Tory Democracy. The Fourth Party, he observed, began as an 'escapade' and had no positive policy other than to harass Gladstone. It would, he thought, be hard to discern any clear or consistent programme embodied either in the antics of the 'Fourth Party,' the teachings of the young Disraeli, or the 'vague radicalism' of Lord Randolph's Dartford speech. 'The trouble is,' wrote Rosebery, 'that there are and always have been men who believe that so long as they call themselves Tories, they may blamelessly and harmlessly preach what doctrines they please.' Rosebery concluded his book on Lord Randolph by asserting that his place in history was as a political prodigy, not as the exponent of the philosophy of a Tory Democracy which, as early as 1906, just over ten years after Lord Randolph's death, was already forgotten.

The fact is that Winston Churchill's father was a 'lone wolf' or a 'shooting star' in politics. He was, Mr James believes, 'a naturally neurotic personality' who made as many enemies as he made friends. Lord Ripon described him as an 'unprincipled mountebank'; Lord Cranbrook doubted if he possessed a balanced mind; Queen Victoria noted in her journal, after Salisbury had told her that Lord Randolph was to be Chancellor of the Exchequer and Leader of the House, 'he is so mad and

odd, and he also has ill health.' Salisbury himself once observed:
'The Mahdi [leader of the Sudanese Dervishes] pretends to be
half mad and is very sane in reality; Randolph occupies exactly
the converse position.' Salisbury also remarked tartly that
Randolph's temperament was 'essentially feminine' and 'I have
never been able to get on with women.'

Lord Randolph was a spoilt child and rarely a happy man. His
latest biographer, who says this, notes that he was always on edge,
always on the move. Lord Rosebery tells us that he was eccentric
and petulant in his youth. His success when he resigned the
chairmanship of the Council of the National Union of Conservative Associations and was later reinstated went to his head. Lord
Rosebery attributes his incomplete political success partly to his
ill health and partly to the fact that he was 'in the wrong party.'
As to that, a careful reading of Winston Churchill's biography
leaves one with the impression that the biographer felt much the
same. But it was not easy for Winston to say so in a way which
would have carried conviction with his readers, when he had set
out to be an impartial biographer, lighting events with the calm
lamp of history, since he himself had just moved over from the
Conservative to the Liberal ranks. But he touched only slightly
on his father's neurotic character and state of health, since he
had a profound distaste for revealing the skeletons in family
cupboards.

Reviewing the evidence, I think one is bound to conclude that
Lord Randolph's failure was due as much as anything to his
eccentricity in personality and in judgment: one of those eccentrics who make British history tolerable and entertaining, like
Charles James Fox. He could never have become the deferential
servant of any party or any Cabinet. His restless behaviour and
overbearing manner alienated his colleagues and caused him to
quarrel with his friends. With more tact and less rashness he
might easily have gained his way in the Cabinet of 1886, but
instead Lord Randolph gave the impression of being wholly out
of sympathy with the rest of the Cabinet and of intriguing
against, or interfering with, the Foreign Secretary. It was,

observed Lord Rosebery with justice, his conduct rather than his policy that offended his colleagues.

A number of minor errors have been detected in Winston Churchill's biography of his father, such as over the time when letters were posted. But these are not significant in a book which was written more than sixty years ago. Nor does it seem to me right to criticize the biography because it was not an intimate psychological study in the modern manner. Winston Churchill was writing a political biography after the manner of his own era and trying to interpret his father's case, using, as far as possible, his own words. No one, after reading it, can imagine, as some thought at the time, that Lord Randolph was the incarnation of evil or that he was as mad as Queen Victoria and Lord Salisbury thought. He emerges as a scintillating orator, a generous-minded politician, a capable Minister. Thus the story can still be read with pleasure and profit by all who are attracted by political history, even if its argument fails in the end to carry complete conviction.

6

The World Crisis—I

TWELVE million men were killed in the world war which began in August 1914 and ended in November 1918; this fact alone justified the title commonly bestowed upon it, before a second grim conflict obscured its memory, that of the Great War. Winston Churchill's four volumes about this war, which he called *The World Crisis* (and were supplemented by his book *The Unknown War: the Eastern Front*) form a classical book which absorbs its reader today, not merely because it describes in powerful and moving language and with much intimate knowledge a story of battle and political struggle but because it lights up the follies of mankind.

But is it history? The first volume was published in April 1923, a year after Churchill had ceased to hold office following the fall of Lloyd George as Prime Minister of a coalition government. The last two volumes, though not published until March 1927, had in fact largely been completed by 1925, and the delay arose solely because in that year Churchill had again been given a principal ministerial office in Stanley Baldwin's Conservative Government. Thus this immense book was written with Churchill's usual astonishing speed while his memory of events and of the controversies which those events provoked was still extremely warm. When in 1931 he published an abridged and slightly revised edition of the entire work within the confines of one 800-page volume he explained that he had 'pruned a mass of technical detail and some personal justifications' which did not seem to him then as important as they had done ten years earlier. From October 1911 until May 1915 Churchill served as First

Lord of the Admiralty and thus had been responsible for the preparation for and waging of war; from July 1917 until the end of the war he was Minister of Munitions under Lloyd George. His conduct in the first, though not in the second capacity, was violently and astringently criticized both at the time and afterwards by fellow politicians, by serving officers, by journalists, and by some historians. So inevitably the book is in part autobiographical and is concerned—to a large but by no means excessive extent—with self-justification.

Churchill himself recognized that.

> I must [he wrote in the second volume] at the outset disclaim the position of the historian. It is not for me with my record and special point of view to pronounce a final conclusion. That must be left to others and at other times. . . . I present it as a contribution to history. . . .

Writing about the position of Turkey in the first volume, he remarked: 'I do not claim that my view was the wisest, but only to expose it to historical judgment.' On the other hand, in the introduction to his third volume, he somewhat shifted his position. He had just been reading for the first time Daniel Defoe's *Memoirs of a Cavalier:*

> In this delightful work [he observed] the author hangs the chronicle and discussion of great military events upon the thread of the personal experiences of an individual. I was immensely encouraged to find that I had been unconsciously following with halting steps the example of so great a master of narrative.

In fact it did not prove so necessary for him to justify himself in the two later volumes of the four as it had been in the first two volumes which were chiefly concerned with the period when he was in charge of the Admiralty and had been responsible for the launching of the naval operation in the Dardanelles that ultimately failed. Thus much of this great book is not merely, as he said, a contribution to history, upon which professional historians have drawn freely as an indispensable source, but also comprises a historical narrative of a high order. Churchill himself, however, was modest in the claims he made for this kind of writing:

> I set myself at each stage to answer the questions 'What happened, and Why?' I seek to guide the reader to those points where the course of events is being decided, whether it be on a battlefield, in a conning tower, in Council, in Parliament, in a lobby, a laboratory, or a workshop. Such a method is no substitute for history, but it may be an aid both to the writing and to the study of history.

Throughout his book Churchill aimed to discover and keep in mind what was happening 'on the other side of the hill.' Immediately after the war finished, even before Churchill himself started writing, many books were being published by men who had taken part in it: in the end there was hardly a single eminent figure from the German Emperor downwards to poetic subalterns who did not write his memoirs. The German commander in the Gallipoli campaign, for example, did so; so did Admiral Scheer, who was to succeed Pohl as the German Chief of Naval Staff. Sir John French, the first commander-in-chief of the British army in France, hastened into the battle of words in spite of the disapproval of King George V. It has indeed been said that of all the leading characters in the Great War only Marshal Joffre failed to write his memoirs. Much historical evidence in the form of private letters (those, for example, of Lord Fisher and Lord Haig) has also been published recently, long after Churchill's volumes appeared. At long last the official archives have been thrown open. These sources, of course, were not available to Churchill, but he did carefully examine everything that he could lay his hands on at the time when he was writing. French was his only language, but where translations of foreign books were not available he had many passages translated into English at his own expense for his own use.

Writing about the battle of the Dogger Bank of December 1914, Churchill observed in a footnote: 'I have followed in the main the account given by the official historian . . . corrected and supplemented by other first-class information.' Not only did Churchill read voraciously but because of his position in the political world he had access to information from many who had played a prominent part in the war. For instance, Sir Ian Hamilton, the British army commander in the Gallipoli campaign, was his personal friend. So was T. E. Lawrence, the almost legendary hero of the Middle East. Thus Churchill was able to draw on a vast amount of material to supplement his own memories and his own collection of official documents. He did not keep a diary, as Earl Haig did and as Lord Alanbrooke was to do in the second world war, and we know (from Lord Butler) that he did not approve of a man busily engaged at the centre of affairs occupying his time in this way. For he could recognize, no man better, that impressions jotted down in the heat of the moment or late at night after a convivial evening are liable to be emotionally distorted. But during the war he was a relatively young man and therefore his recollections of those years were exceptionally lucid: on few points have they been controverted by later historians. His opinions and interpretations have been questioned, but rarely his facts.

Is the book disqualified as history because of the personal explanations and judgments it contains? Surely not. For the historian is not concerned merely with the accumulation and sifting of facts but also with drawing his own conclusions from them. Military historians today, more than fifty years after the Great War was fought, are far from shy in examining and condemning the decisions of dead statesmen about their strategy or of dead soldiers and sailors about their tactics. Maybe because of the enormous accumulation of information of one kind or another in recent years, historians really know rather more than Churchill did when he was writing his book in the nineteen-twenties. But it is hard for modern historians to recapture, by merely exercising their imaginations, the feeling of those times or the force of the personalities involved. Indeed few historians are noted for their imaginative gifts, since, if they possessed

[72]

them, they would probably not be historians. For example, after June 1918 Churchill (as he wrote) 'managed to be present at almost every important battle during the rest of the war,' though he was neither a serving officer nor a Service Minister. He was thus in a position to record the atmosphere as well as examine the facts. His gift for exposition, for disentangling the essential from the ephemera of politics and war as he looked back upon the panorama in which he had featured only in a few scenes, makes the purely historical part of his narrative glow as vividly as that of a Gibbon or a Macaulay and outshine the dull lights shed by lesser writers.

One singular quality of this remarkable book is Churchill's ability to sketch, usually in only a few sentences, the characters of the men who played the principal parts, whether they were friends or enemies. Most of these men, unlike Churchill himself, were already old when the war began. Churchill was a raw second lieutenant in the Sudan when he first met Lord Kitchener, who was Secretary of State for War while he was at the Admiralty. Now at sixty-four Kitchener tried to apply the lessons he had learned in dealing with the barbarians in the Middle East or amateur marksmen on the South African veldt to the highly professional trench warfare on the western front. Joffre and French were both sixty-one. Helmuth von Moltke, the German Chief of Staff, was sixty-six and Fisher, when Churchill brought him back to the Admiralty as First Sea Lord, was seventy-four. Even Hamilton was sixty-one. But what is so surprising about Churchill's character sketches of these old men is that they are so free from malice. All of them had their oddities. Kitchener never married. Fisher thought in capital letters. Joffre, 'slow-thinking, phlegmatic, bucolic,' had a fetish for punctual meals. Churchill does not concern himself with their private lives, but evaluates them as statesmen, soldiers, and sailors. Some of his Cabinet colleagues treated him abominably (I shall return to this in the next chapter) but one would scarcely realize it from reading *The World Crisis*.

Most of the first two volumes deal with the British navy and the repercussions upon it of political and military events. The book opens by setting the scene:

> It was the custom in the palmy days of Queen Victoria for statesmen to expatiate upon the glories of the British Empire, and to rejoice in that protecting Providence which has preserved us through so many dangers and brought us at length into a secure prosperous age. Little did they know that the worst perils had still to be encountered and that the greatest triumphs were yet to be won.

That age looks even more distant to us now. The British never thought of themselves other than as a Great Power. Their government was still proclaiming—and almost upholding— what it called a two-power standard, which meant that it aimed to make its navy almost twice as strong as any other navy, equal in strength to its nearest rivals, those of France and Russia combined. Though war clouds floated over Europe and Africa, scene of a scramble for colonies by rival European powers, 'the British Government did not believe in the approach of a Great War, and were determined to prevent it.' A political settlement had been reached with the old enemy, France, by 1904. It was therefore a matter for surprise and concern that Germany should not merely threaten the peace, but should have the impertinence to start building enough warships to undermine the two-power standard. When in 1905 the German Emperor delivered a provocative speech at Tangier and frightened the French Government of the day, Great Britain stood firm and turned the scales to isolate Germany. Again in 1908 the Austro-Hungarian empire, allied with Germany, rocked the boat by the annexation of the Balkan provinces of Bosnia and Herzegovina, though by 1910 the annexation was accepted.

As late as 1909 Churchill and Lloyd George as radical members of Asquith's Liberal Cabinet had resisted new armaments. The First Lord of the Admiralty, Reginald McKenna, had wanted to construct additional 'Dreadnought' battleships. Though Churchill said that four were enough, in the end eight were

agreed to—a programme which, according to Sir Llewellyn
Woodward in his book *Great Britain and the German Navy*, 'had
a reassuring effect on British public opinion.' But by 1911
Churchill himself had been invited to take over the Admiralty
with instructions to overhaul its war staff and was soon engaged
in the building competition with Germany with the object of
maintaining a sixty per cent superiority in capital ships. Woodward, who has examined the question closely, does not differ
from Churchill's account in *The World Crisis*. He shows that the
proposal for a year's holiday from competitive building, put
forward by Churchill in 1912, was never practicable. It was one
of Churchill's responses to the news of a new German naval
law providing for a substantial increase in building. Though
Churchill's enthusiasm for a 'naval holiday' was genuine enough,
it soon subsided after a rebuff from the German Emperor and
Churchill then concentrated on outbuilding the Germans.

For three years Churchill worked unremittingly to get the
British navy ready for war. He realized that a British expeditionary force would have to be carried to France if Great Britain
were allied with her; that a distant but not a close blockade of
Germany would have to be maintained; and that the security of
the Channel ports was of the first importance. In July 1914 a test
mobilization was organized by Churchill instead of the usual
manoeuvres in the North Sea; thus every vessel was at its war
station when, following the Germans' violation of Belgian
neutrality, war was declared on Germany by Great Britain at
midnight on 4 August 1914. Churchill relates how, ten months
later, after he had been removed from the Admiralty, Lord
Kitchener, usually taciturn to an extreme, paid him a ceremonial
visit and said: 'Well, at any rate there is one thing they cannot
take from you: the Fleet was ready.'

When the war came, Churchill ran the naval war and Kitchener,
as Secretary of State for War, ran the land war. There was
little co-ordination either by the War Cabinet or the Committee
of Imperial Defence, a body created by Balfour in 1904. Kitchener
had enormous prestige and was a Field Marshal. His dictatorship

at the War Office was therefore accepted, though it had the notable defect of his always carrying plans in his own head and making little use of his staff. But Churchill, though he had been trained as a regular officer, had never reached above the rank of subaltern and had never served in the Navy. Yet he dominated the Admiralty by his personality, eloquence, and vigour—though not without ruffling the feelings of the Sea Lords. Admiral Sir Francis Bridgeman, who had been Churchill's first appointment as First Sea Lord before the war, had been retired in a cloud of acrimony after he had threatened to complain to the Prime Minister about Churchill's handling of the Board of Admiralty. Sir John Jellicoe, whom Churchill put in command of the Home Fleet when war came, said the First Lord out-argued his other colleagues on the Board of Admiralty; Lord Esher wrote that he was 'impatient of opinions that did not coincide with his own.' Lord Fisher, who was brought back to the Admiralty on Churchill's own insistence, wrote to Jellicoe in December 1914 that 'Winston has so monopolized all initiative in the Admiralty ... that my colleagues are only the First Lord's Registry.' One would hardly grasp this from reading the first volume of *The World Crisis* for Churchill stresses his consultations and, in particular, his co-operation with Fisher; but one needs to remember that First Lords were not expected to occupy themselves with strategy or tactics or even the structure of warships, but to push the department's estimates past the Treasury, Cabinet and House of Commons. Churchill, however, led because he was a born leader.

Churchill justly asserts that in the first months of the war of 1914–1918 the British navy accomplished all it set out to achieve. The dispositions of the fleet were made so as to cover troop convoys, to protect trade, and above all to 'muzzle' the German High Sea Fleet. At first roving German cruisers menaced merchant vessels over a wide area, but gradually they were all destroyed. Thirteen British army divisions were safely transported to France by the end of November. On 28 August 1914 a successful action, fought in the Heligoland Bight, in which

Admiral David Beatty distinguished himself, confirmed British command of the North Sea. Churchill mocks at Admiral Scheer's disappointment expressed in a book published after the war that the Grand Fleet had not immediately come out and challenged the ardent German sailors to battle. The German fleet, Churchill points out, remained during the first months of the war in river mouths and harbours fully protected by minefields and submarines, and if the Germans had really believed that the British fleet would attack them there, 'they must have rated our intelligence very low.' For as Churchill wrote in another context, Admiral Sir John Jellicoe, as commander of the Home Fleets, was the only man on either side who could have lost the war in an afternoon.

Churchill defends the navy against a number of accusations made about its actions during the first months of the conflict. He deals with the escape of the Goeben, a fast German battle-cruiser, which was stationed in the Mediterranean when war broke out and might, it was feared, interfere with the ferrying of French colonial troops across from north Africa. Although this ship was shadowed and there was a superior British naval force in the Mediterranean, it was allowed to sail safely through the Dardanelles and its arrival off Turkey encouraged that country (which had already signed a secret agreement with Germany) to enter the war. Churchill faithfully sets out the facts about this episode, as a historian should, and leaves his readers to form their own judgments. Other historians have concluded that the Admiralty was gravely at fault in not sending clear and direct instructions to the commanders concerned after war was declared and in previously dispatching badly drafted and contradictory telegrams. It was also in error in not distributing the intelligence it had available. Churchill was not himself personally concerned with drafting these instructions. Nevertheless he had assumed control over naval operations and shares the blame.

The next episode he describes which needs defence is what was known as the battle of Coronel, a lonely spot on the west coast of Chile. At the outset of the war Admiral von Spee was in command of a German squadron in the Pacific; lacking bases there, he sent one of his cruisers, the Emden, into the Indian Ocean, where it did much damage to shipping before it was finally sunk by an Australian cruiser. The rest of the squadron, including the powerful cruisers, Scharnhorst and Gneisenau, he himself led across the world to the coasts of South America. The British Admiralty rightly anticipated his intention and warned Rear-Admiral Cradock, who commanded the South American station, but it reinforced him only with an old and slow battleship, the Canopus, which alone of his ships was capable of outgunning the German cruisers, while it countermanded Cradock's orders to a fast and well-armed cruiser, the Defence, then east of South America, to join him. Here Churchill drops the mantle of the historian. 'I cannot accept,' he writes, 'for the Admiralty any share in the responsibility for what followed.' What followed was that Cradock interpreted his orders to mean he must quickly find and attack von Spee at all costs: he therefore left the old Canopus behind. On 1 November 1914 in 'thick and wicked weather' Cradock's squadron ran into von Spee, was outgunned, and wiped out: Cradock himself did not survive to tell the tale, or explain his action. For von Spee it was, in Lord Fisher's words, 'like shooting pheasants.' But five weeks later von Spee himself accidentally ran into a superior British squadron, containing two battle-cruisers under Admiral Sturdee, which was coaling in the Falkland islands. Von Spee and his ships, equally outgunned, met their doom.

The official historian blamed the Admiralty for the disaster at Coronel first because it had failed to concentrate its forces against von Spee and secondly because once again Cradock's instructions were not at all clear. Cradock was a courageous officer who evidently believed that it was his duty to tackle von Spee whatever the odds. The argument is a complicated one. But Churchill admitted that faulty wording of naval messages 'ran through much of the Naval Staff work in those early days.' Yet Churchill himself was a master of words and had been installed in the Admiralty in 1911 to overhaul the naval staff.

In a third episode, the battle of the Dogger Bank, Churchill found no need to apologize for the Admiralty. It had long been recognized that there was a danger of raids by fast German battle-cruisers across the North Sea. On 15–16 December 1914, though the Admiralty had been warned by its intelligence, which was excellent throughout the war, the brilliant Admiral von Hipper created alarm by shelling Hartlepool, Scarborough and Whitby, killing 500 civilians and narrowly escaping British revenge by the protection of bad weather. At the end of January 1915 von Hipper came out again, more modestly aiming this time to destroy fishing boats off Dogger Bank. Admiral Beatty's battle-cruiser squadron, stationed at Rosyth in the Firth of Forth, and Commodore Tyrwhitt's squadron of light cruisers and destroyers at Harwich sailed out to the attack. The two battle-cruiser squadrons met with a British superiority of five to four. The German warship Blücher was overwhelmed and sunk, but Beatty's flagship, the Lion, was seriously damaged. Because of this damage at the crucial stage in the battle he was no longer able to give orders and such orders as he gave earlier were misunderstood by his second in command. Churchill follows the official account and more or less lays the blame for failure to inflict greater damage on the admirals. At the same time he was perturbed by the fact that the Grand Fleet stationed under Jellicoe at Scapa Flow in the Orkneys had no time to reach the area of the battle. He tried to persuade Jellicoe at least to leave the Orkneys for the Firth of Forth. Jellicoe, always exceptionally sensitive to danger from submarines (so sensitive that at one time he took his fleet away to Ireland because of an unfounded report of the presence of a submarine off Scapa Flow), brusquely rejected Churchill's suggestion. Churchill noted that when in 1917 Beatty became commander-in-chief the Grand Fleet was in fact moved to the Firth of Forth.

So much for the naval operations at the beginning of the war. Afterwards the two battle fleets glared at each other across the North Sea only once venturing an encounter at Jutland, a meeting which Churchill describes purely as a historian, for by then he had left the Admiralty. The Germans as the weaker naval power concentrated henceforward on the destruction of commerce, culminating in the unrestricted submarine or U-boat warfare which was to bring in the United States of America as an associated power. But there remained the 'side-shows' or secondary matters into which Churchill was drawn while he was still at the Admiralty and which are recounted in the first two volumes of *The World Crisis*.

To speak historically of these events as secondary matters is perhaps to undervalue them, though they may have appeared to be such at the time in comparison with the maintenance of Great Britain's command of the sea. For the first was Churchill's dispatch more or less on his own authority of marines to Ostend and Antwerp; the second was his contribution in an odd way to the development of the tank, a novel weapon of war; and the third was his initiation of the Gallipoli operation, the failure of which has been a subject of controversy ever since.

In 1913 Churchill had proposed to the Committee of Imperial Defence the formation of three marine brigades, one consisting of regulars and two of volunteers or reservists. His idea was that these brigades could be used to assist in home defence during the early stages of the war. However they were not needed at home. When in August huge German armies were thrusting on Paris, in accordance with the Schlieffen plan, following a right-hand sweep through Belgium, the Belgian army had been obliged to withdraw behind the fortified lines of Antwerp where it threatened the German line of communications. Churchill then conceived the idea of dispatching a naval brigade to Ostend 'in the hopes that it would attract the attention of the enemy and give him the impression that larger forces would follow from the sea.' The troops landed on 26 August and were withdrawn less than a week later. The arrival of an unspecified British force at Ostend (in fact consisting of two thousand men) was announced by Churchill in the House of Commons. The German high command was well aware that British trained reserves were small. None the less, as Cruttwell wrote, their advent at Ostend 'greatly alarmed German headquarters.' The German operations branch recounted how 'one day countless British troops were said to have landed at Ostend and to be marching on Antwerp.' On 5 September Colonel Hentsch, a special envoy of the German supreme command, informed the 1st Army of General Kluck which had been assigned to outflank Paris: 'The English are disembarking fresh troops continuously on the Belgian coast.' The Belgians also made a sortie from Antwerp. Thus the German flank army was convinced that it was menaced and these events— more than a fantastic rumour of the arrival of Russian troops on the western front—have even been said to have contributed to the German decision to carry out a general retreat following the battle of the Marne. That, Churchill observed with historical precision, was 'clearly an exaggeration.' But his severest critics do not deny that the landing of the marines at Ostend was a fertile exercise in psychological warfare.

After the battle of the Marne it was the hope of the Allies that Antwerp could continue to hold out and unsettle the Germans. Preparations were hastily completed to send British and French reinforcements to support the garrison. But unexpectedly at the beginning of October the Belgian Government decided to leave Antwerp for Ostend. Churchill, when consulted, at once offered to dispatch a brigade of marines to the city while he himself was sent on behalf of the British Government to investigate the situation on the spot and if possible to persuade the Belgians to fight on. When informed of the approach of the relieving forces, the Belgians agreed to continue their resistance. This was felt to be all the more important because Sir John French, the British commander-in-chief, was then planning to strike on the German right.

In fact only three British naval and marine brigades arrived before the city fell, its fortifications having been pounded to pieces by German heavy artillery. The resistance had been prolonged for merely five days, but it was enough to help save the Channel ports, as Churchill argues, from destruction.

Churchill's behaviour at Antwerp subsequently came in for

much criticism. He was mocked at because, after his arrival there on 4 October, he himself offered to take over command of the British forces in the town and to resign his position as First Lord of the Admiralty, an offer which the Prime Minister, Asquith, refused. Secondly he was condemned because two and a half battalions of marines failed to get away with the others after the Belgian army had withdrawn from Antwerp and were interned in Holland. Thirdly it was said that the naval reinforcements were so poorly equipped and so badly trained as to have little fighting value. Yet of all those concerned with the waging of war on the side of the Allies—Joffre, Kitchener, and the rest—who might have been expected to arrange for the relief of Antwerp only Churchill achieved anything at all: only the British navy acted with sufficient promptitude to make any difference to the defenders, and the moral support it gave to the dispirited Belgians was genuine. Further it is claimed that the Belgians had already played their part in delaying a German advance upon the Channel ports before Churchill arrived. Still the fact remained that his influence extended the resistance without imperilling the Belgian army; and it is hard to see how he was to be blamed for the internment of some of the marines after he himself had in fact left the city.

About the invention of the tank it is necessary to say little. For many years the question of who invented the tank was one of those mires into which ardent controversialists sink. Churchill recounts how British seaplanes were employed to guard the docks and therefore help at the beginning of the Great War with the aerial defence of England. Some of these naval aircraft were established at Dunkirk and use was made of the armoured motor cars to enable advanced air bases to be set up fifty miles inward from the French coast. The Germans proceeded to cut gaps in the roads which the armoured cars were unable to cross. Churchill then raised the question whether a way could be found by which armoured vehicles could overcome trenches. Thus 'the needs and activities of the naval aeroplanes,' Churchill wrote in the first volume of *The World Crisis* 'led directly to the development of the armoured car, and the armoured car led directly to the birth of the tank, which was in essence only an armoured car capable of crossing trenches.' In September 1914, at Churchill's request, designs for tanks or cognate vehicles were made by a firm that did work for the Admiralty. When at the end of the war Churchill became Minister of Munitions he pushed forward with the production of tanks, which had taken two years to come into being. But the truth was that even by the time the war ended the tanks employed by the British army were too few in number and too primitive in design to be decisive weapons of war. Nevertheless, like the arrival of the British marines at Ostend and Antwerp, they had a striking moral effect on the enemy. And as Napoleon observed, in war the moral to the material is as three to one.

Churchill the historian recognized and wrote in *The World Crisis* that Churchill the First Lord of the Admiralty had taken upon himself duties not strictly coming within his sphere. There is always, as he well knew, an unanswerable case for doing nothing, 'especially for doing nothing yourself.' 'Looking back with after-knowledge and increasing years,' he wrote, 'I seem to have been too ready to undertake tasks which were hazardous or even forlorn'—the air defence of Great Britain, the Dunkirk guerrilla (another attempt, as at Ostend, to confuse the enemy in September 1914), the defence of Antwerp, the unauthorized experiments with tanks. A fertile imagination, a gift for persuasion, an unwillingness to be baulked by events all turned Churchill into a source of scandal to Service chiefs in two years. They whispered their resentment at his extra-mural activities to politicians and allowed it to colour their memoirs. Churchill the historian understood all that, but was unrepentant.

I now turn to Churchill's account of the Gallipoli campaign. At the end of 1914 Churchill wrote to the Prime Minister reviewing the war situation. He expressed the view that neither side possessed the strength to penetrate the other's lines on the western front, which was now frozen into a state of trench warfare. He asked: 'Are there not other alternatives than sending out armies to chew barbed wire in Flanders?' He first suggested the seizure of the island of Borkum in the North Sea as a preliminary to a decisive campaign in the Baltic. The idea of sending a British fleet into the Baltic was enthusiastically favoured, if insufficiently studied, by the aged Lord Fisher who, at Churchill's request, had returned to the Admiralty as First Sea Lord at the end of October. But the difficulties appeared insuperable and Churchill turned to another scheme, originally put forward earlier when Turkey first declared war on the Allies, for an amphibious operation against Turkey to influence and rally the Balkans and assist Russia. It had then been suggested that the best way of defending the Suez Canal, which it was wrongly feared would be attacked by the Turks, would be to assault the Gallipoli peninsula which guarded the entry to the Dardanelles straits leading to the Sea of Marmara and Constantinople: it was estimated that an army of only 60,000 men would be required for such a project. When Churchill was assured, however, that no troops of any sort were available, Vice-Admiral Carden, who commanded at the Dardanelles, was asked whether he thought it was feasible to force the Straits with warships alone. Carden answered that 'they might be forced by extended operations with a large number of ships.' Accordingly a plan was drawn up and the project approved by the War Council on 28 January 1915. Arthur Balfour observed that day that he 'found it difficult to imagine a more helpful project.' Fisher, who still hankered after the Baltic scheme, was opposed to such an action in the Dardanelles without adequate support from the army; Admiral Sir Henry Jackson was cautious and believed troops would be required at some stage; and, since Churchill wrote his book, it has emerged that the lower echelon of Admiralty experts, including the historians Corbett and Richmond, all along pressed for the dispatch of a military force. Lord Kitchener, secretive, taciturn, and reserved, though seemingly an 'easterner' at heart, blew hot and cold, but eventually agreed to send the 29th Division, a first-class division formed from regular units, to the eastern Mediterranean. He took the view that if the Navy failed to force the Dardanelles, then the Army would have to finish the job.

On 19 February 1915 the naval bombardment of the outer forts began and by 2 March the whole of the outer defences of the Dardanelles had been destroyed by naval gunfire. After that, however, the operations slowed down. Naval landing parties met effective resistance; indirect fire on the inner forts did little damage owing to inadequate spotting for the artillery; howitzers shelled the British warships and compelled them to keep moving. On 18 March Admiral de Robeck, who had replaced Carden in the command, sent the whole Allied fleet into an attack on the Narrows. The inner forts were practically silenced, but two British battle-cruisers struck enemy mines which had been missed by the sweepers and before nightfall the action was called off. In addition a French battleship had been sunk and three other British vessels were badly damaged. But there were only sixty-one British casualties. Churchill himself assumed that the naval attack would be renewed later after better minesweeping; but by now General Ian Hamilton with the 29th Division and other troops amounting to some 50,000 men had arrived on the scene and after consultations with de Robeck they between them decided to abandon the purely naval assault and to let the army attempt a landing on the beaches of Gallipoli.

Hamilton and his troops had been rushed out. Kitchener had finally overcome his hesitations and decided to see the thing through to the end. But neither strategic appreciations nor proper plans had been made; the soldiers had not been tactically loaded into the transports; Hamilton was provided with sketchy orders and an inaccurate map. Understandably he decided to withdraw his forces from the Aegean islands to Alexandria to re-form. This gave the enemy time to prepare for the expected land assault. General Liman von Sanders took over the command and the Turks were reinforced with men and guns. When finally on 25 April British, French and Dominion troops landed on the Gallipoli peninsula they sustained heavy losses. Though by 9 May they had secured footholds at several points, they were soon bogged down and Hamilton was demanding reinforcements. It had been in no real sense a combined operation that would have needed more elaborate planning, for the absence of which Churchill himself was partly at fault. When the army action had been reduced more or less to a standstill, de Robeck asked if he should resume a naval attack in support of the army. Not only did the Admiralty refuse him permission, but proceeded to withdraw from the Dardanelles his best battleship, the Queen Elizabeth, through fear of German submarines.

Four days later what Churchill called a 'sulphurous meeting' of the War Council was held in London. Kitchener complained about the withdrawal of the Queen Elizabeth. Fisher announced that he had been opposed to the Dardanelles operation from the start and next day he resigned. Churchill was awarded the blame. Asquith, under pressure from Lloyd George, formed a Coalition Government with the Conservatives and Balfour replaced Churchill at the Admiralty. Churchill agreed to take the sinecure post of Chancellor of the Duchy of Lancaster on the understanding that he would still be a member of the War Council; for he wanted to help see the Dardanelles campaign through to a successful conclusion. But in spite of large reinforcements which arrived in the theatre after some delay and a fresh landing in August at Suvla bay, it was eventually resolved to abandon the whole campaign. By the end of the year the remaining Allied forces had been withdrawn from the peninsula without loss. But the British and French soldiers who had taken part suffered over 250,000 casualties out of a total of 489,000 men engaged.

In *The World Crisis* Churchill defends the decision to undertake the purely naval attack on the Dardanelles first because it was a worth-while operation to help our Russian allies that could be carried out with surplus resources after all other naval needs in the war had been fully provided; for the most part the warships that were risked were 'valueless for any other purpose'; and history shows—the evidence of von Sanders's memoirs alone indicates it—that the naval attack in March came extremely near to success. The Turks then fully expected a breakthrough would be achieved and the Sultan's Court was ready to withdraw from Constantinople to Asia Minor. At one stage the long-range guns of the Turkish forts had scarcely any shells left. Turkish opinions collected after the war indicated, so Churchill wrote, that if the attack of 18 March had been renewed it would have ended in victory. As it was, the interval that supervened before the army could be brought in eliminated all chances of surprise and enabled the Turks to reinforce their defences.

Churchill's part in the Gallipoli operation was not only condemned at the time and cost him his place at the Admiralty, but his account has since been criticized adversely by various modern historians. Robert Rhodes James wrote in 1965:

> Very recently opinion has been hardening against Churchill's part in its initiation. As new information slowly emerges it is being widely realized that *The World Crisis* is an incomplete account, which has hitherto received an inadequate analysis.

In fact long before this both the official Australian historian of the campaign, Bean, and General J. F. C. Fuller, a military historian of some standing, had been extremely critical, Fuller maintaining that 'Mr Churchill forced his Dardanelles card on the Government and the Government was incapable of playing the hand.' An American writer, Trumbull Higgins, had argued that expert opinion at the Admiralty never in fact approved of the naval attempt, as Churchill contends in *The World Crisis* that it did, though incidentally Higgins admits that the responsibility for the failure of the campaign cannot be laid on Churchill's shoulders alone. Llewellyn Woodward questions whether a purely naval operation could possibly have had valuable results without a landing on the Gallipoli peninsula. Finally A. J. P. Taylor asks whether even had the operation been a success, it would have been a worth-while contribution to winning the war; for the Germans would have fought on even if Turkey had been knocked out.

In his book Churchill writes less as an historian than as one who expounded the course of events for submission to future historical judgment. Naturally one can agree with Mr James that *The World Crisis* does not offer a complete account; but the fact remains that the purely naval operation very nearly achieved its purpose. It cost few casualties apart from the loss of obsolete battleships. The British Government could have called it off in the spring, but did not elect to do so. It was Lord Kitchener who in the end—and, it can be argued, belatedly—decided to go the whole hog with the army, launching a totally unprepared and unthought-out campaign, which finally cost over a quarter of a million casualties. (It may be added in historical retrospect that it also inflicted 300,000 Turkish casualties and that such a bill was not excessive compared with the total losses on the western front.)

As to the question whether the attempt was worth-while at all, many responsible people believed that it was both at the time and since. Von Falkenhayn, the Chief of the German General Staff, thought it would greatly have helped Russia (and it was in fact an appeal from Russia that first induced Churchill to propose and support it). Duff Cooper, who was not merely a historian but also himself became a Service Minister, wrote in his biography of Haig that 'the effect would certainly have been prodigious both by its influence on enemy and neutral psychology and by enabling the Allies of the west to join hands with Russia.' Arthur Balfour, a former Prime Minister and Foreign Secretary, had, as we have seen, 'found it difficult to imagine a more helpful operation.' Both Lord Ismay, a professional soldier and Captain Roskill, a distinguished naval historian, were convinced that Churchill's strategic ideas in the Great War were afterwards vindicated. It has well been observed by another historian that 'Sir Winston had the one strategic idea in the war. He did not believe in throwing away masses of people to be massacred.'

If any one man is to be condemned for the failure of the Dardanelles campaign it is surely Kitchener, not Churchill. First he refused the use of land forces altogether, leaving it to the Navy to try its luck; then, because he feared that Allied prestige would suffer in the East, he insisted on the continuation of the attempt, which required opposed landings on the beaches, and finally threw in reinforcements too few or too late. His latest

biographer does not attempt to defend either the initial delays
or the entirely inadequate appreciation and planning at the War
Office. Churchill recalls how in the middle of July 1915 he had
written in a general appreciation of the situation that 'we have
always sent two-thirds of what was necessary a month too late.'

But Churchill himself blamed no one. In his book he 'tried to
show . . . the interplay of forces and sequence of events in this
tragedy.' He realized that many more documents would be
forthcoming and that tormenting controversies would follow.
He expounded the 'appalling difficulties and cruel embarrass-
ments' of the actors in the tragedy. And writing as a historian in
1949 he added this:

> I was ruined for the time being in 1915 over the Dardanelles,
> and a supreme enterprise was cast away through my trying
> to carry out a major and combined operation of war from a
> subordinate position.

The historical lessons were learned in the second world war;
and that they were so learned was due at least in part to the clear,
if understandably partial, account of what had happened set out
in *The World Crisis*. Seldom do historians fulfil as useful a
purpose as that.

7

The World Crisis—II

THE book, *The World Crisis,* contains two of the finest battle pieces which Churchill ever wrote, that on the battle of the Marne and that on the battle of Jutland. It is no doubt proof that Churchill primarily envisaged his book as an apologia that in the first volume, as he originally wrote it, the battle of the Marne was mentioned only incidentally. But after the whole of *The World Crisis* had been completed and it had emerged as one of the major historical writings on the Great War, Churchill determined in revising it for the one-volume edition of 1931 to add a full account, observing: 'One must suppose upon the whole that the Marne was the greatest battle ever fought in the world.'

When I first read Churchill's descriptions of these two battles—so clear, so concise, and so persuasive—some twenty-five years ago, they made an indelible impression upon my mind; I cannot believe that anyone who enjoys the reading of history can fail even now to be excited by them. The Marne, as Churchill said, decided the war. It was there that the plan blessed by the celebrated German general, the elder von Moltke, of surprising the French by a swift and sweeping offensive through Belgium, ground to a halt. Churchill himself, writing before the Great War, had forecast that within twenty days of its outbreak the French would be driven back towards Paris and that within forty days they would be able to launch a counter-offensive, and this was what happened. Churchill's account of the battle has been criticized because he is said to have given too much credit for the victory to General Galliéni, the military governor of Paris.

It is asserted that it was always the intention of Marshal Joffre to counter-attack the Germans after they had outrun their line of communications.

The original German plan had been to outflank Paris, but it had afterwards been decided that the German armies, once they were stretched across France as far as the Vosges mountains had not the resources to envelop this fortified capital city. The army on the German right, the First Army under General von Kluck, therefore moved down east of Paris and thus presented a target for an attack by Galliéni to whom Joffre had given control of the fresh French Sixth Army. On the evening of 4 September 1914 Galliéni, in a telephone conversation with Joffre, obtained his permission to attack von Kluck's army north of the River Marne. On 5 September, in what was called the battle of the Ourcq, Galliéni struck. The French assault not merely deranged von Kluck's army but also the German Third Army under Bulow, which had followed the First Army in echelon. In wheeling to the right to confront the danger from Paris a gap was opened between these two German armies into which later the British expeditionary force was able to thrust. Thus a long British retreat changed into a sudden and unexpected advance. Meanwhile Joffre had given orders for a general offensive starting on 6 September on the 200-mile front between Paris and the Swiss frontier. It lasted for three days. Though few lives were lost on either side, everywhere the Germans were pinned down. Churchill quotes Colonel Bauer, a German staff officer: 'Desperate panic seized the entire army . . . [the younger] Moltke completely collapsed.' Another German staff officer, Colonel Hentsch, whom Churchill called 'a peripatetic focus of defeat,' was sent by Moltke with the power to order withdrawal from the Marne to the Aisne. Obeying this order, five of the seven German armies engaged proceeded to retreat.

In war, as in life, single episodes are liable to be decisive. But in battles it is the commanders-in-chief who receive the blame for defeat and therefore deserve to claim the credit for victory. No doubt Joffre always intended a counter-offensive when the opportunity presented itself. Yet he had envisaged abandoning Paris and declaring it an open town, while he had earlier told Sir John French that he did not contemplate a battle on the Marne. When von Kluck exposed himself to the flank attack from Paris Galliéni set the battle in motion, just as the arrival of Colonel Hentsch, with plenary authority from Moltke to order a German retirement, brought it to its strange end.

There is another curious episode connected with the battle of the Marne: before the battle the German supreme command had withdrawn two of its best corps, including one regular Guards division, from the French front and sent it to the Russian front on the eve of the battle of Tannenberg which was about to be fought in east Prussia. In fact these two corps arrived too late to take part in the battle and were not wanted anyway. The decision to withdraw this force was taken, according to Churchill, because the younger Moltke believed that the battle in France had already been won. This explanation, however, is now said to have been invented afterwards.

The British expeditionary force under Sir John French advanced forty miles during the battle of the Marne and, in Churchill's words, 'probed its way into the German liver.' Yet it had nearly not been there at all. A fortnight before the battle it had been compelled to retreat from Mons and General French had been infuriated with the neighbouring French general (Lanrezac) for not giving him sufficient notice of his intention to retire and thus, as he considered, leaving him in the lurch. In consequence the British commander-in-chief had seriously considered retiring towards Havre to refit, which would have meant cutting his army off completely from the French. Kitchener was so perturbed by this idea that he himself had gone to Paris wearing the uniform of a field-marshal and ordered French to meet him there, Kitchener's object being to dissuade French from his intention. Churchill, who was a personal friend of French, had laboured by letter to make him change his mind and it is also said that one of his staff officers, Henry Wilson, 'cajoled him' into doing so. But, in spite of what Churchill says in *The World Crisis*, it appears that Kitchener's intervention was decisive.

In writing about the battle of Jutland, as about the battle of the Marne, Churchill aimed to give a completely impartial account. Nevertheless although the battle took place a year after he himself had left the Admiralty he was indirectly involved in it; for he had approved the appointment of Sir John Jellicoe as commander-in-chief and was responsible before the war for planning the resources of the Grand Fleet including its armament and munitions. Just as he has subsequently been accused of being unfair to Joffre in his story of the Marne, so he has been said to have done less than justice to Jellicoe in writing about Jutland; indeed Jellicoe himself resented what Churchill wrote.

The battle was unique, for it was the only one during the war in which the two great fleets actually met and fired at one another. Yet in fact neither fleet was prepared to fight it out to the finish. Jellicoe, as Churchill relates, had informed the Admiralty soon after the war began that he did not intend to jeopardize the integrity of his fleet by taking dangerous tactical risks: 'If, for instance, the enemy's battlefleet were to turn away from an advancing fleet, I should assume that his intention was to lead us over mines and submarines, and I should refuse to be so drawn.' As his conduct at Scapa Flow showed, Jellicoe was possessed by an almost pathological dread of submarines and mines; and the events in the Dardanelles and elsewhere merely served to heighten his fears. The German high command, now under the bold Admiral Scheer, though it was ready to trail its coat, equally had no intention of risking being blown to pieces by a superior enemy.

In the last week of May 1916 Admiralty intelligence discovered that the German fleet was coming out and on this occasion Jellicoe at Scapa Flow had time to intervene. As far as he could, he kept control of all dispositions in his own hand. The two fleets which put to sea on 30 May constituted, in Churchill's words, 'the culminating manifestation of naval force in the history of the world.' On the afternoon of 31 May the battle-cruisers of the two fleets ran into each other, the British which had been sent ahead under Beatty, the Germans under Hipper. A running fight ensued. Although Beatty had six ships and the Germans only five, Hipper had the best of the combat: two British battle-cruisers were sunk beneath the waves and Beatty's flagship, the Lion, was set on fire. Moreover the Fifth Battle Squadron, consisting of four fast Dreadnought battleships which Jellicoe had given Beatty as reinforcements, failed until too late to take part in the contest. This Churchill attributes (rightly, as is clear from Professor Marder's account) to misunderstandings between the two admirals. Hipper then fell back with the intention of drawing the remaining British battle-cruisers, still fighting gallantly, on to the guns of the main German fleet; but Beatty, in Churchill's view, tried to lead Hipper and the German battle fleet up to Jellicoe.

Such were the preliminaries of the contest. Jellicoe knew what was happening and had now to deploy his fleet for battle. He could deploy from column into line either on the right or starboard division of his fleet (nearer to the approach of his enemy) or on his left or port division; or, according to Churchill, he might also have deployed on his centre, taking the lead with his own flagship. In fact he decided to deploy on the port division, while Beatty had to steam across the front of the line of battle to take his position in the van. The Fifth Battle Squadron of fast battleships, which had arrived too late to help Beatty in his battle with Hipper, was not even able to do that and took up a position in the rear and again therefore played virtually no part in the proceedings. During the ensuing engagement, which lasted about ten minutes, yet another British battle-cruiser was sunk. But Scheer found the pace too hot for him and made off south-westward covering his retirement by a torpedo attack and smoke screens and soon disappeared into the mist. Yet he still had to get back home. So twenty minutes later he turned his fleet round and for a second time charged into the Grand Fleet. He had hoped, Churchill thought, to get across its tail: 'Instead of this he ran right into the centre of the British fleet, which was certainly the last thing he sought.' Nevertheless he successfully repeated his previous manœuvre, if with less aplomb than the first time, and leaving his tired battle-cruisers to cover his retreat again drew off westwards: 'The range opened, the Fleets separated, and Scheer vanished from Jellicoe's view—this time for ever.'

It was now nearly dark and the Germans were far from home. Jellicoe rejected the idea of a night action, hoping to renew the battle in the morning. He set off on a course which would have enabled him to catch the German High Sea Fleet if it attempted to make for Heligoland or the mouth of the river Ems. In fact Scheer made for home by way of the Horn Reef which Churchill claims was his shortest and *prima facie* his most likely route. (Churchill does not mention that Jellicoe dispatched a mine-layer to the Horn Reef and sent a flotilla to report.) The German battle fleet crossed to the rear of the British Grand Fleet in the course of the night. Though firing took place between the lighter units of the two fleets and though Jellicoe received a report from the Admiralty which indicated that the Germans were making for the Horn Reef, he decided to disregard these pieces of evidence and continued to steam southward. During the night British destroyers to the rear of the Grand Fleet suffered heavily as the Germans worked their way past them. Before day broke they were out of reach of the British battleships. 'The Germans loudly proclaimed a victory,' wrote Churchill. 'There was no victory for anyone, but they had good reason to be content with their young navy . . . The British battle fleet was never seriously in action.'

Churchill offers various reasons for the disappointing result of the battle from the British point of view. The British losses he attributes to the fact that the German armour was better distributed on their ships, whereas the magazines of the British battle-cruisers were insufficiently protected. Moreover British naval constructors had not taken sufficient account before the war of the plunging character of enemy gunfire. (In technical phrase-ology the magazines were not flash-tight.) Finally the British armour-piercing shells were inferior. As to the tactics, Jellicoe's caution is not, in so many words, impugned: 'The ponderous, poignant responsibilities borne successfully, if not triumphantly, by Sir John Jellicoe during two years of faithful command, constitute unanswerable claims to the lasting respect of the nation.' This combination of magnanimity spiced with a touch of irony is Churchill at his most typical. Equally he defends himself for approving Jellicoe's enunciation of his tactics in 1914, arguing that the circumstances at Jutland were different. Certainly the German battle fleet carried no mines and was accompanied by no submarines. Apart from torpedoes, these were the weapons that Jellicoe feared most.

Churchill's suggestion that Jellicoe could have deployed more rapidly on his flagship before the first encounter with Scheer has not been accepted by naval opinion and, according to Jellicoe himself, would merely have bunched the fleet badly in case of torpedo attack. The contradictory and, in one case, unreliable, nature of the intelligence received by Jellicoe during the night after the battle makes it difficult to blame him, as Churchill does by implication, for failing to grasp the direction in which the German High Sea Fleet was really heading. Churchill has also been criticized by Jellicoe's admirers for being too kind to Beatty. But, on the whole, Churchill sets out the essential facts and arguments about the battle fairly enough; and few today would hail Jellicoe as one of the great captains of Britain's once famous navy.

These were the two big set battles of the war in western Europe in which British forces took part. There were also of course long, expensive and fruitless offensives by both sides; Champagne-Artois and Champagne-Loos in 1915, Verdun and the battles of the Somme in 1916–1917, and the battle of Passchendaele in 1917, but, in Churchill's view, these cannot properly be called battles since a battle is a climax in war when 'the whole of the resources of either side that can be brought to bear are, during the course of a single episode, concentrated upon the enemy.' Both as a Minister and as a private member of parliament

Churchill had protested about the extravagant expenditure of lives in these drawn-out offensives which belonged to the war of attrition. He reiterates this opinion in *The World Crisis:* 'There was surely no policy in *seeking* offensives with immature formations or during the period when no answer to the machine-gun existed.' Churchill relates the doubts of the Prime Minister and how he had vainly tried to restrain Haig, but had been compelled to give way. Churchill is particularly critical of Passchendaele which was fought by Haig to help the then dispirited French and also with the aim of clearing the Belgian coast of Germans and thus checking the submarine menace still at its height. Churchill refutes the second motive—saying that submarines could operate just as successfully from German harbours—but there seems no doubt that the First Lord of the Admiralty had asked Haig for such an offensive. Churchill also claims that the disastrous defeat of the Italians at Caporetto in October 1917 might have been averted if the British military authorities had not neglected the Italian front for the sake of Passchendaele. But it can be argued that it is just as likely that if the British and French forces had been sent to Italy they would have been engulfed in the Italian defeat.

Churchill pays tribute to the persistence of Douglas Haig who took over from Churchill's friend, French, at the end of 1915 and endured his ordeal with 'phlegm, temper and fortitude'; but Churchill does not mince words about the offensives. The first battle of the Somme was extremely costly in lives and achieved an advance of two-and-a-half miles; at the time Churchill described it as 'a welter of slaughter which gained no strategic advantage of any kind and left the British and French armies weaker than the Germans.' The second battle of the Somme, promoted by the upstart French General Nivelle, who had the idea he could break through the German lines with the aid of artillery, received the approval both of Haig and Lloyd George. Nivelle had in 1916 distinguished himself by recapturing Fort Douaumont during the battle for Verdun. Nivelle, Churchill observes, 'had not only captured Fort Douaumont, but he had an English mother': thus he spoke excellent English and so captivated Lloyd George that to Haig's annoyance the Prime Minister placed the general direction of the campaign in Nivelle's hands. Haig played his part loyally, but it was another disaster; Nivelle was dismissed and French troops mutinied. Nivelle's costly offensive (April 1917) was followed by the Passchendaele offensive in the autumn, planned by Haig as a preliminary to reconquering Belgium and to relieve pressure on the French; this was followed by the battle of Cambrai (November 1917) in which nearly 400 tanks were used to open the attack without any artillery preparation. A penetration of six miles was effected, 10,000 prisoners were taken, and 200 guns captured. But as there were no reserves, the Germans were able to carry out a decisive counter-attack.

Churchill's broad descriptions of these Allied offensives—and of Ludendorff's final series of fruitless assaults on the western front in 1918—have not been confuted, but the argument that he sustained about them has not been generally accepted by historians; for he maintains that such offensives were wasteful mistakes and that it would have been wiser to have stood on the defensive until more tanks were ready, meanwhile concentrating British efforts on other fronts, for example in Italy and the Balkans. Churchill argues that in every one of these offensives the attacker lost much more heavily than the defender and that during the offensives of 1915–1917 the Allies suffered larger casualties than the Germans. Churchill set out his case in a chapter called 'The Blood Test' published in 1927 and remaining unaltered in 1931 and 1939. His figures were challenged by Sir Charles Oman, the military historian, in a book entitled *The World Crisis: A Criticism* published in 1927. Oman asserted that Churchill had underestimated the German losses in the battle of the Somme. Somewhat similar figures to Oman's are given in Cyril Fall's recent *History of the Great War*. The official history, too, contends that the German casualties on the western front exceeded those of the French and British combined. Churchill also maintains that in the battle of Verdun, where the Germans took the offensive, their losses were as 3 to 2; but Cruttwell in another book on the war asserts that they were about equal. These statistical arguments are highly complicated and have not been satisfactorily resolved by historians even today; but if, as seems likely from the facts presented by the latest historians of the Great War, Churchill's figures were wrong, then it weakens his case and the case of 'the Easterners' against 'the Westerners' in their criticisms of the strategy of the Allies in the war of 1914–1918.

The case for the Westerners, as put forward, for example by General Callwell, was that the French front was the German's weakest not their strongest point. Here the Allies were operating on inner lines close to their bases. 'Here the British and French troops were easily assembled and defeat there meant disaster for the Germans.' If it is true that Haig—or Falkenhayn (in command at Verdun)—elected to attack their enemy at their strongest points, it was because a break-through at these points would have been decisive and might have won the war. It was because fresh American troops were known to be coming to take their places on the French front that General Ludendorff, brought from his triumphs in Russia to take command of the German armies, launched in the spring of 1918 'the greatest onslaught in the history of the world.' Here in fact the last battle was won by the Allies and victory gained.

Since Churchill wrote *The World Crisis* another world war has been fought with himself as British Prime Minister and Minister of Defence and in that war many kinds of alternative campaigns, or side-shows, if you like, to the waging of war in France were tried: the Norwegian campaign, the Libyan and Tunisian campaigns, the campaign in East Africa, the Sicilian and Italian campaigns, the Greek campaign. Nevertheless in the end the decisive campaign in the west had still to be fought in France where American and British troops landed on D-day in 1944. By then the German armies had been weakened in Russia; yet they had stopped the Allied advance in Italy and still put up a tremendous battle in France and on their own western frontiers.

On the other hand, in 1917 Russia had already been knocked out of the war and it is difficult to believe, even if the other campaigns in the Middle East, at Salonika and in Italy had gone better than they did, that the Germans could have been defeated by 1918 without the war of attrition in France. That was Haig's belief from which he never swerved. History, it has been said, repeats itself with differences and it is the differences that make all the difference. Nevertheless the events of the war of 1939–1945 may be said to shed light on the historical argument about the earlier war.

In order to break the deadlock on the western front Churchill advocated not only action in other theatres of war but the exploitation of new weapons. We have seen how when he was at the Admiralty he authorized experiments with caterpillar vehicles, the forerunners of the tank. In the last year-and-a-half of the war he did all he could to press on with the production of tanks. He had consistently stressed the importance of doing so. In a speech delivered as a private member during a secret session of the House of Commons in May 1917, he had pointed out that the Allies not only possessed no preponderance in artillery or superiority in the air but they had not yet got the number of tanks they needed nor had they discovered any other mechanical means of piercing fortified lines defended by German troops. He had therefore pleaded against 'fresh, bloody and disastrous adventures before the Americans came.' That speech impressed Lloyd George and persuaded him to invite Churchill to join his coalition government. After Churchill entered that government he wrote, in December 1917, a paper for the War Cabinet urging 'an unprecedented development of mechanical and aeronautical war' and in March 1918 he wrote another paper in which he advocated the employment of novel methods to overcome physical and mechanical difficulties: 'Gas,' he wrote, 'will give you one of these. Tanks, if we develop them could give us at least two of the highest order.' Thus, as the war was drawing towards its end, tanks were still 'undeveloped,' though Churchill planned by April 1919 to produce over 3,000 tanks of various kinds. But in September 1918, in the last campaign, the British Tank Corps had only 600 or 700 tanks to use in action. On 18 July the French General Mangin had successfully counter-attacked the Germans with 330 small tanks and when in September the British at last forced the Germans to abandon the line of the Somme 100 tanks were in use. But they still frequently broke down through mechanical defects.

It may well have been as a historian that Churchill looked on this problem of breaking the military deadlock; for in the history of war it has invariably been the invention of new weapons—from the scythed chariot to the stirruped cavalry horse, from the long bow to the bayonet, from the Maxim gun to the modern heavy tank—that has enabled armies to achieve surprise and win unexpected victories. The first use of poison gas by the Germans and the first proper use of tanks by the British at Cambrai both had the merit of surprise. Churchill realized that it was only by such methods that the obstacles presented by barbed wire entanglements, by trenches and pill-boxes protected by machine-gun fire might be overcome.

In a fine historical chapter in which he described how un-restricted submarine warfare, one of the Germans' surprise weapons, was defeated by novel methods such as Q ships, submarine nets, depth charges, and horned mines, Churchill illustrated this historical point (though he paid full tribute to Lloyd George's insistence, in the teeth of Admiralty resistance, on regular escorted convoys). As Minister of Munitions Churchill hoped to apply mechanical devices and inventions to the defeat of the Germans on land as had been done at sea.

I have discussed how Churchill as a historian analysed the events of the first world war, how he described the emergence of the costly military stalemate in France, and how he had advocated attempts to defeat the Germans and their allies on other fronts and to overcome trench warfare by new weapons. In this book Churchill does not probe into political questions in detail, though he outlines the German mistakes which led to their defeat: he saw that the entry of the United States into the war was the crucial fact. 'Either Russian endurance or German impatience,' he wrote, 'was required to secure entry of the United States and both were forthcoming.' He considered that the German General Staff committed three critical errors: the first was the invasion of Belgium, the second unlimited submarine warfare, and the third the 1918 offensive in France; but for the latter the Germans might have gained a negotiated peace.

As to the conduct of individuals, though it is claimed that Churchill was unfair to Joffre and Jellicoe, in fact he did not gainsay their motives and put the case for what they did or failed to do. He thought that President Wilson would have been wiser to lead his country into the war in 1915 and hints that Jellicoe might have displayed greater acumen. But to everyone he was as fair as most historians are and he praised the high services of men to the State. He does not, for example, complain about the way in which Lord Fisher behaved to him, though it was Fisher's resignation as First Sea Lord, the post to which Churchill had brought him back in the teeth of misgivings, that brought down the Government. Churchill even suggested that it was in part the munitions shortage that caused this. Yet in a letter that Churchill wrote to Kitchener on 21 May 1915 he said that Fisher 'went mad' and had 'a fit of megalomania.' The astonishing letter that Fisher wrote to Asquith demanding dictatorial control of the Admiralty as the price of his return is sufficient proof of that. But in his book Churchill stresses Fisher's splendid work for the navy. At the time of the Gallipoli campaign Churchill received a letter from Ian Hamilton dated 12 March 1915 in the course of which Hamilton wrote 'I must not in loyalty tell you too much of my War Office conversation.' Churchill did not comment, as he well might have done, on how odd it was that there should be secrets between the head of the War Office and the head of the Admiralty on the eve of a combined operation.

Lord Beaverbrook, who because of his friendship with Bonar Law, leader of the Conservative party, knew what was happening behind the scenes, wrote that Churchill was wrong about the reasons he gave for the fall of the Government in May 1915 and 'was ignorant of what was going on and kept in the dark by his colleagues.' Asquith in fact deliberately made Churchill the scapegoat for the failure at the Dardanelles. After he resigned office at the end of 1915 he sought a command overseas and Sir John French as commander-in-chief was willing to give him a brigade. Little did he know that this was countermanded by Asquith himself and that it was Haig who instead made him a battalion commander of the Scots Fusiliers. When, after the elaborate intrigue that brought down Asquith, Lloyd George became Prime Minister, not only did he refuse to bring his old friend and colleague back into the Government but denied him a command in East Africa. Lloyd George said that he had to consider the 'feelings of widows and orphans of Gallipoli' and blamed Churchill for bringing Turkey into the war against the Allies. It was only when Lloyd George, partly because of the brilliance of Churchill's speech in the secret session, decided it was safer to invite Churchill to join the Government then to leave him as a critic outside it, that the Prime Minister took courage to offer him a post either at the Air Ministry or Ministry of Munitions. Writing about this offer, Churchill observed that Bonar Law 'who had always been a friend' returned a stiff answer to Conservative protests over his appointment. In fact, as Beaverbrook showed clearly, Bonar Law had never been Churchill's friend and had been largely responsible for his dismissal by Asquith from the Admiralty in 1915. When Lloyd George wanted to bring back Churchill, Bonar Law had resisted it as best he could and had only been eventually induced to agree out of loyalty to Lloyd George. For these and other men, such as Sir Henry Wilson who at the end of the war became Chief of the Imperial General Staff and was a notorious intriguer, Churchill has in *The World Crisis* little but words of praise on account of their high services. Some of these men were dead when Churchill wrote, but he honoured their memories; those who were still alive did not share Churchill's magnanimity; indeed he had to put up with virulent attacks not merely for what he did but for what he wrote.

The book contains some fine phrases and was carefully written: 'The old world in its sunset was fair to see,' he wrote of the pre-1914 era; of von Spee's adventures in the Pacific where he had not means of repairing or refuelling his ships, Churchill wrote: 'He was a cut flower in a vase, fair to see, yet bound to die and die very soon if the water was not renewed.' Of the tank he said: 'The air was the first cause that took us to Dunkirk. The armoured car was the child of the air and the Tank its grandchild.' 'The invasion of Belgium and the unlimited U-boat war were both resorted to on expert dictation as the only means of victory. They proved the direct cause of ruin.' Of General Monro who advised the evacuation of Gallipoli: 'He came, he saw, he capitulated.'

This was the first of Churchill's books in which he made use of his friend Eddie Marsh, an aesthetic Civil Servant who considered himself an expert on poetry and prose, to work on his syntax and punctuation. Churchill did not regard himself, as we have seen, either as a master of prose style or a master historian; he aimed to present to his readers the facts and his interpretation of them clearly as he saw them, but he attached importance to the judgments of future historians who examined what he had written. According to T. E. Lawrence in a letter he wrote to Marsh, Churchill had told him that *The World Crisis* was 'a pot-boiler'. 'Some pot!' Lawrence added, 'I suppose he realizes that he's the only high person since Thucydides and Clarendon who has put his generation imaginatively in his debt.' It seems to me that other generations who appreciate history may feel the same.

8

The Aftermath

CHURCHILL'S account of the four years after the
Great War is called *The Aftermath*, when he served as a
Minister in Lloyd George's Government, which had
gained an overwhelming victory in the election of 1918. It
does not strike me as one of his very best books. It is clear and
lively and entertaining about politics, but there is some decline
in his style of writing: the rhetoric at points is too florid. In it his
purpose was 'to present a general view of the scene—albeit from
a personal angle—and still more to trace through a labyrinth
of innumerable happenings the unique and inexorable sequence
of cause and effect.' That was a lofty and laudable aim. To realize
it would have needed, apart from memories of what had been
said and done, the examination of hundreds of books, newspapers,
and other writings offering evidence to be refined. In fact the
'personal angle' predominates. Churchill is concerned in the book
chiefly with four main happenings: the demobilization of the
British army, the Allied intervention in Russia, the evolution of
the Irish Free State, and the Chanak crisis which brought Great
Britain to the verge of war with Turkey.

In his preface Churchill writes that he was sure that 'there is
scarcely any period about which more has been recorded, more
has been forgotten and less is understood than the four years that
followed the Armistice' of November 1918. 'It is hard,' he
added, 'to realize that victory beyond the dreams of hope led
only to weakness, discontent, faction, and disappointment.' It is
the theme of all who have written since Churchill did about
those post-war years. Men longed for a brave world. 'Humanity,'

General Smuts declared in 1919, 'has struck its tents and is once more on the march.' In his novel *The Undying Fire* that H. G. Wells published early in the same year, his hero proclaimed that 'this war has torn away the veil of illusion from millions of men . . . mankind is coming of age.' The war had cost altogether twelve million lives. The four million men who came back to Great Britain from the wars looked to the community to provide good homes and decent jobs: they did not think of themselves as heroes but they reckoned they had 'done their bit'; while workers who had stayed behind the lines watched with eagerness the 'red sky in the morning' in revolutionary Russia and conceived of a millennium. On the other hand, in the middle classes (always expanding and being renovated) scepticism and tolerance were the keynotes of the new age. Novel forms of literature and styles of painting became the vogue. It was the era of the emancipation of women, of 'flappers,' of jazz, though Churchill was not concerned with these. But it was not long before the grander aspirations met with disillusionment. By 1921 unemployment and unrest were growing. Even the peace settlement proved unsatisfactory to many and ultimately the treaties came to be regarded not as forming a charter for the self-determination of peoples but an unwise and even Carthaginian peace.

Churchill scarcely fulfilled the promise held out in his preface of picturing this transformation from hope to disappointment. He dwelt on neither the unemployment and poverty of 1921 nor the changes in intellectual ideals and tastes. He writes in terms of a wider world, the world of the politician whose mind is absorbed in the solving of problems related to foreign affairs. In his concluding chapter he says: 'The story of the human race is War' though he ends his book in an optimistic vein, expressing the view, fervently maintained at the time by old and young alike, that such instruments as the League of Nations, the Dawes Agreement (settling reparations due from defeated Germany), the Treaty of Locarno for mutual security between Great Britain, France, Germany, and Italy, and the Kellogg Pact, proclaiming the outlawry of war, together meant the birth of

an entirely new spirit in international affairs, foreshadowing
reconciliation and permanent peace.

Looking back on the history of Lloyd George's peace-time
coalition government, as we now can, we appreciate that it had
solid achievements to its credit, particularly the speed with
which the peace was made, largely through the ingenuity,
persistence and gifts for negotiation possessed by the British
Prime Minister. The Cabinet contained extremely able statesmen—apart from Lloyd George and Churchill, there were
Balfour, Curzon, Austen Chamberlain, Lord Birkenhead, all
men of stature and loyal to the Prime Minister's leadership. Yet
Lloyd George, the Liberal, indeed the radical demagogue, was
dependent for his power on a Conservative majority. When the
Coalition Government fell (partly under the impulse of Bonar
Law, the one Conservative of standing who was outside it) the
cause of the Liberal party, to which Churchill himself belonged
for nearly twenty years, was broken for ever. Yet men who had
taken part in politics during the inter-war years became conscious
that with all its faults it had been an exceptional government.
The Prime Ministers who followed Lloyd George—Bonar Law,
Stanley Baldwin, Ramsay MacDonald, and Neville Chamberlain
—had neither Lloyd George's instinct for leadership nor his
ability to hold together a top-class Cabinet. To some (Robert
Boothby, for example) these men were pygmies. The fall of Lloyd
George, not because of his inability to grapple with the economic
and social questions of the time but because he had offended the
rank-and-file of the Conservative party over his handling of
foreign and imperial problems, had come to be regarded as a
retrograde stage in inter-war history.

And yet it was difficult for Churchill at the time when he was
writing this book to realize that. In 1924 Churchill had become a
leading member of Stanley Baldwin's Cabinet and had in effect
returned to the Conservative party which he had left in 1904.
The writing of contemporary history has many advantages:
indeed it has been argued that it is the only genuine kind of
history since all the facts are available, all the actors can speak,

the atmosphere is vivid and does not need to be reconstituted merely from documents, whereas history written later always has to rely on incomplete evidence. At the same time, however, those who write so closely to events can scarcely expect to see them in perspective. In *The Aftermath* Churchill was still moved by the passions and disappointments he had experienced as a Cabinet Minister, though he was sufficient of a historian to recognize that as time marched on, the peace treaties of 1919 and the Irish settlement would be regarded in a different light.

After the election which Churchill thought had 'woefully cheapened Britain,' he was appointed Secretary of State for War and also for the Air. He was confronted with mutinies and riots because the rank-and-file of the army was discontented with the arrangements for demobilization which had allowed 'key men' to return to civil life first, regardless of their length of service. Churchill promptly put the matter right by pushing through a fairer scheme. It was one of the few occasions when men learn from history, for the same mistakes were not repeated after the war of 1939–1945; no doubt Churchill's book (apart from his then being Prime Minister himself) contributed to the changed policy. Churchill describes his own attitude to the proposed hanging of the Kaiser for war guilt and to ending the economic blockade of Germany. He defends the peace settlement, though obviously he had limited admiration for President Woodrow Wilson or for Lord Curzon, who succeeded Balfour as Foreign Secretary. He was generous in victory and respected enemies who had fought so hard.

But while, as is clear from all his writings, Churchill felt kindly towards nationalist aspirations, whether in the Sudan, South Africa, Poland or Ireland—he believed, he observed in this book, that nationalism had replaced religion as the strongest motive force of mankind—he was not able to sympathize with the search by Russian underdogs for a fuller and better life. Looking back now, we can see the revolution of 1917 looming from far off; it was presaged by the events of 1905 and even in the superb plays of Chekov (though these were scarcely known at

that time in England). There was resentment, especially among
the French, that the Bolshevik leaders, having overthrown
Kerensky's Provisional Government, had abandoned the Allies
at their time of peril; though, as Churchill admits, the treaty of
Brest-Litovsk, which finally took Russia out of the war against
Germany, was 'a peace dictated by force of arms.' Not even the
greatest admirer of Churchill as a historical writer could agree
that his account in this book of the Russian revolution and of the
aims of Lenin is an impartial one. David Lloyd George, who was
always more critical of Churchill than Churchill was of him
(though they were on first-name terms all their lives) speaks not
merely of his friend's 'genuine distaste for Communism' but
asserts that he was revolted at the wholesale elimination of the
Grand Dukes in Russia by the Bolsheviks since he himself had
ducal blood flowing in his veins. This passage from Lloyd
George's *Truth about the Peace Treaties* reads to me like nonsense.
Before the war, at the time of the Liberal crisis over the House of
Lords, Churchill had used words about the English peerage so
virulent that they would have come equally appropriately from
Oliver Cromwell. Indeed both in British and French history it
has often been the aristocrats who have furnished the most
radical leaders (like Mirabeau), though no doubt it was difficult
for Lloyd George, himself a self-made Welsh solicitor, to see
matters that way. The truth was, I think, that Churchill hated
cruelty in any form and therefore detested the 'Red Terror' in
Russia as he also in this same book condemned the methods of
assassination employed by the Irish Republican Army against
the English soldiers and police. He was therefore shocked by the
figure of some 1,700,000 victims of the Red Terror which was
being put about in the nineteen-twenties by the critics of the
Bolshevik regime. This figure has never in fact been substantiated
by subsequent historians.

Another point to which Churchill gave insufficient emphasis
was that atrocities were committed on both sides. He was content
to observe that the Red Terror had provoked a White Terror.
Yet the American General William S. Graves, who commanded

American troops in Siberia in 1919, went so far as to assert that 'the anti-Bolsheviks killed one hundred people in Eastern Siberia to every one killed by the Bolsheviks.' Figures of atrocities are never satisfactory or convincing. But civil war is usually the most cruel kind of war and one knows that atrocities were committed on both sides during the French Revolution. So in the period 1917–1920 there was a 'White Terror' and a 'Red Terror' which were the inevitable concomitants of internecine conflict. Nor does Churchill in this book and in his book *The Eastern Front* take sufficient account of Russian history and the sufferings of the peasantry under the autocratic Tsars. It might perhaps be said of Churchill, as it was of Burke during the French Revolution, that he pitied the plumage but forgot the dying bird.

Lloyd George says in his book that Churchill was 'the most formidable and irrepressible protagonist of an anti-Bolshevik war' and that at the end of 1918 he advocated intervention to establish a democratic government in Russia. But whatever Churchill's emotions were, he explains perfectly fairly in *The Aftermath* the difficulties of the Allies at the close of the war against Germany—not, it must be remembered, until the middle of November 1918—since as long as that war lasted they had been involved in commitments in Russia and on the Russian borders in the hope of continuing to distract the Germans on the eastern front. Not only had British arms been piled up at Murmansk and Archangel but a Czechoslovak army had been formed in eastern Russia to which the Allies owed moral obligations. Moreover Churchill was by no means the only European statesman anxious to restore stability to Russia and prevent the spread of Red revolution into Germany. The French leaders, including Clemenceau, were bitter towards the Russians who, they thought, had betrayed them. In the British Cabinet Lord Curzon was also the advocate of intervention at any rate in Georgia. And Lloyd George himself had proposed to the Supreme Allied Council as late as May 1919 to send material support to the White Russian Government in Siberia.

Lloyd George asserts that in February 1919 Churchill 'very

adroitly seized the opportunity created by the absence of President Wilson and myself to go over to Paris and urge his plans
with regard to Russia on the consideration of the French, the
American and the British delegates.' But Lloyd George omits to
write that he himself had first sent Churchill to Paris to explain
the Cabinet's views and it was understandable that the British
Secretary of State for War was intimately concerned with future
British military commitments in Russia. Churchill was always a
man of action, whether as a Service Minister or before the war
as a radical reformer at the Board of Trade or Home Office.
He urged his own views, but acquiesced in the conditions for
helping anti-Bolshevik elements that Lloyd George himself
proposed. For though afterwards Lloyd George maintained that
he was always opposed to any form of intervention, the fact was
that during 1919 it was by no means clear to him or any other
British Minister that the Bolsheviks were going to win the war.
It was not until the beginning of 1920 that it became obvious that
the Bolsheviks were winning and then it remained only to
consider the position of the Poles whose independence had been
guaranteed by the peace treaties. Churchill shows that he was a
consistent advocate of encouraging the Poles to go on fighting the
Bolsheviks. He prints several memoranda that he wrote at the
time so that future historians have not lacked material for inter-
preting his views. In the end with the aid of the French General
Weygand and 'the Miracle of the Vistula' the war was brought to
an end and a temporary period of peace and independence
followed for turbulent Poland.

One small point in Churchill's story of the events in Russia
illuminates his attitude to history. He describes in some detail
the death of Admiral Koltchak who was, on the whole, the most
successful of the White Russian leaders. Koltchak in the end was
handed over to the Bolsheviks by the Czechoslovak legionaries
who for a time had co-operated with him in Siberia, though they
had never trusted him. Nevertheless he had been promised a safe-
conduct across the frontier into the Far East. Churchill wrote of
this tragic episode—for the Bolsheviks at once shot the Admiral

—'it is a pity that the magnificent record of the Czecho-slovak army corps should have been marred by the surrender of Koltchak. It seems for a while these legionaries *forsook the stage of History* . . .' To Churchill history was, or should be, heroic. Men can be measured by their attitude to events. When they betray their principles—in this case the principle of loyalty to an ally—then history will be their judge. In his later years, as we shall see, Churchill constantly asked the question: how will history judge our conduct?

In the part of his book which he devotes to the Irish question Churchill includes a brief and somewhat impressionistic historical account of the events that preceded the signing of the treaty or settlement in which he himself was deeply involved. Although Churchill left the War Office for the Colonial Office in January 1921, and therefore became constitutionally responsible for Ireland, he explains that it was not until a year had elapsed that he became a principal in Irish affairs, conducting all the negotiations with the Irish leaders and handling the debates in the House of Commons. From April 1921 until then, the Prime Minister himself had concentrated his single-minded attention on finding an Irish settlement, and although Churchill had been one of the British delegates during the long and troublesome negotiations with the Sinn Feiners, he writes about the preceding events more as a historian than an autobiographer.

Churchill's account of this turning-point in Irish history has been severely criticized. In the first place, it is argued that just as in his descriptions of the Red Terror in Russia, he allowed himself to be inspired by political passion rather than by impartial historical judgment, so in his summary of the course of the civil war in Ireland during 1919–1921 he is too one-sided. He speaks, for example, of 'the murder campaign' that 'grew and spread in Ireland' during 1920. This campaign followed the meeting of the Sinn Fein Congress in Dublin in 1919, where the claim was put forward for complete political independence for the whole of Ireland, and the later refusal of the southern Irish to accept the Government of Ireland Bill of 1920 which aimed to establish separate legislatures with limited powers both in Dublin and Belfast. Irish historians take the view that the guerrilla campaign launched by the Sinn Feiners was the only means at their disposal for enforcing their legitimate demand for independence upon Westminster; they argue that since the Sinn Fein movement had been outlawed by the British Government, its leaders threatened with arrest, and all nationalist activities proscribed as illegal, if the movement was to maintain its momentum the Sinn Feiners had no alternative but to fight with such weapons as they possessed. They speak of a few thousand dedicated men ready to risk their lives in the cause of Irish freedom against the superior forces of British police and British soldiers. But the policy of the Lloyd George Government was that the rebellion had to be suppressed before negotiations could be opened.

In order to reinforce the police not only were considerable numbers of additional troops sent to Ireland from England but a special auxiliary police force, selected, according to Churchill, from the best type of British ex-officers, was recruited: these became known because of their dark caps and khaki uniforms as the Black-and-Tans. In grappling with murder, Churchill wrote, these men developed 'a very strong counter-terrorist activity' and he added that 'obviously there can be no defence for such conduct'—'except the kind of attack to which it was the reply.'

But both many Englishmen in parliament and in the press at the time and most historians have found it hard to justify the methods of the Black-and-Tans. And it is difficult not to feel that Churchill is disingenuous. For example, he relates the famous episode known as Bloody Sunday when fourteen unarmed Black-and-Tan officers were shot to death in Dublin, but omits to explain that this was in part a reprisal for the Mayor of Dublin who starved himself to death in a British prison or that the Black-and-Tans responded on the same day by shooting dead and injuring players and innocent members of the crowd at a football match in Croke Park. Nor does it appear that the

[113]

Black-and-Tans were such a select force as Churchill implies: Lloyd George subsequently admitted that many of them had to be dismissed or prosecuted for 'deplorable offences.'

Although in November 1920 Lloyd George claimed in a speech that 'we have murder by the throat' the methods of the Black-and-Tans were repudiated and 'authorized reprisals' substituted as a regular policy, a method which, Churchill says, was 'far less effective than the rough-and-ready measures of the special police.' But now both sides were reaching the end of their tether. The British commander-in-chief in Ireland was demanding more troops and martial law; Michael Collins, the leader of the Irish Republican Army, admitted that his men were being harried beyond endurance. So eventually after a number of informal contacts had been established and King George V had appealed for reconciliation when he opened the Belfast Parliament in July 1921, a truce was concluded and Eamon De Valera, the president of the self-constituted Irish republic, was invited to a conference in London.

Churchill's description of Lloyd George's behaviour to De Valera during these London meetings in July 1921 has been questioned by Frank Pakenham (afterwards Lord Longford) in his book *Peace by Ordeal* in which he had access to information from the Irish side. Churchill suggests that Lloyd George deliberately set out to embarrass or discomfort his Irish visitor; whereas Pakenham records that all the British Prime Minister's efforts were conciliatory and that he tried to appeal personally to De Valera as a fellow Celt. Nothing in fact came of the meeting. But in October 1921 other Irish leaders arrived in London in search of a settlement, though De Valera himself significantly remained in Ireland; Churchill as Colonial Secretary was one of the British delegates.

Although Churchill took an active part in the complicated negotiations that preceded the agreement that was accepted by both sides on 6 December 1921, he gives little historical detail. Lloyd George was determined that the Irish should remain within the Empire or Commonwealth of Nations, as it was called in the final treaty; the Irish fought for their independence and for the unity of the whole of Ireland. Lloyd George intended that if the negotiations broke down, it should be over an Irish refusal to recognize King and Commonwealth, while Arthur Griffith, leader of the Irish delegation, wanted the breakdown to be—if it came—over the position of Ulster. Griffith was in fact outmanœuvred by Lloyd George; for Lloyd George promised that if Ulster refused to accept the rule of Dublin, then a boundary commission would be set up which might reduce the size of Ulster virtually to an unmanageable economic unit. None of these subtleties are mentioned by Churchill. On the contrary, he airily dismissed the whole negotiations lasting for two months with the phrase 'futilities and rigmarol.' He highlights the final drama. Lloyd George presented the Irish delegation with an ultimatum on 5 December 1921: 'They must settle now; they must sign the agreement for a Treaty in the form in which after all these weeks it had attained, or else quit; and further, that both sides would be free to resume whatever warfare they could wage against one another.' Churchill also emphasizes that the treaty—disliked by Bonar Law and much of the Conservative Party, though approved by its leader, Austen Chamberlain, who had replaced Bonar Law earlier in the year, 'was fatal to the Prime Minister. Within a year he had been driven from power.'

De Valera was opposed to the draft treaty and resigned after it had been approved by a mere seven votes in the Sinn Fein parliament or Dail. Churchill was now concerned with the implementation of the treaty and with the re-establishment of peace throughout Ireland. In the 1921 meetings he had reached a friendly relationship with Michael Collins, the leader of the Irish Republican Army. They both shared the outlook of soldiers and Churchill appreciated a man who had fought for national independence. The Sinn Feiners were split among themselves. A 'high-souled fanatic,' Rory O'Connor, who was determined that Ireland should be an independent republic, seized and fortified the Law Courts in Dublin. At the same time there were vendettas and counter-vendettas in Belfast. The most dangerous situation arose, however, when Irish republican forces occupied two villages inside Ulster. Churchill warned Collins that if the Irish Republican Army invaded Ulster 'we should throw them out.' In fact a military demonstration proved sufficient to put a bloodless end to this particular incident. And by October 1922, when Lloyd George's Government resigned, 'the strength and power of the Irish Free State was firmly erected on the basis of the Treaty.'

But the Treaty left a host of victims. Arthur Griffith suddenly died; Michael Collins was assassinated; Rory O'Connor was shot without trial; Sir Henry Wilson, an Ulster M.P. and former Chief of the Imperial General Staff, was murdered by Irishmen on the steps of his London home. Lloyd George and the Conservative leaders who supported him in the Irish negotiations were to lose office in 1922, Lloyd George for ever. Only Churchill himself and the irreconcilable De Valera lived on to witness the final complete separation of the Irish Free State from the British Commonwealth in 1949. But it was ironical that the formula proposed in 1921 by De Valera of 'external association' was adopted twenty-eight years later by a Commonwealth conference which, as David Thomson had written, 'might have served to keep Ireland within the Commonwealth.' Yet, to quote A. J. P. Taylor, 'for all practical purposes, the Union ended on December 6, 1921, and the unity of Ireland with it.'

In describing the events that followed the agreement concluded on that date Churchill quotes extensively from letters he wrote to the various participants including Collins and Craig, the Ulster leader. They throw light on the story. The note of hope on which he concluded his narrative has hardly been realized. Churchill himself was to live to regret the intransigence of the Irish. For in 1940 De Valera's Government refused to allow the use of Southern Irish bases in the anti-German submarine campaign at a time of crisis in British history and indeed, Churchill thought, 'by following a rigorous neutrality repudiated the terms of the treaty of 1921.'

In *The Aftermath* Churchill describes how after one of the debates in the House of Commons on Ireland (at the time when Ulster was still threatened by the Irish Republican Army) he and Lloyd George met Bonar Law in the lobby. The former Conservative leader, who had urged strong action in his speech, 'manifested intense passion. As far as I can remember, he said "you have disarmed us today. If you act up to your words, well and good, but if not . . ." ' He then walked abruptly away. Bonar Law, though Churchill writes that his health was then 'restored,' must have been a sick man, for three years later he died of cancer. But in Bonar Law the Conservative party had found a possible leader of an alternative government if the Lloyd George Coalition should break up. Sir George Younger, the Conservative party chairman, was already murmuring 'Isn't it time we had a government of our own?' But who would have guessed, even in the spring of 1922, that the last nail would be thrust into the coffin of the Coalition not by any domestic crisis (the economic situation had improved after the depression of 1921) nor trouble over Ireland, Russia, or Germany, but over so distant and obscure a matter as British policy in the Near East?

Like the Irish embroglio, the preliminaries to this story are complex. Churchill does his best to simplify them. Broadly it began with the question of reaching a peace settlement with the Turks who had fought against the Allies in the Great War. The statesmen at Versailles were at first absorbed in the German settlement and it was not until August 1920 that a treaty was signed at Sèvres. By the terms of this treaty the Turkish State became a shrivelled corpse, the pathetic remnant of the once mighty Ottoman empire. In the form of mandates, France, Italy, Great Britain and Greece all received large slices of former Turkish territory. The Americans wisely refused a mandate for Armenia. The Allies dealt with a puppet constitutional and parliamentary regime under the Sultan which had been set up in Constantinople. (Both Lloyd George and Lord Curzon, the Foreign Secretary, had wanted to expel the Turks from Europe but had been overruled by Churchill and other members of the

Cabinet.) A neutral zone was established covering the Dardanelles and Sea of Marmara, and a rival Turkish nationalist
government under Mustafa Kemal, the hero of Gallipoli, was
soon in being in Angora.

The Turkish National Assembly in Angora refused to acquiesce
in the humiliating terms of the treaty of Sèvres and even before
it had been signed by the Sultan's Government British outposts
were being attacked by Kemalist forces. The Allies, fully committed elsewhere, had no army to cope with these recalcitrant
Turks. France and Italy hastened to come to terms with Kemal.
The Greeks had been allowed by the Allies to land troops in
Smyrna as early as May 1919 (though without the knowledge of
the Italians), which Churchill called 'a rash and fatal step,' and
they now offered to provide the men needed to uphold the treaty.
This appeared all right so long as Venizelos, the friend of Great
Britain, ruled Greece. But in October 1920 his master, King
Alexander, died, bitten by a pet monkey. Churchill compares the
incident to the escape of the Goeben in 1914 as exemplifying the
place of the fortuitous in history. The British Government did
not trust King Constantine, the former Germanophil, who was
now enthusiastically welcomed back to the Greek throne. Indeed
the Allies were reluctant to recognize the new government and
decided in February 1921 to revise the treaty of Sèvres in the
Turkish favour.

Nevertheless the Greeks fought on. King Constantine himself
took command in Smyrna. The Allies declared themselves
neutral in this Turko-Greek war. Constantine was at first
successful, but in September 1921 sustained defeat. Next year
he proposed in desperation to occupy Constantinople, thus
protecting the withdrawal of the Greek army from Asia Minor.
But the Allies vetoed this move. By the autumn of 1922 the
Greeks had been crushed; the Kemalist forces occupied Smyrna,
set the town on fire, and massacred its Christian inhabitants.

The British Cabinet was divided over Turkey. Lloyd George
himself was strongly pro-Greek. Edward Montagu, the Secretary
of State for India, had been pro-Turk (being anxious not to

alienate the Muslims). Curzon was neutral and, according to Churchill, 'ineffectual.' Stanley Baldwin wanted peace at almost any price. The compromise reached after the fall of Venizelos was to bring pressure to bear on both sides to make peace. But the victorious Mustafa Kemal was not easily intimidated. The crisis came in September 1922 when Kemalist forces menaced a smaller British force, commanded by General Sir Charles Harington, in the neutral zone. The French withdrew their support; and at Chanak, south of the Dardanelles, British troops were confronted by triumphant and fanatic Turks. On the other hand, the British Mediterranean fleet was there in support and Kemal was a wise statesman. Though Harington was empowered by the British Government to present an ultimatum to the Turks to quit the neutral zone within a brief space of time, he did not use it: an armistice was agreed and peace negotiations were reopened which culminated in the revised treaty of Lausanne in 1923.

Churchill was one of the most energetic members of the inner ring in the Cabinet which was determined to combine firmness with conciliation. It was he who was asked to draft on 15 September a *communiqué* on the course of events, a *communiqué* which was read with consternation in Canada and Australia before their governments had received official information about the crisis from London. It was said that appeals had been made to them before in fact the appeals had been received. Churchill was again criticized as a war-monger and as being guilty of giving offence to the Dominions whose help would have been needed had hostilities actually broken out. Thus Lloyd George, Churchill and in fact the whole Government were accused of dragging the British Empire to the verge of war less than four years after the Great War had ended. Bonar Law wrote a letter to *The Times* saying 'We cannot act alone as policemen of the world.' And thus the death knell of the Coalition was sounded.

The Aftermath is essentially an autobiographical book; but it contributes to history because it pictures, often in succinct language, some of the atmosphere of the epoch, notably in the

Cabinet, which it is difficult for a historian writing a generation or two afterwards to imagine or revive. It is neither a complete chronicle of events nor does it analyse the fundamental reasons for the downfall of the Coalition which consisted of so many capable Ministers and had no mean record. But Churchill does not hesitate to expound such errors as were committed. Lloyd George, who also wrote his own apologia, was above all an eclectic statesman who concentrated on solving each problem separately as it arose. Possibly, if one interprets *The Aftermath* correctly, the troubles in Ireland and the Balkans might have been averted if Lloyd George himself had made up his mind more quickly and intervened earlier. We have to remember that all his life Winston Churchill was the personal friend of Lloyd George, whom he liked and admired. He did not much care for Curzon, the Foreign Secretary. No doubt these personal factors need to be taken into account in assessing the value of *The Aftermath* as a historical document.

9

The Eastern Front

DURING the ten years between 1929 and 1939 when Winston Churchill was out of office his output of historical writing was prodigious. In February 1931 he produced the abridged and revised one-volume edition of his *World Crisis* to which he added an account of the battle of the Marne. He wrote his book on *The Eastern Front* (published in the United States under the title of *The Unknown War*) as an appendage or companion piece to his *World Crisis;* this he finished in the autumn of 1931. He wrote his four volumes on *Marlborough: His Life and Times* (completed in August 1938) and before the war of 1939 began he had drafted, as has already been related, some 500,000 words as the basis for his *History of the English-speaking Peoples* for which he was under contract.

But that was by no means all. In October 1930 he published his autobiographical book *My Early Life: a Roving Commission* and in addition there appeared in November 1932 and September 1937 two collections of essays or articles which he had contributed to magazines and newspapers under the titles respectively of *Thoughts and Adventures* and *Great Contemporaries*: one or two of these articles he had even dictated as he was driven by car from Westerham to the House of Commons. The latter book consisted of articles he had written on various occasions during the previous eight years. Admittedly the last three books were drawn from the rich store of his capacious memory: none the less, to have seen through the press no fewer than six books (one of them in four volumes) and to have dictated the equivalent of another four-volume book was an astonishing record. Not only

E

was all of this extremely readable but much of it was a valuable deployment of historical knowledge. For example, the book on *The Eastern Front* is at present, as American scholars on Russia admit even today, the only easily accessible and lively account of the last war fought by Tsarist Russia.

It was during the first part of this period that I myself worked as a historical assistant to Churchill, though I was only specifically engaged on the *Marlborough*. But one would not have imagined in those days that his house, Chartwell Manor, was a factory of books. Quite the contrary. During those years Churchill went on a lecture tour in the United States; he had a street accident in New York from which it took him, in spite of his habitual toughness, some months fully to recover. At Chartwell he occupied many of his daylight hours in painting or building activities. He never hurried over his lunch or dinner. He attended the House of Commons from time to time and visited many parts of the country to deliver public speeches first on India and then on the German danger and the need for rearmament. It is true that all the books were dictated and that this method contributed to the rapid outpouring of thousands of words. Yet, as I have described in an earlier chapter, each book and each chapter went through many drafts all of which Churchill personally revised and sometimes largely rewrote. Little of his writing can be described as superficial: the rhetoric might be embroidery but it was never the windiness of Ramsay MacDonald, Churchill's contemporary bête noire. Though he had assistants—such as Lieutenant-Colonel Charles Hordern, who put an immense amount of work into the preparation of *The Eastern Front*— every word of Churchill's books was his own; his assistants were there to provide him with intellectual sustenance and support and to check the accuracy of the final achievement.

I received the impression that *The Eastern Front* was written primarily to earn money. Of course one might apply that remark to any of his books, but of some books it could be said more obviously than of others. His project for retelling Bible stories in modern terms, which fortunately never saw the light, was such a one. The *Randolph Churchill* and the *Marlborough* were, however, written out of a genuine sense of family piety and some of his other books were inspired by an understandable desire for self-justification. In writing, military history was his métier, and he was anxious to discover the causes and character of the fighting on the eastern front during the Great War of 1914–1918 which had been taking place while he himself and the British Cabinet were absorbed with the west—except for the Dardanelles expedition in which he was personally involved.

As his books go, that on *The Eastern Front* is comparatively short, fewer than 400 pages. Most of the first nine chapters are devoted to the causes of the war and the preparations that were made on both sides. Then follows an illuminating account of the battles. The book comes to a somewhat abrupt end with a brief description of the final Russian political collapse. I suspect that Churchill had become bored with it and was eager to turn to his *Marlborough*, which he had to some extent been playing with while *The Eastern Front* was in the process of dictation. This ability to write two books at once is unusual even among university professors whose duty it is to research and write.

Churchill's story of the origins of the war opens with a chapter called 'The Dusk of the Habsburg' in which he outlines the recent political history of the Austro-Hungarian empire or Dual Monarchy presided over by the veteran Francis Joseph. He sketches the decay of Austria and the decrepitude of Turkey; he recalls the ambitions of the Balkan countries under the Austrian yoke and the ambition of the Poles for the reconstitution of their nation partitioned in the eighteenth century between Russia, Prussia, and Austria. He gives a thumbnail sketch of Francis Joseph who, he says, bore his tragedies with stoicism—the execution of his brother Maximilian, the suicide of his son Rudolf, and the misalliance of his nephew Francis Ferdinand. He also sketches the fire-eating Conrad von Hötzendorff, who was to become the Austrian commander-in-chief, and Count Aerenthal, the Austrian Foreign Minister. He goes on to relate the series of European crises: the annexation of Bosnia, the

[123]

episode of Agadir in French Morocco, and the two Balkan wars which presaged the world war that broke out in 1914.

It is curious that Churchill does not in these introductory chapters deal either with the character of the Tsar, that weak but autocratic figure who was dominated by his strong-minded wife, or with the political and economic background in Tsarist Russia. Indeed it is not until he reaches the end of his story that he castigates 'the fond, obstinate husband and father, the absolute monarch obviously devoid of all the qualities of a national ruler in time of crisis.' Yet if one can measure events in terms of personalities, it can hardly be doubted that the Tsar Nicholas, as much as the Emperor Francis Joseph or the Kaiser Wilhelm II, played a leading part in the coming of the war and the defeat of his empire.

Since Churchill wrote this book a vast amount of research has been done on the origins of the war of 1914 and many volumes have been written about it by historians of all nationalities. But it may be doubted if many western historians would differ materially from Churchill's account except on points of detail. The ambitions of military circles in Austria, epitomized by Conrad, to crush Serbian irredentism for all time, and of the German military staff to expand the Bismarckian empire with the campaign envisaged by Count Schlieffen, created an explosive atmosphere. The murder on 28 June 1914 of the heir to the Austrian throne in the streets of Sarajevo, capital of Bosnia, by the Black Hand organization, whose leader was the head of Serbian Intelligence, provided the opportunity. When the Austrian Ministers presented their ultimatum to Serbia demanding under threat of war humiliating concessions because of Serbian complicity in the crime, Wilhelm II, whose government had been allied with Austria since 1879, sent Vienna on 7 July a 'blank cheque' promising the military aid that might be needed if Russia with its Pan-Slav ideals should intervene on the Serbian behalf. Thus it was only a question whether at the last moment commonsense or fear would avert a world conflagration as it had done after the annexation of Bosnia or the dispatch of the German gunboat to Agadir. (Incidentally with regard to the annexation of Bosnia Churchill appears to be in error: it seems that the first approach for a deal between Russia and Austria in 1908 came from the Russian side, from her Foreign Minister Izvolski and not from Aerenthal, although it is plain, as Churchill says, that Aerenthal deceived Izvolski about his ultimate intentions.)

The ultimatum from Austria to Serbia was dispatched on 23 July 1914. The Kaiser had anticipated a victory without war, as over Bosnia. In fact the Serbian Government virtually accepted the conditions of the Austrian ultimatum and when the Kaiser learned the nature of the Serbian reply late on the morning of 28 July at Potsdam, eighteen miles from Berlin, he said that 'with it every reason for war is removed . . .' But on that very same day the Emperor Francis Joseph had been persuaded to sign a declaration of war and Austro-Hungarian troops began to invade Serbia. Churchill points out astutely that the German authorities in Berlin who wanted war deliberately withheld the Serbian reply from the Kaiser at Potsdam as long as they could—for some twelve hours. On the other hand, there seems little substance in the story which Churchill copied from the American historian, B. E. Schmitt, that Count Berchtold (who had succeeded Aerenthal as the Austrian Foreign Minister and who was as responsible as any one individual for the coming of the war) deceived Francis Joseph into believing that the fighting had already begun in order to induce him to sign the declaration of war.

'Up to this stage,' Churchill wrote, 'it had not been certain that Germany and Austria would not gain another bloodless victory such as had rewarded Aerenthal five years before.' But on this occasion 'Germany found herself almost immediately in the presence of a sombre fatalism in the "Entente" Powers. There was a feeling in Paris and London that Germany meant to have war and meant to have it now. If she did not, it was easy to find half a dozen solutions. Grey indefatigably proposed a conference of the Powers and begged all parties to be reasonable.' The invasion of Serbia provoked Russia into action and on 29

July the Tsar was persuaded to sign two ukases, one for partial, the other for full mobilization. Though Churchill is cautious on the subject, later historians have shown that the Tsar signed both, though afterwards he cancelled the ukase for general mobilization. The Russian war machine took time to wind up. Eventually at four o'clock in the afternoon of 30 July a new ukase for general mobilization was issued. The Germans answered by sending an ultimatum demanding that the Russians should cease every war measure against Austria-Hungary within twelve hours. Then on 1 August Germany declared war on Russia. German mobilization began next day; on 3 August Germany declared war on France and on 4 August England declared war on Germany. Thus the first world war began.

'We must not allow ourselves,' Churchill wrote, 'to be baffled by the immense volume of knowledge now accessible upon the immediate coming of the war.' It was not, he says, a case of 'spontaneous combustion.' Germany by deliberately encouraging Austria with the 'blank cheque' and later by deliberately violating the neutrality of Belgium in order to attack France, was 'the main culprit.' In his analysis of the causes of the Great War Churchill relied largely on the book on *The Coming of the War* by Bernadotte E. Schmitt. Another book, also by an American historian, S. B. Fay, appeared at about the same time and was more favourable to the Central Powers. Fay insisted that 'Germany did not plot a European war, did not want one, and made genuine, though too belated efforts, to avoid one.' He also argued that it was the hasty Russian mobilization, assented to on 29 July and ordered on 30 July, while Germany was still trying to bring Austria to accept a mediation proposal, that finally rendered the European war inevitable. Finally Fay claimed that Russia was partly responsible for the Austro-Serbian conflict because of the frequent encouragement which she had given to Belgrade. But all that scarcely invalidates Churchill's case. The German 'blank cheque' had been given. The Kaiser had been prevented from seeing the submissive Serbian answer to the Austrian ultimatum until it was too late for him to act. The Tsar held his hand for twenty-four hours in spite of the pressure from his generals and in fact tried to use his personal influence with his cousin the Kaiser to maintain peace. But by then the Austrians had unleashed their army on Serbia. Russian involvement brought in France. The Schlieffen plan required, once war was declared, the violation of Belgium and the invasion of France.

A criticism was made by the Italian historian, Luigi Albertini, who examined the origins of the war more minutely than any modern historian, of the attempts made by Sir Edward Grey, Churchill's colleague in the Cabinet, to avert the final conflict. He suggests that if Grey, as British Foreign Secretary, had only warned the Germans earlier that were France to be attacked, Great Britain might be obliged to come in on the French side, this would have damped German military fervour. There does not seem much substance in this. It is perfectly true that on 29 July Grey did warn the German ambassador in London in an unofficial conversation and that this warning came too late to help—for Austria was already at war, backed by Germany. Albertini argued that Grey should have conveyed the warning sooner, before the ultimatum to Serbia expired. Churchill in effect anticipated this criticism in *The World Crisis,* for he says there that because the British Cabinet was so overwhelmingly pacific at the time of the Austrian ultimatum it would have been impossible then for Grey to have given such a warning without going against the feelings of the majority of British Ministers. Albertini, however, controverts Churchill and urges that if Grey was able to deliver such a warning on 29 July, he could equally have done so a few days earlier. Fay, in reviewing Albertini's book, supported Churchill.

So much for the immediate origins of the war. Churchill then goes on to examine the military situation of the Central Powers and to analyse their strategic plans. 'In the west,' he writes, 'the armies were too big for the country, in the east the country was too big for the armies.' Yet, as we now know, before Russia was knocked out of the war, well over 15,000,000 Russians were mobilized. Germany planned to stand on the defensive in the East while concentrating her main effort initially against France. The Austrians were committed to their assault on Serbia, but Conrad was obliged to weaken his army there in order to strengthen the Galician front against the Russians. He envisaged a combined Austro-German offensive from Galicia and East Prussia to cut off the Russians in the Polish salient. But for Conrad everything fell apart. The Serbians resisted firmly and drove the Austrians back; the Germans were too weak immediately to engage in an offensive upon the Russians. When Moltke later withdrew German divisions from the western front—where he believed victory was assured—in order to strengthen the eastern front, he contributed to the loss of the battle of the Marne and thus disrupted the Schlieffen plan.

As a historian Churchill was critical of the Austrian offensive plans, as he was of the French offensive plan known as Plan XVII. He argued that it would have been wiser in both cases if they had allowed the invaders 'to test for themselves the then unmeasured power of modern firearms.' Instead of that 'both were nearly destroyed at the very beginning of the war by precipitate offensives.'

When Churchill turns to his descriptions of the battles on the eastern front, he disentangles pretty effectively the complicated course of events. In the so-called battle of Lemberg on the Galician front (comprising in fact seven separate battles) the Austrians at first made progress against the Russians on their right or northern flank but, after heavy casualties had been suffered by both sides, called off the offensive and began a general retreat on 9–11 September. In Serbia the Austrians lost in casualties some 227,000 men out of a total of 450,000 engaged. Thus the Austrians by dividing their armies and attacking on two fronts experienced a serious rebuff. Meanwhile on the East Prussian front the Russians with a superiority of nearly 3 to 1 over the weak German forces under General von Prittwitz attempted with two Armies, the 1st under Rennenkampf and the 2nd under Samsonov, to force their way into Germany, and thus give relief to the French on the western front. A battle took place at Gumbinnen on 20 August in which seven German divisions fought eight Russian divisions of Rennenkampf's army; the result of the contest, according to Churchill, was 'piebald,' by which he meant drawn. However Professor Cyril Falls is of the opinion that the Russians won that battle, for the German corps commander, Mackensen, 'fled in panic.' Prittwitz, faced by the Russian 'steam-roller,' also lost his nerve and spoke to Moltke of retiring behind the Vistula, which might have been fatal. Moltke then superseded Prittwitz and dispatched the retired Titan, Von Hindenburg, with General von Ludendorff as his Chief of Staff—'a prodigy of mental energy cast in military form,' Churchill called him in another book—to take command on the eastern front, to whom he sent reinforcements from France. The battle of Tannenberg followed in the last week of August 1914.

Samsonov's 2nd Russian army, cut off from the 1st Russian army by the Masurian lakes* was virtually wiped out by the German 8th Army under its new commanders and Samsonov himself committed suicide. The battle of Tannenberg was as crucial on the eastern front as the battle of Marne was on the western front. Henceforward, though the Russians defeated the Austrians, they never defeated the Germans.

Churchill as a military historian is always careful to pay tribute wherever he feels that tribute is due. He commends, for example, Conrad's 'force of will' in concentrating his armies against the Russians even after one of them had suffered an initial defeat on the Galician front. Equally he praises the arrangements made by General von Prittwitz in face of an original setback at the hands of an immensely larger Russian invading force. Churchill describes how when Hindenburg and Ludendorff arrived at the headquarters of the 8th Army all the

---

* Various explanations have been offered for Rennenkampf's failure to support Samsonov. Churchill blames the overall commander-in-chief, Jilinski, who was afterwards removed. Other historians believe that Rennenkampf was a traitor.

plans for the battle of Tannenberg had already been arranged, and this has been accepted by all later English writers. Though Ludendorff was to claim the credit for the victory, in fact all the movements which enabled the 8th Army to concentrate against Samsonov had been ordered by Prittwitz on the initiative of Colonel Max Hoffmann, his First General Staff Officer. And Churchill also argues that what ensured the ultimate victory was the fact that one of the corps commanders, General von François, disobeyed Ludendorff's orders to attack prematurely without artillery preparation. Max Hoffmann, with whose accounts of the battle of Tannenberg Churchill was presumably familiar, and who should have known what he was talking about, gives a rather different explanation why the attack by von François was delayed.

After the battle of Tannenberg Hindenburg and Ludendorff planned to defeat the other Russian army on the East Prussian front under the command of Rennenkampf. 'The double battles of the Eighth German Army under Hindenburg and Ludendorff against the superior armies of Samsonov and Rennenkampf are not only a military classic but an epitome of the art of war.' Thus Churchill prefaces his account of the first battle of the Masurian lakes. The Germans gathered together seventeen divisions (including the four divisions which Moltke had withdrawn from the western front, for which Churchill criticized him in *The World Crisis*) to attack Rennenkampf's army of some twenty-four divisions. Eight German divisions were assigned to a frontal offensive, while seven under the command of von François, the 'real hero' of Tannenberg, were ordered to execute a turning movement. On 9 September the Russian left flank was successfully turned. Under the cover of a counter-attack by two divisions Rennenkampf managed to escape to the line of the river Niemen. The Russian commander-in-chief on this front, Jilinski, accused Rennenkampf of cowardice, but was himself relieved of his command.

Meanwhile the Russians had completed a victory on the Galician front. One-third of the Austro-Hungarian army had been wiped out. 'Conrad,' says Churchill, 'broke their hearts and used them up in three weeks.' He argues that this army, composed of men of many nationalities, needed the most careful handling. Conrad's aggressive qualities—his 'lion-heart'—were not suited to playing upon so delicate an instrument. Had he been in the seat of Moltke, Churchill writes, with the Schlieffen plan to execute, he might have been hailed in the history books as an outstanding captain; as it was, he contributed to the doom of the empire of Francis Joseph.

The Germans, ever-prompt (as in the war of 1939-1945) to come to the aid of their distressed allies, hastened to assist the beaten Austrians. Falkenhayn, whom Churchill commends as an outstanding strategist, withdrew four corps from the 8th Army to form a 9th Army north of Cracow which was also placed under the command of Hindenburg and Ludendorff. Both sides contemplated an offensive. The Russians largely reinforced their armies, having been pressed again to give relief to the French on the western front. The Austro-German forces, though numerically much inferior, attacked first on 28 September with the object of crossing the Vistula and threatening Warsaw. Though the Germans came within twelve miles of Warsaw, the weight of the Russian numbers finally told: after nearly three weeks Hindenburg and Ludendorff ordered the retirement of the 9th Army from Poland into Silesia. The Germans blamed the Austrians for the setback: 'Whereas the German troops were equal to two or three times their number of Russians, it was obvious that the Austrian armies were incapable of fighting the Russians man for man.' Churchill admired equally the way in which the Russians aided their French allies and the Germans had come to the rescue of the Austrians.

Churchill describes how the war continued much on this pattern. After stalemate developed on the western front, the German high command decided to reinforce the eastern front and in the late winter of 1914-1915 a second battle of the Masurian lakes took place. Again the Russians were outmanœuvred, but clung on because of their superior numbers. The invasion

[131]

of Germany was prevented, though once again the Austrians were defeated, losing 100,000 prisoners. Falkenhayn, says Churchill, was an 'inveterate westerner'—not for Churchill a term of praise since he himself was an inveterate easterner—but he claims that his mind was changed by the Dardanelles campaign. Thus a new offensive was prepared by the German 11th Army on the Tarnow–Gorlice area of Galicia. Just after the British troops landed in Gallipoli the German 11th Army launched its offensive and completely broke through the Russian front in Galicia.

On 25 May 1915 the Italians declared war on Austria (though they did not declare war on Germany until August). A combination of events—the failure of a Turkish campaign in the Caucasus, the British assault on the Dardanelles, the Italian entry into the war—inspired the Germans to press their offensive in the east. A new 12th Army was formed. Under its attack Warsaw was evacuated on 5 August by the Russians who in the year's campaigning sustained nearly a million casualties and lost a further 750,000 prisoners. On 5 September 1915 the Tsar himself assumed personal command of all his armies.

Falkenhayn now decided to knock Serbia out of the war with the assistance of the Bulgarians, who were anxious to help defeat their former enemies in the earlier Balkan war. On 9 October Belgrade at last fell. The German successes on the eastern front had thus been shattering. They were operating on inner lines with the aid of a well-organized railway system that enabled them to move their troops rapidly from one front to another. The Allied riposte was feeble. A French General, Sarrail, had taken command of Anglo-French forces shipped from Gallipoli to Salonika on 5 October, but they had made no progress. Churchill marvelled that the naval assault on the Dardanelles was not resumed. 'The Admirals and Generals,' he wrote, 'had their way.' 'The fleet continued idle at the Dardanelles. The armies shattered themselves against the German defence in France. The Bulgarians carried an army of 300,000 men to join our enemies and Serbia as a factor in the war was obliterated.' Thus, writing fifteen years afterwards, Churchill still thought bitterly of the failure of the Dardanelles campaign, which he, as much as any man, had been responsible for organizing and for which he had been so virulently blamed as almost to ruin his career as a statesman. As a historian he can scarcely be condemned for writing in an emotive way.

David Lloyd George stated in his memoirs that by July 1915 the Russians had ceased to fight with any hope of victory. Evidently Churchill felt much the same, for he writes extremely briefly about the events of 1916 when the Russian imperial army sang its swan song. After the fall of Warsaw in the late summer of 1915 the Russians had withdrawn from the Polish salient to a line running southward from Riga through Kovno, Grodno and Brest-Litovsk to Kamenetz north of the Rumanian frontier. The Russian front was more or less stabilized because General Falkenhayn had decided to concentrate the main German effort in the west and a prolonged offensive had been opened in February with the aim of capturing Verdun, a fortress redolent with historical meaning for the French army. Two months later General Conrad von Hötzendorff, anxious to win a laurel against a less recalcitrant enemy than the Russians, had determined— contrary to the wishes of his German colleague Falkenhayn— to direct an offensive upon the Italians in the mountains of the Trentino. By May 1916 the Austrian armies were achieving progress towards Verona.

Although the Russians now lacked both a real supreme commander and a competent Chief of Staff, they responded to the appeals of their French and Italian allies, who were both severely pressed, to begin an assault from their new line so as to draw off some of the steam from the German offensive in France and the Austrian attack on Northern Italy. The Russians, who now possessed more guns and ammunition than before and stood in a better position, had already planned to take up the offensive again; but in answer to these pleas from their allies they elected to make a big demonstration on their south-western front immediately. The commander-in-chief there was General Brusilov, who had earlier distinguished himself against the Austrians in

Galicia and was now again facing a weakened Austrian section of his enemy's line since troops and artillery had been withdrawn to Italy. This premature offensive, which had been preceded by a very brief artillery preparation, successfully created surprise. The Austro-Hungarian divisions retreated towards Lemberg; and Brusilov, whose own account of the campaign survives in a book translated as *A Soldier's Note-book*, claimed that he took 450,000 prisoners and inflicted 1,500,000 casualties. That was certainly an exaggeration, but his was a considerable victory. Once again, however, wherever the Russians encountered German troops they met with effective resistance. The Germans hastened to restore the situation. Conrad was obliged to give up his campaign in Italy and to obey German orders. In the same summer of 1916 Rumania came into the war on the side of the western allies. These two facts—Brusilov's victory and the Rumanian entry into the war—brought about the downfall of Falkenhayn, especially as the Germans had failed to obtain a break-through at Verdun. Henceforward Hindenburg and Ludendorff, the German architects of victory on the eastern front, were transferred to direct the war in the west. In any case Brusilov's offensive proved to be the last major effort by the Russians. And the revolution when it broke out in March 1917 was the prelude to Russia's total disappearance from the world war.

Churchill's book has been criticized, fairly, I think, because it relates the history of the war on the eastern front almost entirely from the German point of view. This no doubt was because his information about it came largely from German sources. The German story (unlike the Austrian or the Russian) was one of continual and astonishing victories over a more numerous enemy, while the defeated rarely write long books as apologias. A completely new phase in Russian history then opened and Russian historians—and, for that matter, American and British historians—showed themselves more concerned with describing the long-range causes of the Bolshevik revolution than the course of the last imperial war. Admittedly the two important books by Lieutenant-General Golovine, who had been on the Russian General Staff, were not published until after *The Eastern Front* had appeared.

Another criticism that may be made about the book is that Churchill concentrated his attention almost exclusively upon the strategic and tactical aspects of the war and to a far lesser extent on the personalities involved—his full sketch of Von Hindenburg, the German commander-in-chief, for instance, is not to be found here but in another of his books, *Great Contemporaries*. It seems a pity that he did not attempt to analyse more closely the deeper reasons for the Russian failure in the war, which were as much moral, political, social and economic as military. In his *War Memoirs* Lloyd George rightly stressed the Russians' lack of adequate arms and equipment as the principal reason for their defeats in 1915. (Lloyd George was at the time equally concerned about the course of events on the eastern front and, like Churchill and Sir Maurice Hankey, the Secretary to the War Cabinet, was himself an 'easterner', though he consistently advocated an Allied front in Salonika rather than Gallipoli.) Inexhaustible man-power, he argued, was not everything. On 22 February 1915 Lloyd George warned the British War Cabinet of grave Russian deficiencies—even of rifles. The great retreat of 1915, he wrote, was 'entirely due to Russian inferiority in artillery, rifles and ammunition of all kinds.' This munition shortage, he said at the time, was 'bleeding the Russian armies to death.' By 1916 when the Russian position in that respect materially improved, it was too late to avert the revolution, for by then the armies were demoralized. Golovine emphasizes that although the morale of the Russian army was high when the war began it had already collapsed by 1915 and the removal by the Tsar of the Grand Duke Nicholas from his post as commander-in-chief in September 1915 was a fatal step.

In his book Churchill tends to be rather romantic about the Russians. He dedicated it 'to our faithful allies and comrades in the Russian imperial armies.' He admired the way in which on every occasion the Tsar promptly responded to the appeals for help from his allies—in 1914, 1915, and 1916—which generally meant the launching of offensives with insufficient preparation and often too little ammunition. As Cruttwell remarked, chivalrous gestures are not everything. Churchill takes too little account of the incompetence and corruption of the Russian General Staff whose lack of planning made it easy to embrace chivalrous gestures.

But whatever defects may be found in Churchill's book as a complete historical survey of the subject, it is an invaluable and illuminating guide to the general course of the military campaigns, especially those of 1914 and 1915. Churchill drew upon his own strategic appreciation acquired from his position in the British Government at the time and from the studies he had made of the war as a whole in *The World Crisis*. Books written about these campaigns by the actors who took part in them, notably the memoirs of Ludendorff and Brusilov and to a lesser extent those of Hoffmann, are incomprehensible except to the most dedicated students of military history. Churchill distilled the essence of his narrative from them, using all the facility he had acquired from constantly writing on cognate subjects, and thus enabled his readers to understand the true nature of the war on this front and the problems faced by the commanders on both sides. But it must be confessed that even in Churchill's own book on these campaigns, spread over so huge a geographical area and involving so many millions of soldiers, the detail at times becomes oppressive and requires the reader to struggle to locate places on the maps and to long for occasional relief from the complex movements of armies, corps and divisions.

The book is not altogether free from the predilections of the author. Though in theory Churchill started to write about it as an impartial historian anxious to find out what had actually happened on the eastern front in 1914–1916, he could not fail to recall the frustrations of the 'easterners' in the British Government who felt both at the time and in retrospect that what they had attempted to do in order to relieve the German menace to Imperial Russia had always proved to be too little and too late.

That applied equally to the Gallipoli campaign and to Lloyd George's scheme to animate the Balkans from Salonika. Also Churchill's feelings about the 'betrayal' of their allies by the new Russian Bolshevik Government causes him to highlight the romantic sacrifices of the Tsar's armies. So once again it is right to regard this swiftly written book of Churchill's not merely as an extremely useful and informative essay on military and political history but also as a significant sidelight thrown upon his own career and attitudes as a statesman in time of war.

10

Marlborough: His Life and Times

FROM the time that he was a young man Winston Churchill had been pressed to write a biography of his ancestor, John Churchill, the first Duke of Marlborough. The subject appealed to him both because of his devotion to his family and because of the Duke's fame as a soldier. Churchill's cousin, the ninth Duke, had promised that Churchill should have exclusive access to the vast quantity of material in the muniment room at Blenheim Palace and had denied permission to the popular historian, George Macaulay Trevelyan, who in the nineteen-twenties planned a book on the reign of Queen Anne, to examine these papers, at any rate until Churchill had finished with them.

After the fall of Stanley Baldwin's Government Churchill approached this task with gusto. He had never attempted anything like it before and indeed, apart from Macaulay's *History of England,* had read comparatively little about the first Duke of Marlborough's life or times. But he felt sure that his deep knowledge of war and politics and his gift for narrative would stand him in good stead. So he signed a contract and projected a two-volume book.

He was understandably determined from the first to make the best case he could for his ancestor. This was not to be an essay in the impartial writing of history but the biography of a hero. The difficulty was, as he knew, that historians—or at any rate the general public who read history—had tended to accept the kind of criticism of the first Duke of Marlborough's political morality and personal habits that had been enshrined in Macaulay's *History:* that is to say, the accusation that he had betrayed his master, King James II, in the revolution of 1688, that he had equally conspired against King William III with the very king, exiled across the English Channel, whom he had previously deserted, and that he was unscrupulous in the pursuit of wealth and power, mean and avaricious until the end of his days.

Churchill therefore arranged to gather together every scrap of evidence that would throw light on the reasons for his hero's political behaviour and prepared to marshal every argument based on morality or expediency that would promote a convincing case on his behalf. From the first it was his intention not merely to defend but to attack. He therefore planned an assault on the veracity of Lord Macaulay. For this he already possessed one piece of ammunition in a book called *Paradoxes and Puzzles* by John Paget which had been presented to him by Lord Rosebery. Paget had been a Victorian barrister who vividly exposed some of Macaulay's historical mistakes, but once Churchill began to investigate the subject closely he discovered that it was even more complicated than he had imagined and that the material was formidable. Consequently the first volume of the biography, which takes the story down to 1702 when Marlborough became Captain-General of the British army and a first Minister under Queen Anne, is a curious mixture of brilliant advocacy and detailed argument. Because of its length the whole biography eventually burgeoned into four volumes.

At times Churchill found the historical minutiae in which he was thus involved hard going—and he was worried about it for his readers' sakes—though he enjoyed the intellectual challenges that were presented. He wrote in his preface: 'In this work I am compelled before reaching the great period of his [Marlborough's] life to plough through years of struggle and to meet a host of sneers, calumnies and grave accusations.' He did not find any great difficulty in offering a justification for John Churchill's

[139]

decision to desert his master, King James II, when he was second-in-command of the King's army at the time of the invasion by William of Orange in 1688. He showed that John Churchill had already indicated to the King his dislike of his policies and that he was but one of the King's former servants who was drawn into the 'national conspiracy' against their bigoted Roman Catholic monarch.

Nevertheless John Churchill's conduct went against the grain of his biographer. For Winston Churchill himself was always intensely loyal both to his monarch and to his fellow Ministers. Lloyd George once said that there are no friendships at the top, but Winston himself was a generous friend. Consider, for example, his behaviour towards the eccentric Lord Beaverbrook and the senile Lloyd George during the second world war, and the fact that in none of his historical writings, as I have noted earlier, does he speak unkindly even of men like Lord Fisher and Bonar Law who treated him badly. When at the very period he was writing this book Churchill himself was ostracized by former friends in the Conservative Party because he differed from them over India he felt his treatment rather sadly. Like the first Duke of Marlborough, he himself had been the subject of calumny. Yet, on the other hand, he did not altogether care for the idea of an officer deserting his post in the face of an enemy, as John Churchill did, though admittedly it was an enemy in a civil war.

Winston Churchill found even more distasteful Marlborough's political behaviour after James II had fled from his kingdom and William of Orange had taken his place. For how could one justify the 'betrayal' of James II if within a few years of that event Marlborough started, as he did, to seek his pardon from the very King he had betrayed, and from his followers the Jacobites? So Churchill was obliged to write that 'no complete justification will be found' for Marlborough's conduct after 1688. But Churchill aimed to argue with detailed supporting proof that the foundations on which some of the accusations of Marlborough's disloyalty were based were extremely weak: in

particular to question the story told by Lord Macaulay that
Marlborough had given intelligence to the King of France, when
England was at war with France, of a planned combined operation by British forces against the port of Brest in 1694. Churchill
was able to cast doubts on the value of the sources for this
accusation, especially on the authenticity of the so-called memoirs
of King James II and on a collection of Jacobite documents (the
Nairne papers) that had ultimately found their way into the
Bodleian Library at Oxford.

Much of Churchill's argument about this matter has been
accepted as valid by later historians. Nevertheless it is troublesome to his admirers to have to admit that Winston Churchill
in his understandable effort to provide the completest apologia
for his hero exaggerates a good case. Malcolm V. Hay, a Roman
Catholic author, exposed a few errors in a booklet entitled
Winston Churchill and James II published in 1934, soon after
the appearance of the first volume of the *Marlborough*. The
errors were not of much significance and did not really invalidate
the essential arguments; but, to give one instance of this tendency
to exaggerate, Churchill asserts on the evidence of a letter
discovered in Windsor Castle that James II himself had never
written memoirs beyond the year 1660 and therefore what was
later published under his name could not be treated as first-class
authority for Marlborough's relations with the exiled Court at a
subsequent date. Sir Keith Feiling, the distinguished historian
who was consulted by Churchill about this book, pointed out to
him that even if James himself had not written all the memoirs
published under his name he had undoubtedly left personal
papers that he had written over the years. It is, I think, pretty
clear if one reads the book known as J. S. Clarke's *Life of James II*
that it derived to a large extent from James's own writings. An
American editor of a newly discovered version of James's
memoirs to 1660 (writing in 1962) has expressed the considered
opinion that James continued to write memoirs at least until
1684. And in fact King James II told Cardinal Bouillon (who was
writing a life of Marshal Turenne) in 1695 that 'he had already

[141]

written pretty exactly year by year in English the memoirs of his own life.' The source for this statement is to be found in A. M. Ramsay's *Histoire du Vicomte de Turenne* published in Paris in 1735. It was hardly Winston Churchill's fault that nobody drew his attention to this admittedly obscure book. But it shows how dangerous it can be to be over-emphatic in a historical argument.

Still Churchill was, I think, entirely successful in indicating that nearly all the evidence for Marlborough's alleged treacheries, on which Lord Macaulay had dilated, came from much the same dubious Jacobite sources; and the Jacobites, as Churchill argues, had every motive for wishing to persuade the King of France that they possessed influential supporters in England. If, in fact, Marlborough, who was not then a member of the Government, did reveal to any Jacobite agent information about the proposed operations against Brest, he certainly could not have done so before he was quite sure that the intelligence had already reached Versailles from other sources. The undoubted historical fact is that most leading English politicians at the time (including Cabinet Ministers) sent polite messages from England to King James as a form of insurance in case William of Orange's growing unpopularity with his English subjects should provoke a successful counter-revolution.

Churchill tends to overpaint the blackness of King James's villainy, as Malcolm Hay pointed out. A good case can be made out for this King. Nor does Churchill show enthusiasm for William III, though he recognizes his tolerance and devotion to duty. He suggests that if William had made more use of Marlborough's services in the nine years' war against France, the whole history of Europe might have been changed. That is to exercise hindsight. It could not have been easy for King William to detect Marlborough's military genius at the beginning of the reign; and the King had every reason for distrusting English courtiers and politicians.

The technique of daubing villains black in order to heighten the virtues of the hero is characteristic of melodrama. Churchill does not fall into so obvious a trap—any more than he did in his unique novel—and just as in his earlier books on the history of warfare he is generous to the commanders on the other side, from the Khalifa to Michael Collins, so in sketching the characters of Marlborough's political opponents including Robert Harley and the Earl of Shrewsbury he is reasonably fair. But he paints with a full brush.

When Churchill moves on from the long, complicated and slightly discreditable story of Marlborough's rise to power at the age of fifty-two, he feels more comfortable. When King William III died, what Churchill called 'the sunshine day' arrived for Queen Anne, the two Marlboroughs and their friend, Sidney Godolphin (who had become Lord Treasurer). It was the prelude to an era of victories by Marlborough and the final defeat of King Louis XIV of France, whom Churchill rightly compares with such other disturbers of the European peace as Napoleon I and Kaiser Wilhelm II of Germany. The story then becomes one of the elaborate preparations for the War of the Spanish Succession (1701-1715), the military campaigns ranging from the Danube to the Ebro, the diplomatic aspects of the war, and the internal political crises in England. Louis XIV had asserted the right of his grandson, Philip of Anjou, to succeed to the entire Spanish empire, the dead Spanish king having written a will in his favour. That would have upset the balance of power and made the French the masters of Europe. Thus the English, Dutch and Austrian Habsburgs (who also laid claim to the Spanish inheritance) banded together to form a Grand Alliance against Louis XIV. Here then was a war which affected the whole of Europe, and though it was not strictly comparable with the war of 1914-1918, such questions as the holding of a supreme command and the working out of an overall military and naval strategy had their affinities with what happened during the period fifteen years before Churchill started thinking about Marlborough.

Naturally it is easy enough to be anachronistic in the writing of history, but certain principles in the conduct of war and politics remain much the same in all epochs. There is no question

[143]

that it was Churchill's profound knowledge and experience in the actual working of such matters that gave his book on Marlborough its outstanding quality. He could perceive exactly how the minds of statesmen and commanders moved in those far-off times. To give one instance of this. Just before he started writing, Lewis Namier had published his revolutionary studies of English political history in the eighteenth century, which transformed the character of academic research into modern parliamentary history for at least a generation. By a minute analysis of individual members of parliament in the mid-eighteenth-century House of Commons Namier demonstrated precisely how the political system then functioned. Some historians have attempted to apply the Namier techniques to the reign of Queen Anne and have argued that it is misleading to speak of a two-party system since it was, they say, a multi-party system or system of groups. Churchill understood perfectly clearly that the two main parties of Whigs and Tories contained many different shades of opinion, moderate as well as extreme; also that there were cross-benchers, non-party men and men who changed sides. Moreover he was fully aware that both Marlborough and Queen Anne disliked the party system and preferred to have a coalition government as an instrument for waging the war against France—just as a coalition was to be needed to wage the wars against Germany in the twentieth century. Nevertheless Churchill perceived that a distinct government party and a distinct opposition existed and that the general elections (such as that of 1702) were fought on party lines. Two books by university historians published in 1967 have shown that Churchill was correct in his view; they point out that the two-party system was a reality in the reign of Queen Anne—whatever Namier may have shown to have developed fifty years later—and that elections were fiercely contested by the two parties. Thus Churchill is not anachronistic in his description of politics in the reign of Queen Anne.

In the political sphere Churchill is shrewd on men's motives and policies, though he is less happy when he writes about women. He pictures the reign of Queen Anne as on the whole the greatest period in British history and portrays the ruler as 'a great Queen championed by a great Constable.' Anne was as stubborn as a mule and had a mind of her own, but it is rather absurd to speak of her as a great Queen; as to her reign being the greatest period in English history, that is a question of personal opinion which can hardly be subjected to an objective appraisal. Many historians would prefer the reign of Queen Elizabeth I; others might even look back to King Alfred; and today not a few who were contemporaries of Churchill might regard 1940 when he himself became Prime Minister as the greatest period in English history. For then we stood alone; we were never alone during the wars against Louis XIV.

Another advantage that Churchill possessed in writing his biography was that he learned as he went along and, having learnt, was able to convey to his readers what he had found out. I do not believe that either the military or naval advisers who helped him to write his history knew much about the period when they began to work for him; so they discovered and explained to Churchill the differences between the art of war in the early eighteenth century and at the time when he was writing. At sea there was the question of how necessary naval bases were in the days of sailing ships; on land the use of cavalry and its relationship with the infantry in the times of the flintlock musket and ring bayonet before the invention of the machine-gun. So Churchill was able to describe in a clear and practical way the technical characteristics of eighteenth-century warfare, while he explained the problems of a commander-in-chief or a chief of staff in the light of his own knowledge and experience. No one who worked for him could fail to be impressed by his rapid grasp of detail and the manner in which he wove it into his historical narrative. Those who are lucky enough to enjoy such gifts are never pedestrian historians.

In relating the life of the first Duke of Marlborough after 1702 Churchill was in his element. For now his hero was serene and not troubled by scruples but only by the obstructions of his allies and colleagues, which, after all, is the usual price of political life. Churchill shows clearly that Marlborough from the very outset of his campaigns was determined to bring the French to battle rather than become bogged down in the reduction of fortresses. In this he differed from his predecessor, William III, and also from Louis XIV's able general, Sebastien Vauban, who wrote that the successful carrying through of sieges was the finest way of waging war. But in the early stages of the war Marlborough's plans were frustrated by the Dutch. Churchill believed that Marlborough, after much dispute, had been appointed Deputy Captain-General of the Dutch armies at a salary of £10,000 a year as well as commander of the English forces in the Netherlands and of the troops in British pay. In fact research into the Dutch archives since Churchill wrote indicates that he never held any other position than that of commander of the Anglo-Dutch forces when they served together in the field. In any case he was certainly not a supreme commander or Generalissimo in the modern sense. He had to take the advice of Dutch deputies who were sent to represent the States-General with their armies as well as to conciliate the Dutch generals who resented his position. However he was a master of the art of diplomacy. Only by overcoming or side-stepping obstacles was he able finally to gain his military aims.

In the campaign of 1702 Marlborough cleared the line of the river Meuse of his French enemy and in 1703 at Dutch request he took Bonn on the Lower Rhine. But he was not allowed to fight a battle even when he had manœuvred an excellent opportunity to strike the French army in the flank, while in 1703 the disobedience of a Dutch general prevented Marlborough from capturing Antwerp or Ostend or both and thus clearing his communications with England. So it was that in 1704 he decided to lead his own troops across Germany to the Danube and thus relieve the Emperor who was menaced by French armies *en route* to Vienna. Churchill disentangles with skill the military and diplomatic preparations for this brilliant military enterprise and pays tribute to the Dutch who in the end allowed Marlborough to carry some of the soldiers who were in their pay far from their frontiers. In recounting this campaign which culminated in the battle of Blenheim, one of the most notable victories for British arms in the eighteenth century, Churchill does not omit to consider the human aspects of the story and describes with art and humour Marlborough's delicate relations with Prince Eugene of Savoy, the Austrian commander, and the Margrave of Baden, a veteran German general of touchy disposition. By the skilful and ingenious use of numerous maps Churchill pictures the advance of Marlborough's army—the 'scarlet caterpillar' as he calls it—crawling across Europe and illuminates the tactical aspects of the campaign ending with the battles of Schellenberg and Blenheim, which 'changed the political aspect of the world.'

Churchill rightly did not concentrate solely on the campaigns in which Marlborough himself fought but places them in a wider strategical setting. He shows how at home Marlborough had to contend with Tory critics who believed that the war might be won mainly by the exertion of sea-power and the subsidizing of German and Scandinavian troops. Churchill himself was to hear similar arguments often deployed in his own lifetime, for example by politicians who remained convinced that 'economic sanctions' would bring down a determined government without threat of war. It seems to me, however, that Churchill did not always emphasize sufficiently the significant broadening of the war aims of the Grand Alliance which formed an essential part of the treaty concluded by it with Portugal to bring that kingdom into the war of the Spanish succession in 1703. The Portuguese were willing to open Lisbon as a base to the Allies and to provide a contingent of soldiers for war in Spain on the understanding that a French Bourbon prince should never be allowed to rule in Madrid. The original terms of the Grand Alliance had envisaged a partition of the Spanish empire between the Bourbons and the Habsburgs. And there is little doubt that after the defeat at Blenheim, and certainly after Marlborough's later victory at Ramillies in 1706, the French King would have been willing to make peace on some such terms. (Peace feelers were held out to Marlborough in the autumn of 1705.) But from 1703 onwards the parrot cry was repeated in Vienna and in London that 'there can be no peace without Spain'—in other words that the whole of the Spanish empire had to be forcibly transferred to the Habsburg claimant.

Winston Churchill was of course fully aware that in times of world war all sorts of promises are made to enlist fresh allies, promises which are usually hard to fulfil and are always the source of embarrassment in negotiating peace treaties. He could vividly remember the secret treaties concluded during the Great War which had been so much disliked by President Wilson and the Americans and yet had to be honoured at Versailles. Marlborough was a leading member of the government which unwisely committed itself to this widening of the war aims of the Grand Alliance. Churchill says that 'the English Cabinet and Nottingham, the Tory Secretary of State, were directly responsible' for the resolve. Yet Marlborough might surely have made his own opinion felt had he wished since he was responsible for carrying out the decision. Statesmen are rarely distinguished for foresight. Marlborough was no exception. The alliance of Portugal was not worth the high price paid for it; and the cry of 'no peace without Spain' was, as much as any one cause, to be responsible in the end for Marlborough's own political downfall.

Churchill writes that Marlborough always regarded the campaigns in the Iberian peninsula as a 'side-show.' The French, Marlborough believed, could only be defeated in battle and the battles—with the exception of Blenheim—had to be fought on the fields of Flanders. Thus Marlborough appeared to adopt a different view from that held by his biographer in the Great War. (Churchill would not have admitted this: he compares the march to the Danube with operations against Turkey in the Great War.) Admittedly the war of the Spanish succession was not being fought in the age of the machine-gun, barbed wire, or trench warfare; but traditionally it was the scene of sieges and counter-sieges, a campaigning area in which cleverly sited fortresses had to be reduced one by one before field armies could progress. In fact the sieges of towns and citadels required a kind of trench warfare, while to break through fortified lines was by no means easy with the primitive weapons of that time. Thus Marlborough's critics had a case when they argued that the war might be won more cheaply by naval pressure and amphibious operations in the Mediterranean. There is no question, as Churchill shows, that Marlborough interested himself in the Mediterranean theatre even when he was absorbed in operations elsewhere; but the division of the resources of the Allies between the various theatres of the war, Italy, Germany, and Spain as well as Portugal and the Netherlands, was a constant cause of weakness. The French and their Spanish allies were generally fighting upon the defensive on inner lines and therefore—granted that the extended war aims of the Grand Alliance precluded a compromise peace— were able to prolong the struggle for twelve years, in spite of their inferiority in manpower and financial resources. Churchill does not neglect these problems. Indeed no historian was better equipped than he was to cope with them. One cannot help but feel, however, that it was in finding tactical rather than strategic solutions, both in war and in politics, that his hero was supreme.

After the battle of Blenheim Marlborough pursued what proved to be an over-ambitious scheme for an offensive along the valley of the Moselle which would take him through Lorraine into France and 'might carry him far on the road to Paris.' The scheme foundered because of lack of German co-operation and Marlborough was compelled to bring back his army to the Netherlands. The effort was made, even if it proved fruitless. 'Still,' writes Churchill, 'in every war someone at the summit of intellect and authority had to try and try very hard.' Marlborough was 'deserted in Germany' and 'fettered in Holland.' Later, while he pierced the fortified lines of Brabant, he failed to bring the French to battle on the river Dyle. These failures in 1705 partly obliterated the memory of Blenheim.

Meanwhile in England Marlborough was harassed by political problems. Though he and his friend Godolphin still preferred

[149]

the idea of a coalition government after a general election in 1705 had cost the Tories seats, pressure was brought to bear on Queen Anne to employ more Whigs. Marlborough's wife, Sarah, was the Whig agent at Court: 'she not only overrated her influence on public matters with the Queen,' writes Churchill, 'but she mistook its character. She sought to win by argument, voluble and vociferous, what had hitherto been the freehold property of love.' In fact—Churchill perhaps does not emphasize this sufficiently—Sarah's influence with the Queen declined almost immediately she came to the throne because she insisted on treating Anne with a familiarity which few people can put up with from old friends when they have attained positions of authority. It was Marlborough's victories that sustained his political position, not the former friendship of Princess Anne with his wife during the reign of King Charles II. Even that appeared to be in danger in 1705 since because of his failures during the campaigning season he was deemed to be 'a mortified adventurer.'

However, 1706 was again a year of victory. At first Marlborough had envisaged another daring scheme—to lead an army to Italy. Instead he was able to fight the battle of Ramillies in the Netherlands which opened the way to the complete submission of the Spanish Netherlands (Belgium) to the Grand Alliance. The battle of Ramillies was won by Marlborough's reinforcement of his left wing with the bulk of his cavalry after an unexpected success had been obtained in the first minutes of the battle by the deft use of artillery. Marlborough himself took part in the actual fighting on the left and nearly lost his life. In this year a political compromise was reached with the Queen when she gave an important appointment to the Marlboroughs' son-in-law, the third Earl of Sunderland. Also in that year the final stages of the union between England and Scotland were completed.

Difficulties arose in Belgium because of the rival claims between the Austrian Habsburgs and the Dutch to control the territory. Partly for this reason in 1707 Marlborough planned yet another bold operation for an invasion of France from the south by an amphibious movement against the naval base of Toulon in the Mediterranean. 'In the winter of 1706–7 Marlborough's central aim became the siege of Toulon,' writes Churchill. Prince Eugene of Savoy was persuaded, against his will, to lead an army thence from northern Italy and a British fleet co-operated from the sea. This plan reminds one of the scheme for the invasion of southern France in the second world war which became abortive after D-day. Eugene's march took longer than had been expected; when he arrived at Toulon it had been reinforced by the French; and in spite of pressure from the British Admiral Eugene refused in July to pursue the assault. After the army withdrew the British fleet smashed up the port—as far as the cannon of those days permitted—and the English command of the Mediterranean remained unchallenged for the rest of the war.

Eugene had regarded his task as an impossible one; certainly his heart was never in it. Eugene's apologists have found plenty of excuses for his failure. The Duke of Savoy, who was nominally in command, was blamed; Eugene's delay in leaving Turin is explained by his wish to confuse the French about where he was going; Marlborough is condemned for pursuing an *idée fixe* which was never practicable. One writer even ridiculously suggests that Marlborough's support for the Duke of Savoy at this time 'may not have been altogether disinterested' because the Duke had presented him with a set of paintings (not by Titian, as Churchill in fact states) with 'nude figures in diverse lewd and lascivious postures.' The Austrian conclusion of a separate military agreement with France over Italy, known as the treaty of Milan, is also defended as a wise decision, although Churchill regards it as a betrayal of the Grand Alliance.

1708 began with the rupture of an attempt to break up the British Government by the Tories. Queen Anne was fed up with being hectored by Sarah Marlborough on behalf of the Whigs and was tiring of the war. But in spite of ill success in 1707 (the French had won a victory at Almanza in Spain, decisive for the future of the war in the Iberian peninsula, and another French army had penetrated a defensive line in Germany) Marlborough's reputation still stood high enough to defeat the intrigues of Robert Harley, 'Robin the trickster,' who was the Secretary of State. Marlborough added to his laurels by winning in July the battle of Oudenarde, although because he placed Prince Eugene, who was serving with him as a volunteer, in charge of the allied right wing, Eugene gained much of the credit. Churchill compares this victory to the battle of Tannenberg which was fresh in his mind. Like the Russians at Tannenberg, the French were threatened with encirclement, though the numbers involved were smaller and 'with the weapons that shot not more than a hundred yards' it was impossible to cover gaps in the encircling brigades. One does not feel that Churchill was altogether fair to the commander-in-chief, Marshal Vendôme, in his account of the battle. At Ramillies to clinch the victory Marlborough personally led a cavalry charge on the left wing in which he was 'transported by the energy of his war vision and passion.' Eugene was not at Ramillies and no one but Marlborough himself was in general control of the battle. At Oudenarde Churchill blames Vendôme for leading the fighting at a critical stage of the battle on his left wing and thus losing control of the battle. Yet, as one can see from Churchill's own narrative, if the French had been able to thrust through on their left, they might have gained the victory. For that very reason Marlborough had dispatched two lots of reinforcements to Eugene from the other wing. Moreover Vendôme had the right to suppose that the Duke of Burgundy, who was nominally his superior, was in a position to control the battle from his headquarters to the rear. In fact Vendôme's messages to Burgundy were ignored or disregarded and when his own exertions came to nothing, his army was encircled. But he had not behaved very differently from Marlborough at Ramillies.

After this defeat Vendôme wisely withdrew to the fortress of Ghent where he interfered with the allied lines of communication between the United Netherlands and the French frontier and perplexed the Dutch. Marlborough himself wanted to mask the great fortress of Lille and, with support from the sea at Abbeville, thrust straight into the heart of France. This bold scheme was altogether too much for Prince Eugene, just as the Toulon operation had been, for he was 'a land animal.' Needless to say, Eugene's admirers criticize Winston Churchill for not paying sufficient credit to Eugene in 1708. 'Eugene's strategic views,' it is said, 'found general acceptance among the allied generals'— other than Marlborough—for what that was worth. Eugene's mere presence in the Netherlands, it is affirmed, prevented the war 'going sour.' He outshone Marlborough and had none of his 'hankering after personal gain.' But one does not believe that close reading of Churchill's book will convert the impartial reader from the belief that Marlborough possessed the more commanding and more daring military genius.

Churchill compared the decision to engage upon the long and difficult siege of Lille with the costly offensives on the western front during the Great War which were preferred to 'so-called eccentric alternatives' and quotes Kitchener's saying, 'One cannot wage war as one ought, but only as one can.' The fall of the citadel of Lille on 9 December 1708, and the recapture of Ghent, put the seal on a year of victory, and thus Marlborough reached the peak of his career as a soldier. It was then that peace should have been made between the allies and France. Marlborough himself put out secret peace feelers through his nephew, the Duke of Berwick, who was a French Marshal. Marlborough was promised a gratuity of two million livres by the French Government if peace were concluded, but the Whig Government insisted on 'no peace without Spain' and Marlborough supported this. That insistence prevented peace, for the Spaniards had acquired an intense loyalty to their French monarch, Philip V. Marlborough was also distrusted by the Dutch because the Habsburg Emperor had astutely offered him the Governor-Generalship of the former Spanish Netherlands at a large salary once he had conquered them as a result of the battle of Oudenarde. The Dutch were kept in the war by the promise of a large barrier of fortresses in the former Spanish Netherlands, while the Austrians went on fighting so as to gain the entire Spanish inheritance. Hence the making of peace was prevented on all sides.

The French were in a grave position and were willing to make peace. Churchill argues that Marlborough was the prisoner of the Whigs, but himself really yearned for peace. While the allies were demanding that one of the terms of a peace treaty should be that King Louis XIV must compel his grandson to abandon Spain, Marlborough thought it would have been wiser for the allies themselves to drive Philip V out of Spain and volunteered to achieve this himself in the space of six months. Thus either way the war would have continued beyond 1709 for another year. Churchill's argument that Marlborough desired peace at this time and had no motives for continuing the war any longer does not carry complete conviction. It is never easy to yield up a supreme position, and by wedding himself since 1703 to the doctrine of 'no peace without Spain' Marlborough in effect ensured that the war would have to go on. Churchill found it most distasteful that Marlborough did not jib at being offered money by his French enemies to help them make peace—and was even, later, to remind them of their offer. Nevertheless Churchill also suggests that Marlborough was less interested in acquiring the post of Governor-General of the Netherlands than other historians have believed. Still the fact was that such things were recognized perquisites both in the seventeenth and eighteenth centuries and do not need to be held to Marlborough's discredit if one judges him by his own contemporary standards.

When the peace negotiations broke down, Marlborough and Eugene together fought the battle of Malplaquet against the French. They assaulted the French army when it was in prepared positions and lost twice as many casualties as their enemy, though they won a victory by driving the French from the field. The French decision to fight on, Churchill attributes to 'obscure intrigues in the backstairs' in London. It was also owing to the excessive demands of the allies which aroused French patriotism. Malplaquet brought peace no nearer. Marlborough now asked Queen Anne to give him the Captain-Generalship of the British army for life, a request without a precedent. This request was partly inspired by the decline of his influence in the government

MARLBOROUGH: HIS LIFE AND TIMES

which he served. Queen Anne was tiring of the war and her secret adviser, Robert Harley, was planning to undermine the Government and replace it with a Tory one. The general election of 1710 resulted in a Tory victory. Although Godolphin and Marlborough's other Ministerial colleagues were dismissed from office, he himself agreed to retain his own posts. He was still required as the victorious commander-in-chief and in any case it was thought that if he were insulted enough he would resign voluntarily. Churchill considers that the reason he abstained from resigning was because he patriotically regarded his services as indispensable to the alliance. He did in fact in 1710 and 1711 capture a number of fortresses on the French frontier, but he had no wish to fight another 'murdering battle' like that of Malplaquet. As things turned out, Churchill observes, it would have conduced more to his glory in history if he had been killed at Oudenarde.

The fact is that no man is indispensable, although all statesmen and most generals think that they are. It is difficult for an impartial reader not to feel that the successive temptations experienced by Marlborough—the two million livres (later raised to four million) offered to him as a peace-maker, the £60,000 a year salary as Governor-General, the possibility of being created Captain-General for life—influenced him towards clinging to his position. But his continuation in service contributed little to his own or his country's future. In fact the Tory Government negotiated a separate peace with France behind his back and at the end of 1711 Queen Anne dismissed him under circumstances of the utmost humiliation.

Churchill does not complain of the terms of the Treaty of Utrecht which ended the war, but he censures the 'mean and treacherous manner' in which the war was concluded. These are dangerous words, for his hero too has been accused of meanness and treachery. Even after his retirement Marlborough continued to send fair messages to the Jacobite exiles while at the same time offering help to the Hanoverian successor to Queen Anne. Though a humane man, Marlborough found it hard to forgive his political enemies. When he was restored to office and power by King George I after the death of Queen Anne he frightened out of England Henry St John, Viscount Bolingbroke, the former Tory Secretary of State (for whom Churchill can find no good words), and pushed for the impeachment of Robert Harley, Earl of Oxford, the former Lord Treasurer, the two men who had driven him from power and deliberately blackened his reputation.

A considerable amount of historical research on the political history of the reign of Queen Anne has been done since Churchill's biography of Marlborough first appeared: the membership of the two Houses of Parliament has been elaborately investigated and the structure of politics in that period freshly examined; but at the time of writing no definitive biographies of Harley or St John have been published. It is possible therefore that Churchill's political account will be modified by future historians. Often Churchill is extremely astute in his dissection of political motives, but he is somewhat romantic when it comes to personal relationships. He speaks, for example, of Marlborough and Eugene as the great 'Twin Captains.' But we know that Eugene was often highly critical of Marlborough's strategy, while, as we have seen, Marlborough was extremely disappointed with Eugene's failure in the Toulon operation on which the Duke had set his heart. A modern historian has also suggested that at one stage at least—at the beginning of 1708—Marlborough was less loyal to his colleague Godolphin than Churchill makes out: it is argued that he might then have been willing to come to terms with Harley at Godolphin's expense. Equally Godolphin refused to back Marlborough when the latter was prepared for a vital trial of strength with the Queen. When Godolphin was forced out of the Government Marlborough did not resign as well. Churchill did not feel much enthusiasm for Marlborough's wife and perhaps gives undue importance to her tactless aliena- tion of Queen Anne in the political history of the reign, but he paints a rosy picture of their married love. He refrains from quoting the passage in the Wentworth papers which asserts that

Marlborough kept a mistress and he was most reluctant to quote the unpublished letters found in Blenheim Palace which show that Sarah Marlborough accused her husband of infidelity (although it is plain there was little in that particular accusation).

To say that at points Churchill tends to romanticize his narrative and to imagine that Marlborough was as dedicated to the service of his country and as generous-minded as the author always was himself are minor criticisms of this book. I used to think that Winston Churchill's life of his father was his finest historical work, but on re-reading the *Marlborough*, I have come to the conclusion that indeed this is his best. When a shortened version appears from which most of the letters have been eliminated it will, I think, stand out even more clearly as a supreme example of historical skill and art. The book is of exceptional quality for three reasons. In the first place, unlike the life of Lord Randolph Churchill, it is not concerned purely with a relatively short and unimportant decade in British political history; nor, unlike *The Eastern Front,* is it exclusively about battles. It also deals to a much larger extent than Churchill's other historical books with the characters and motives of the men and women of an earlier age: in Churchill's books on contemporary history he was far too magnanimous to traduce the living or question their motives. Secondly, the book embodied much historical scholarship. Churchill was able not only to draw on the Marlborough and Sunderland papers at Blenheim Palace, but also on material collected from the Dutch, French and Austrian archives as well as private papers and military diaries put at his disposal. All this material he carefully examined and much of it scrupulously printed. He makes excellent use of contemporary narratives and of German historical research which he had translated for him. Thirdly, it should not be held against Churchill as a historian that he set out to 'whitewash' his ancestor, as is so often said: 'whitewash' is an opprobrious word. He determined from the outset to make out the best case for his hero: how many biographers do otherwise? Yet one can see that certain things in Marlborough's conduct and career went against the grain with him—for example, his reminder to the French of their promise to pay him a large sum of money if he helped them to a favourable peace or his desertion of King James II while holding a leading command in his army. He does not gloss over these unfortunate episodes, but it was Churchill's intention to do the utmost justice to his ancestor which gives his book its extraordinary and undeniable power. G. M. Trevelyan, who was writing his three-volume book on the reign of Queen Anne about the same time as Churchill was embarking on the *Marlborough,* was much more of a recognized historian, being then Regius Professor of Modern History at Cambridge. Yet Trevelyan's book is already largely out of date. It can hardly be doubted that Churchill's *Marlborough* will be read for many years to come and may never be completely superseded as long as British history is read.

11

The Second World War—I

FRANKLIN D. ROOSEVELT, President of the United States of America, wrote to Winston Churchill on 11 September 1939: 'I am glad you did the Marlborough volumes before this thing started—and I much enjoyed reading them.' 'This thing' was the world war of 1939–1945, which was to be the subject of the next book Churchill wrote after he had ceased to be Prime Minister of Great Britain when it ended.

In his preface to the first volume of this six-volume book, dated March 1948, Churchill repeated more or less what he said in the third volume of his *World Crisis*—that he was following the methods of Defoe's *Memoirs of a Cavalier,* as he conceived them, 'in which the author hangs the chronicle and discussion of great military and political events upon the thread of the personal experiences of an individual.' Again, Churchill observed that his book was not 'history' but 'a contribution to history.'

This is in fact truer here than it was of *The World Crisis.* For though Churchill makes good use of documents which became available from the side of the enemy in the war (such as the Nuremberg evidence and the diaries of Count Ciano, the Italian Foreign Minister) *The Second World War* is essentially and avowedly autobiographical. For from the very outset of the war to the eve of the surrender of Japan to the allies Churchill stood at the heart of public affairs. No one who lived through those days in England can judge Churchill with complete impartiality. We English have been fortunate that in our continental wars we

[159]

have had a series of remarkable leaders: Marlborough, the two Pitts, Lloyd George, and then Churchill. Many of the older of us owe a debt of eternal gratitude to a great man. But the last world war began thirty years ago: the younger generation did not experience it or even know of Churchill except as a name. They will be able to measure his achievement in the light of history. Already hundreds of first-class books and valuable documents have seen the light and very few of the facts remain unearthed or events unexplored. A. J. P. Taylor has written that *The Second World War* 'demands a critical examination which it has not yet received' and that 'Churchill's version of the second world war is likely to dominate the writing of its history for many years to come.' It might, I suppose, equally be said that Dr Taylor's 'version' as embodied in the widely read *Oxford History of England* will carry immense weight with this and rising generations who read our history: but Taylor himself also belongs to the old generation, to the pre-war Left. When I, like Taylor, was at Oxford in the nineteen-twenties I remember reading a remark attributed to a Frenchman that 'truth always arrives in time for history,' implying that history needs to be written in calm and complete chronological perspective. Whatever may be the advantages of writing contemporary history, that is to say writing about the times through which one has lived oneself, it is difficult to shake one's mind free of emotions. I therefore declare my interest; and also I am not attempting to analyse this book as a historical document (that would require a wider ranging scholarship than I possess) but merely to say something about what there is in it of a historian's approach.

The first volume entitled *The Gathering Storm* may be said to contain more of pure historical writing than the others—though it is somewhat of an impressionistic pastiche. For during the ten years before the war actually broke out Churchill was in no way responsible for the decisions of the British Government; indeed he was intensely critical of them. The theme of this volume is that it was to be 'an unnecessary war.' From the moment when Hitler attained full power as dictator of National Socialist

Germany in 1933, Churchill regarded Germany as the principal enemy of European peace, as she had been, he thought, in his younger days. Anthony Eden, who was in Ministerial office at the time (he felt obliged to resign as Foreign Secretary in February 1938), called his autobiographical volume *Facing the Dictators*. But Churchill, like Neville Chamberlain, from whose government Eden resigned, was on the whole prepared to conciliate Mussolini, the dictator of Fascist Italy. I well remember listening to a conversation in the garden of Chartwell Manor, I think it must have been in the summer of 1933, in which Churchill, his friend T. E. Lawrence, and Keith Feiling were discussing for hours the rise of Hitler and the progress of German rearmament. That was to be the dominant theme of Churchill's political thinking in the six years before the war began and it is reflected in his book.

Among the long-term factors making for war Churchill discerns the 'malignant and silly' economic clauses of the Treaty of Versailles and the 'insane economic transactions' with Germany that followed. (A case has since been made for them by the late Etienne Mantoux in a book criticizing Keynes's *Economic Consequences of the Peace*.) Churchill also believed that the 'second cardinal tragedy' was the break-up of the Austro-Hungarian empire which had been a stabilizing force in central Europe. The Weimar Republic, which had replaced the Kaiser's empire, was regarded as the creation of the victors. So there arose Fascism, 'the ugly child of Communism,' and Hitlerism fed on the discontents of a ruined middle class. However, up till 1934 the allies who won the war of 1914–1918 were still supreme and the second world war could 'easily have been prevented.'

When and how could it have been prevented? Up to 1932 German statesmen like Stresemann and Brüning were regarded by the former allies as men with whom peaceful dealings could be carried out, although we now know that Stresemann acquiesced in arrangements that were made by General von Seeckt and others in the German Reichswehr—the regular army permitted to Germany by the Treaty of Versailles—to lay the foundations for secret German rearmament. The French military occupation of the Ruhr in 1923 had been violently disapproved in England. It was not until 1933 when Germany (and Japan) left the League of Nations that the hopes of what was rather mis-leadingly called 'collective security' began to be undermined. When Churchill wrote his book *The Aftermath* in 1929 he con-cluded, as we have seen, by expressing his belief in a peaceable future for Europe. It was not until the rise to power of Hitler, therefore, that any question arose of forcibly restraining the revival of German nationalism.

Churchill writes of British 'fatuity and feebleness' in the 'locust years' 1931–1939. But no one suggested that the 'problem of containing Germany in Europe' could have been positively undertaken before Hitler threw down the gauntlet by reoccupying the demilitarized zone of the Rhineland in March 1936 in defiance of his previous promise to respect the freely negotiated terms of the Treaty of Locarno of 1925. Meanwhile Eden was engaged in facing the other dictator, Mussolini, who had launched his war against independent Abyssinia in October 1935. Churchill writes that the 'problem of containing Germany in Europe was henceforth confused and distorted by the fate of Abyssinia.' He considered that pressure brought by the British navy in the Mediterranean could have given teeth to the League of Nations' condemnation of an aggressor and thus cleared that particular problem out of the way. Indeed Churchill thinks it was foolish to arouse the League against Italy unless in the last resort Great Britain was prepared to go to war.

So far as the British people were concerned at the time, that was never practical politics. In this connection I may recall a small experience of my own. At that time I was a leader-writer on the staff of the old *Manchester Guardian* and was assigned the task of writing about the economic sanctions imposed against Italy by fifty members of the League of Nations gathered in Geneva. Whatever wishful thinking we may have engaged in then, these sanctions were a farce. But when I suggested to the editor of the *Manchester Guardian*, who was a profound believer in the virtues of the League of Nations and of 'collective security,' that the newspaper should back the imposition of an oil sanction (in fact this would probably not have worked either) he would not allow it to be advocated, for he feared that its imposition would mean war. Unlike Churchill, that was a risk he was not prepared to take. It was this widespread feeling that war had to be avoided at all costs that made warlike moves so impractical in 1935–1936.

Moreover it is quite clear now, for example from Anthony Eden's memoirs, that when Hitler's troops reoccupied the Rhineland the French, who were alone capable of throwing them out again, had no serious intention of doing so. Churchill's account, which relies on what Flandin, the French Foreign Minister, said to him at the time, is misleading. The French Cabinet was divided and, when Flandin came to London in March 1936, all he proposed was that the League Council should be summoned. The French advocated sanctions by stages and had no thought-out plan for military action. Not only Baldwin, the British Prime Minister, but Eden, the newly appointed Foreign Secretary, were extraordinarily unwilling to undertake positive commitments. So we were certainly in no position to push the French on to a course of action they did not wish to pursue. Moreover the British Labour Party in opposition and most of the Press were determined above all to avert war.

Churchill himself had contributed to this fear of war. In consequence it did not look as if it would be a simple police operation to expel the Germans from the Rhineland. As we now know, from information that has become available since Churchill wrote the first volume of *The Second World War*, he was in fact exaggerating the military strength of the Germans. In a debate in the House of Commons in November 1934, Stanley Baldwin, answering Churchill, maintained that the German air force had not yet attained fifty per cent of the front-line strength of the British air force. Subsequently Hitler himself told Eden in April 1935 that parity had in fact already been reached and on 22 May Baldwin 'confessed' in the Commons that he had made a mistake. In fact no mistake had been made at all. Hitler was lying. It was difficult, however, for Churchill to argue at one and the same time that the Germans were bluffing in 1936—as Taylor believes they were bluffing throughout—and that their air strength was then substantially greater than ours. For it was widely believed that our island could no longer be completely protected by the British navy and that it had become extremely vulnerable to bombing from the air. If the German air strength had in fact been substantially greater than the British, it would have been difficult to stand up to Hitler as many would have liked to do. Thus while it would be wrong to assert that Churchill's political arguments about the unnecessary and avoidable war are invalidated by the historical facts as they are now known, they do certainly modify his account of events in pre-war Europe as an accurate historical narrative.

Should Great Britain, then, have prevented the 'unnecessary war' by standing up to Hitler when, in the autumn of 1938, he launched his campaign to dismember Czechoslovakia, the ally of France, which possessed an army of thirty-five divisions and the important Skoda arms works? By that time Britain had obviously begun to rearm and British public opinion was much less favourable to Germany than it had been in 1936. Churchill does not say this in so many words.

Churchill writes that 'the British and French Cabinets at this time presented a front of over-ripe melons crushed together whereas what was wanted was a gleam of steel.' And in summing up the tragedy of Munich he blames the British Government for encouraging the French on a fatal course, namely the dishonouring of their treaty obligations to Czechoslovakia. What Churchill is saying, in fact, is that it would have been better to resist then than a year later. He admits that it might in any case have meant war. If the war of 1939 was to become 'unnecessary', to undertake the risk of fighting a war in 1938 would have been necessary.

The researches of historians into the state of British and German rearmament in the last year before the war of 1939 suggest that the British benefited materially from the breathing space acquired through war not breaking out in 1938. During that time the Hurricane and Spitfire fighters that won the Battle of Britain were in the process of being formed into squadrons; radar was being improved and extended; anti-aircraft guns and searchlights were being rapidly manufactured; shadow arms factories were being arranged; and conscription was introduced. In the first part of 1939 630 British aircraft were being produced a month, and in September 1939 the figure rose to 780. In September 1938 the sole British contribution of any significance to a war would have been the navy; and its limitations were shown by the part it was later able to play in the Norwegian campaign, when Churchill admitted that Great Britain was still short of cruisers and destroyers (while the expensive and elephantine battleships, as in the war of 1914–1918, could rarely be risked in action for fear of attacks by submarines, mines and bombing aircraft). Churchill observes in the course of his account of the surrender to Germany over Czechoslovakia that 'We must leave this to the judgment of history.' So far as France was concerned, he was thinking of her national honour. For wherever Churchill speaks of the judgment of history, that is what he means. So far as Great Britain was concerned, it was less a question of honour than of practical realities. Here history affords no certain guide, but historians of Great Britain naturally ask themselves the questions, first whether Chamberlain was wise to have taken the lead at all and to have pitted his businessman's brains against the nationalist fanatic; secondly, whether if war had come earlier and events had anticipated themselves (with Czechoslovakia being overwhelmed instead of Poland) the Battle of Britain could then have been won.

Churchill admits that in 1938 Great Britain was 'hideously unprepared for war,' that the air defences even of London were completely inadequate, and that rearmament was forcibly pursued afterwards. But he says that after 1938 the German progress was more rapid still and her expenditure was larger. Subsequent research however indicates that German expenditure was not as big as Churchill says. In the middle of March 1939 the Germans occupied Prague, the capital of Czechoslovakia, and this complete dismemberment of an independent nation opened the eyes of the British public in general to the ruthlessness and relentlessness of Nazi aggression. An almost united country now approved rearmament. In April the Italians occupied Albania, and Churchill, ever eager for action, advocated the occupation of Corfu but discovered that the British Mediterranean fleet was scattered. The sands were running out. Nevertheless Chamberlain feared that Churchill's inclusion in the Cabinet would provoke Hitler. Instead British guarantees were given to Poland, Rumania and Greece and an alliance was concluded with Turkey—even more provocative steps. And on 3 September 1939 the guarantee to Poland led to Great Britain declaring war on Germany. France reluctantly followed. So began the second world war. Churchill entered the War Cabinet and was once again First Lord of the Admiralty.

Churchill showed at once, as he had done in 1914, that he was not going to confine his activities to his own Department, and both the Air Force and Home Office came under the lash of his criticisms. Equally he was reluctant to wage a defensive war. Soon he was advocating plans first to drop mines in the Rhine as a reprisal for the use by the Germans of magnetic mines against British shipping and secondly to mine the territorial waters of Norway so as to interfere with the German importation of iron ore from Sweden. In a memorandum of 16 December 1939, Churchill wrote: 'Humanity rather than legality must be our guide. Of all this history must be the judge. We must now face events.' But these plans were complicated by Russia's unprovoked attack on Finland which had begun at the end of November and aroused indignation both in England and France. Finland surrendered to the Russians on 12 March 1940, and eventually at the beginning of April a new French Government under Paul Reynaud agreed to Churchill's two schemes for the launching of fluvial mines in the Rhine (previously opposed by the French for fear of German retaliation on them) and secondly for the laying of a mine-field in Norwegian territorial waters.

The Norwegian operation was planned for 8 April and small

Anglo-French forces were held ready to meet any violent German reaction by occupying key points in Norway. But by now Hitler 'was ready with a far more powerful and better prepared scheme.' Churchill's account of the Norwegian campaign must be compared carefully with that given in Dr T. K. Derry's official history. 'Having failed to crush the German invasion by naval action,' writes Dr Derry, 'Britain turned to counter-invasion instead.' Attacks on Narvik and Trondheim were successfully repulsed by the Germans and air action against German communications proved abortive. Several conclusions emerge: the first is that British intelligence throughout was shockingly poor; insufficient preparations had been made for the original operation; British reactions to the German invasion of Denmark and Norway were slow and vacillating; incompatible instructions were given to incompatible commanders. It is conceivable that if direct assaults had been daringly made on Narvik and Trondheim they could have been taken. But at Narvik the British military commander refused to do this, while at Trondheim a pincer movement was preferred. Whether, had these ports been occupied at once, they could have been held against the Germans is another question. Narvik was in fact later occupied for a time (by then without much purpose) but it had to be evacuated. There is no doubt about the heroism displayed by the British navy, but to the world in general and to the British people in particular it seemed astonishing that the one arm of war in which the British reckoned themselves supreme should have been successfully defied by the Germans, however severely what existed of a German navy at the time was damaged in the campaign. The Germans threw in all they had and they won. Churchill writes correctly that Britain was 'forestalled, surprised, and outwitted.'

Churchill accepted at the time his full share of responsibility for the failure of the Norwegian campaign. It was, after all, largely his plan. On the eve of the campaign he had been appointed chairman of the Military Co-ordination Committee in place of Lord Chatfield. Later, on 1 May, Chamberlain gave

[167]

Churchill fuller powers. But it was Chamberlain, not Churchill, who was blamed by the public and in the House of Commons for the disaster in Norway. This was partly because, during the period of the so-called phoney or twilight war that lasted, so far as western Europe was concerned, from 3 September to 8 April, Chamberlain had made a speech in which he said very foolishly that Hitler 'had missed the bus.' So on 10 May 1940, the very day on which the Germans unleashed their offensive through Holland and Belgium upon France, Churchill replaced Chamberlain as Prime Minister and formed a National Government, which Chamberlain had been unable to do. Churchill conveys the impression that as First Lord of the Admiralty he suffered obstruction in his plans not, as in 1914, from his own staff but through an inefficiently organized administration at the centre and also of course from the French. After he became Prime Minister (and appointed himself Minister of Defence) he writes 'I was conscious of a profound sense of relief. At last I had the authority to give directions over the whole scene. I felt as if I were walking with destiny and that all my past life had been but a preparation for this hour and for this trial.'

In his second volume *Their Finest Hour* Churchill describes the exciting six months following the Battle of France and culminating in the British victories over the Italians in the desert war in north Africa. Most of the volume is autobiographical. Churchill made a point of putting down in black-and-white all the instructions and advice he gave as Prime Minister and Minister of Defence: this was partly so that no doubts should exist about what he thought and what he wanted done, but also because he was conscious that he was making history and that one day historians would examine his record.

The Battle of France began on 10 May and lasted for barely six weeks. Some half-million British soldiers and airmen took part in it. As soon as the Germans invaded Holland and Belgium the British expeditionary force, in accordance with General Gamelin's 'Plan D', advanced to the line Antwerp–Louvain–Namur–Meuse with the French Seventh Army on its left.

Churchill does not analyse the campaign in any detail except to say that at one time the British General Staff had expressed doubts about the wisdom of plan D and considered it might have been wiser had the British remained in defensive positions along the French–Belgian frontier instead of thrusting forward to the line of the river Dyle in Belgium. The German 4th Army with a powerful force of tanks broke through at Dinant and the German 12th Army at Sedan. Thus the British to the north were compelled to retire. The British official historian is of the opinion that had the British not advanced, they would still have been cut off. Plans were adumbrated by the French generals for attacking what Churchill doubtfully calls the German bulge from north and south, but nothing came of them. On 25 May Lord Gort, in command of the British, decided, according to Churchill, to 'march to the sea' or more precisely to withdraw his army towards Dunkirk, the sole port remaining safely in allied hands. This withdrawal, known as 'the miracle of Dunkirk', took place at the end of May and included a number of French soldiers. On 17 June the French Government, now under the aged and defeatist Marshal Pétain, sought an armistice from the Germans. Churchill explains that the last desperate offer made by him to the French of an indissoluble union between the two nations was not his own idea but that of colleagues in the British Government. So Great Britain was left to fight the Germans alone. The Italians also came in against us and the beaten French on 11 June. Few Americans or other neutrals believed that the British Isles could survive prolonged bombing or invasion by the Germans.

Churchill's method of writing the history of the war is to print many of his own official documents and letters to President Roosevelt but not to print the answers. For example, when one comes to study his relations with General Wavell, the British commander-in-chief in the Middle East in 1940, one has to look at Wavell's official biography or the official history of the war in north Africa to understand the full historical picture. So far as the decision to fight on alone is concerned Churchill is careful to explain that he himself was merely the mouthpiece of his fellow-countrymen in their determination not to surrender to the Germans, though he warned Roosevelt that if the existing Government fell, what he called a Quisling Government (Quisling was the chief collaborator with the Germans in Norway) might come to terms with Hitler. But what seems clear from his documentation is that Churchill himself was convinced at the time that a German invasion of England in the autumn of 1940 was unlikely to succeed. The German military authorities—particularly the German Admiralty—felt much the same. The responsibility for preparing the conditions for invasion was placed by the German navy squarely on the German air force, which thought it was as likely to obtain the surrender of Great Britain by direct bombing attacks as by covering an unwieldy force of military transports trying to negotiate the English Channel at its narrowest point.

Churchill describes Operation Sea Lion, as the Germans called their invasion plan, but fuller and more exact accounts will be found in books entitled *Invasion 1940* by Peter Fleming and *Operation Sea Lion* by Ronald Wheatley. Fleming points out, for example, that no evidence exists to support Churchill's statement that during August the bodies of forty German soldiers were washed up on the shores of England. According to Churchill, Hitler finally suspended the invasion plan on 17 September after the German air force failed to gain supremacy—though Mr Wheatley seems to put that decision ten days later and it was not until 12 October that Hitler finally renounced in writing the idea of invading Britain in 1940. On 27 September even the Battle of London was called off, the Germans abandoning hope of forcing a British surrender by paralysing the capital city. Churchill does not attempt to defend the exaggerated claims put out at the time by the British Air Force and disseminated by the British Broadcasting Corporation. The relative casualties in the contending Air Forces were, he says, 2 to 1 and not 3 to 1. The victorious commander of the fighters in the Battle of Britain was Air Marshal Dowding. Immediately after the battle was won he was retired, to Churchill's displeasure, though he does not mention this fact in the book.

What is historically so remarkable is that during this decisive Battle of Britain, which took place immediately after the British army had been driven from France and the Royal Air Force was fighting for very survival, Churchill himself was busy making plans for continuing the war all over the world and was penning minutes filled with aggressive intentions. The Chiefs of Staff, if not defeatist, were prolific in finding technical difficulties in doing anything much. For example, two months before Italy entered the war they recorded their opinion that nothing practical could be done to increase the powers of resistance of Malta. On 17 June Admiral Dudley Pound, Chief of the Naval Staff, signalled the commander-in-chief in the Mediterranean the tentative proposal that part of the Mediterranean fleet should remove itself from Alexandria to Gibraltar and the rest be brought home round the Cape of Good Hope. These facts are stated in the official naval history. Churchill is less specific. Indeed throughout his book Churchill is so anxious to prove that his relationship with his Staffs and with the Services in general was a happy one—unlike Lloyd George's relations in the previous war—that much is glossed over or omitted that needs to be discovered elsewhere by historians. Churchill is content to show how he contended with the Admiralty for the reinforcement of the fleet, the strengthening of the defences of Malta, and the dispatch of an armoured brigade across the Mediterranean to Egypt. The latter proposal was successfully resisted both by the Admiralty and by General Wavell.

Churchill had his favourites: he often quoted with approval a saying of Lord Fisher that favouritism is the secret of efficiency. He understandably preferred his old friend Frederick Lindemann, as his scientific adviser, to Sir Henry Tizard: here a choice had to be made and if it is true that Tizard thought that Lindemann was incapable of holding an honest opinion about anything, their differences were upon a childish level. Alan Brooke, whose memoirs have rightly been described as a mixture of arrogance and pettiness, was preferred by Churchill to General Wavell. Churchill could not understand Wavell's disposition of his forces and thought that troops should have been brought from East Africa and Palestine and removed from internal security duties to fight in the campaign against the Italians on the Egyptian frontier. Wavell, writes his biographer, was 'far more subtle and complex in character than Churchill' and would 'not surrender his own integrity and independence of judgment.' When Churchill as Minister of Defence drafted instructions for him, Wavell observed that Winston 'clearly did not trust me to run my own show' and proceeded to disregard a good deal of his instructions. Wavell states that Churchill always disliked him personally. If Wavell's attitude to his political chief was as it is represented to be in his biography, the dislike is comprehensible. His biographer admits that General Wavell overestimated the Italians' capabilities. So did the Admirals; and Churchill asserts that he had to overrule a proposal to abandon the Mediterranean altogether and thereby surrender Malta and the whole of North Africa to the Italians. Thus the Chiefs of Staff were wrong in their belief that the invasion of Great Britain was imminent in September and that it might be successful (the Admiralty thought that 100,000 Germans could be landed without interception) and they were equally wrong in supposing that the Italians could overwhelm the British forces in the Mediterranean in October. They were also entirely wrong in their pre-war estimates of the casualties and damage that would be inflicted during the Battle of Britain.

The Chiefs of Staff remarked gloomily that, after the fall of France, Germany 'had most of the cards.' But Churchill consistently envisaged not merely survival but ultimate victory. Retired British generals writing their memoirs frequently complained that Churchill interfered too much. Was it not necessary? Later historians have also criticized him for believing that victory might be won by the bombing of Germany. But in 1940 there was no other possible way. A plan was made to form fifty-five divisions, but as Churchill wrote at the time, 'the fighters are our salvation, but the bombers alone provide the means of victory.'

Of course not everything went well in the last quarter of 1940. The entry of Italy into the war had created new problems and fresh commitments. An attempt to help the 'Free French' under General de Gaulle to establish themselves at Dakar in West Africa had ended in disaster because of poor intelligence. On 28 October Italian troops had invaded Greece from Albania and the British Government was in honour bound—in spite of the many overwhelming calls upon its limited resources—to do what it could to assist an ally and friend. But on the credit side could be counted the brave Greek resistance to the Italian attack, the crippling of the Italian battle fleet at Taranto in November by British torpedo bombers, the abandonment in effect (though this was not yet known) of the German plans to invade England, and the growing distrust between Germany and Russia. On the other hand, a three-power pact between Germany, Japan and Italy was announced to which Russia was invited to adhere, a formidable enough combination even to a Britain led by Churchill. Severe losses were inflicted on British shipping by German submarines in the Battle of the Atlantic which was to continue until the following summer, while the German battle-ship Scheer alone had sunk sixteen British merchant ships. After long negotiations and horse-trading, the American Government had agreed to let the British have fifty old destroyers in exchange for the leasing of naval bases in the West Indies and elsewhere; but the destroyers did not prove to be of much value. It was only slowly that the activities of the Air Force's Coastal Command began to make an impression in the Battle of the Atlantic, vital to British survival.

At the end of the year Churchill was cheered by news of the victories won by General Wavell's Middle East command over the Italians in Africa. The campaign began on 9 December and resulted in the advance of British armed forces into Libya where they captured in succession Sidi Barrani, Bardia, Tobruk and Benghazi. Thousands of Italian prisoners were taken and the

British army and air force proved their superiority. As we have seen, no love was lost between Churchill and Wavell, and Wavell did everything he could to conceal his plans as long as possible from the Prime Minister. Even when Anthony Eden, the Secretary of State for War, visited Egypt in October, Wavell had been reluctant to reveal his secrets. 'I realized,' he wrote, 'Winston's sanguine temperament and desire to have one finger at least in every military pie.' 'I did not want,' he added, 'Winston to make detailed plans for me.' This was a strange way in which to treat the Prime Minister and Minister for Defence. As Wavell's biographer observed, no other general in the second world war dared to keep his plans hidden from Churchill as Wavell did. Nevertheless Churchill praised Wavell for his victories not only in Libya but also in Italian Somaliland and in Abyssinia, where the Emperor, defeated by the Italians in 1935, was restored to his throne by British arms and re-entered his capital in May 1941. Wavell was able to have a laugh at Winston because in reporting the victories in the desert he had spoken as if the Australian Light Horse had engaged in a cavalry charge (when it was in fact mechanized) and had said so in the House of Commons. But Churchill persistently brought pressure to bear on Wavell to reduce his military 'tail' and not rely so much on shipping carrying supplies and reinforcements by the long route round the Cape of Good Hope. After the middle of January Wavell was instructed to subordinate all operations in Libya to the need to furnish aid for Greece, shortly to be attacked by the Germans as well as the Italians. Wavell resented this. He had hoped to make a dash for Tripoli, but that plan was overruled.

No doubt it was because of these difficulties between the Prime Minister and the commander-in-chief in the Middle East that Churchill's historical account of the victory in the desert in 1940–1941 is exiguous. But it was, in fact, the culmination of a remarkably successful year in which Great Britain was fighting the two Fascist dictators alone, though she enjoyed American goodwill after the Presidential election of November 1940 was over. In concluding the second volume of his history Churchill employed an extremely florid style which must certainly jar on the younger modern reader:

> We may, I am sure, rate this tremendous year as the most splendid, as it was the most deadly, year in our long English and British history. It was a great, quaintly organized England that had destroyed the Spanish Armada. A strong flame of conviction and resolve carried us through the twenty-five years' conflict which William III and Marlborough waged against Louis XIV. There was a famous period with Chatham. There was the long struggle against Napoleon in which our survival was secured through the domination of the seas by the British Navy under the classic leadership of Nelson and his associates. A million Britons died in the First World War. But nothing surpasses 1940. By the end of that year this small Island, with its devoted Commonwealth, Dominions and attachments under every sky, had proved itself capable of bearing the whole impact and weight of world destiny. The citadel of the Commonwealth and the Empire could not be stormed. Alone, but upborne by every generous heart-beat of mankind, we had defied the tyrant in the height of his triumph.

This paragraph seems to me to embody all the virtues and all the vices of Churchill's style of historical writing. It is rhetorical, romantic, exaggerated and to a meticulous critic somewhat inaccurate. Yet it is basically true. For 1940 was surely the finest hour in British history.

12

The Second World War—II

DEALING with the period after he took over as British Prime Minister and Minister of Defence in the second world war, Churchill almost ceases to write in any real sense as a detached historian of events, though he is conscious throughout that he is justifying his own actions and decisions before the bar of history. Even as a piece of documentation the book is incomplete. Critics had pointed out in reviewing the first volumes that while Churchill printed many of his own appreciations and instructions he rarely gave the answers or responses he received. In his foreword to the third volume of *The Second World War,* which he called *The Grand Alliance,* he explains that space would not allow him to do this and that in many cases he did not possess the right to do it. In the second place, he was anxious, as far as possible, to avoid retrospective recriminations. Many of the soldiers and statesmen about whom he was writing—General de Gaulle, for example, whom he describes perspicaciously as no friend of England—were still alive and would have to be met again in the course of his political life. So, on the whole, he prefers to let his views emerge from what he wrote at the time.

Again, Churchill does not examine to any large extent what was called 'the home front' during the war, apart from publishing some of his own minutes to Departments on domestic questions. He does not reveal what went on inside the Cabinet—apart from occasions when he discusses its broad approval (or, rarely, disapproval, which he dubs 'obstruction') of the grand strategy of the war. For instance the nature of the rivalry between the Minister of Labour, Ernest Bevin, and Churchill's personal friend Lord Beaverbrook will need to be discovered from their official biographies. Churchill does not dwell on how Beaverbrook constantly threatened to resign office for one reason or another even when Churchill took him to Washington after the crucial phase when the Americans had been forced to enter the war. It is clear from Kenneth Young's book *Churchill and Beaverbrook* that the Prime Minister had a harassing time. Finally, though Churchill gives readers the reasons for the conclusions he reached about the strategy of the war at the time when he reached them, he seldom attempts to defend in the full light of historical retrospect and of later information such decisions as the dispatch of a British expeditionary force to Greece in March 1941 or the heavy concentration of British resources on the war in North Africa, which was questioned at the time by the American Chiefs of Staff.

1941 was the turning point in the world war because on 22 June Hitler attacked his former ally, Soviet Russia, and in December the Japanese without any previous warning launched a bombing attack on the American Pacific Fleet at Pearl Harbour. Since the British Government at once declared that it would ally itself with the Americans against the Japanese and since Hitler, with equal promptitude, announced that he would declare war on the United States in support of the Japanese, the American Government had no choice but to come in as Britain's ally in the war against Germany, even if it was not anxious to do so and was careful to avoid using the word 'ally'.

Churchill, like his military advisers, underestimated the power of resistance of the Russians. Indeed it was commonly thought in British military circles that Hitler would crush the Russians in three months, though it was afterwards asserted that the British intervention in the Balkans in the spring of 1941 gave the Russians a breathing space by delaying the German assault for five weeks. But Churchill had no doubt at all about what the American entry into the world conflict meant: he knew 'we had won the war.'

[177]

During the first six months of 1941 Great Britain was still fighting Germany and Italy unaided except for the American supplies provided by the Lease-Lend agreement approved by the U.S. Congress in March. As early as January Churchill had warned General Wavell: 'We must expect a series of very heavy disastrous blows in the Balkans and probably a general submission there to German aims.' Churchill never had any illusions about the dangerous consequences should the Germans intervene in this theatre in order to sustain the waning prestige of their Italian allies after their defeats in Africa and Greece. But in writing *The Second World War* Churchill was aware that he had been condemned by serving officers and would therefore be criticized by future historians for sending troops to Greece. He remarks that the arguments for concentrating on north-east Africa and 'letting the Balkans slide' had been put in books by various officers 'occupying subordinate positions.' (Such books include those by General Kennedy and General de Guingand.) In fact Churchill is able to demonstrate clearly that the most he ever hoped for was to unite Yugoslavia and Turkey in a common front with the Greeks to bar the southern penetration of the so-called Axis Powers. Thus he proposed a military alliance to Turkey, which was understandably refused. In February 1941 Anthony Eden, the British Foreign Secretary, and Sir John Dill, the Chief of the Imperial General Staff, were sent to the Middle East to arrange 'speedy succour' for the Greeks, to animate the Yugoslavs and spur the Turks to resistance. Churchill warned the British envoys that they must also consider which islands in the Eastern Mediterranean might be 'saved' if their larger efforts failed; and after they arrived in Cairo he reminded them that they were not 'obligated' to give extensive help to the Greeks if that meant 'another Norwegian fiasco.' It was, in fact, not Churchill himself but Eden, Dill, and Wavell, the men on the spot, who advocated sending a British expeditionary force to Greece to try to help withstand the coming German offensive in aid of their Italian allies. Eden telegraphed on 7 March that 'to have fought and suffered in Greece would be less damaging than

to have left Greece to her fate.' However, the military arrangements concluded with the Greeks were muddled and misunderstood. General Papagos, the Greek commander-in-chief,
afterwards maintained in his memoirs that the arrangements had
been dependent on immediate and active Yugoslav support. On
6 April the Germans invaded Greece and Yugoslavia, which at
the very last moment came into the war; on 17 April the Yugoslavs capitulated. General Metaxas, the dictator of Greece, had
suddenly died and his successor as Prime Minister committed
suicide. British forces were immediately compelled to retreat
before the much stronger Germans. Churchill writes that 'Greek
national honour stands undimmed' and that, as to the British
decision to aid the Greeks, 'when our lives have faded, history
will pronounce its cool, detached, and shadowy verdict.'

Some of the British soldiers were evacuated from Greece to the
island of Crete; but the Germans made use of parachute troops
to attack the island and soon captured an ill-defended airfield
near Suda Bay. The British navy successfully prevented landings
from the sea and most of the German airborne forces were
destroyed before the island was lost. Thus Churchill was able to
claim some *kudos* during the final stages of another military
fiasco. But while he does not disclaim his own responsibility for
the political decision, he implicitly blames Wavell for the
omission to fortify Suda Bay or to capture the island of Rhodes
as an offset to the loss of Crete.

It has been urged that the British commanders in the Middle
East were goaded by Churchill into advising ill-judged aggressive
action, but that seems a strange verdict. Certainly Anthony
Eden's subsequent conduct as Prime Minister of Great Britain at
the time of the Suez crisis does not suggest that he was at all
lacking in aggressive intentions. Nor was Wavell, who had just
tasted victory.

Before the fiascos in Greece and Crete Wavell had also
experienced defeat in the western desert at the hands of the
German General Rommel and his Afrika Korps. Rommel,
personally selected by Hitler, had arrived in Tripoli in the middle

[179]

of February with an armoured force nominally to serve under Italian command, but he soon proved to be a genius at this kind of mobile warfare and an inspiration to the Axis forces in the desert. Wavell had inevitably to reduce his strength to provide troops for Greece and he had only one inadequate armoured brigade left in Cyrenaica, the other half of the armoured division having been sent to Greece. Rommel attacked at the end of March. The correspondence printed by Churchill reveals his own optimism which scarcely attuned with Wavell's sombre warnings. Churchill spoke of waiting for the 'tortoise' to stick 'his head out far enough before chopping it off.' He also referred to Tobruk as a 'fortress' and 'a sally port.' Rommel's tactics were to employ his armoured columns to make a rapid penetration across the desert while using anti-tank guns to knock out the British tanks. The British armoured brigade in fact played little part in the battle and the two British Lieutenant-Generals, somewhat incongruously commanding together, allowed themselves to be captured by a German patrol. Benghazi was lost and Tobruk outflanked. Eden judged Rommel's incursion to be 'a major diversion' from the Balkans campaign. Certainly the result was to compel Wavell to withdraw an Australian division earmarked for the British expeditionary force to Greece. Afterwards Eden wrote in his memoirs that 'the defeat in the western desert' was 'not caused by the sudden removal of troops to Greece against the advice of the military commanders, but was due to a faulty appreciation of Rommel's tactics and lack of experienced desert commanders in the forward area.' The official historian, however, takes the view that Wavell's appreciations were not at all at fault and that the inadequacy of the British armoured brigade and the poor use made of it is the main explanation for the defeat.

Wavell had intervened in the battle by giving orders for Tobruk to be held and had then withdrawn to Cairo to cope with other matters. He was soon being pressed to counter a rebellion or revolt in Iraq in May, and faced with a campaign in Syria in June. Wavell did not want to act in Iraq and troops were sent there from India. Afterwards Wavell admitted that Churchill was right and he was wrong over Iraq. In Syria, however, where Axis air forces had arrived and where the 'Free French' had been unable to make any progress against the representatives of the Vichy Government, Wavell organized a masterly campaign which in about five weeks secured allied control of the country.

But in Churchill's mind victory over Rommel was the paramount consideration, for must it not be demonstrated to the entire world that British soldiers and airmen could beat the Germans? 'The tragedy of the evacuation of Greece, the distractions in Iraq and Syria, the dire struggle in Crete,' he writes, 'all paled before the gleam of hope which we attached, and rightly, to victory in the Western Desert.' He personally exerted himself, in the teeth of protests from the Admiralty, to send reinforcements of tanks directly through the Mediterranean to the army there, now under the command of General Beresford-Pierce. An operation called 'Battleaxe' aimed at opening up land communications with Tobruk began on 15 June. The operation was hurriedly mounted for fear that more German troops would soon be coming from Tripoli. In consequence the 7th Armoured Division had no time to organize itself properly or for the tank crews even to accustom themselves to their newly arrived vehicles. So 'Battleaxe' failed, to Churchill's bitter disappointment. The failure of the operation was attributed by Rommel to the inferiority of the British tanks while the British official historian points out that it was difficult to combine the faster British cruiser tanks with the slower infantry tanks in one division without adequate training: it was like 'a three-legged race.' The operation was in fact on a very minor scale. About 25,000 British troops took part in it and the losses on either side were some hundred killed. The whole episode was insignificant compared with the gigantic German offensive against Russia which began on 22 June with 164 German and German satellite divisions attacking 119 Russian divisions with a further 67 in reserve. But Wavell paid the penalty for defeat. On 21 June he was asked to exchange posts with General Auchinleck, the commander-in-chief in India, who had been so obliging over Iraq. Auchinleck was given

[181]

the assistance of a representative of the British War Cabinet as Minister in the Middle East and an Intendant General to co-ordinate supply questions. Neither of these comforts had been furnished to Wavell who in the spring and summer of 1941 had been overwhelmed with responsibilities and pestered with conflicting demands on his limited resources. Churchill was able to claim that Wavell was 'tired out.' Wavell accepted the decision with dignity. To the impartial historian his record speaks for itself.

Though Churchill had many other occupations, victory over Rommel remained at this moment the dominant thought in his mind. In August he met President Roosevelt for the first time and between them they concocted the now forgotten Atlantic Charter; though the United States was not yet in the war, the Charter actually contained a reference to 'the final destruction of the Nazi tyranny.' Churchill also entered into communication with Stalin, the leader of the Bolshevik Russia which he had attempted to strangle at birth. Stalin at once demanded the opening of a second front against the Germans in Europe in 1941, an obvious impossibility. Churchill's friend, Lord Beaverbrook, busied himself with sending supplies to this new ally at much sacrifice. A joint Anglo-Russian occupation of Persia was arranged in order to secure oil supplies and protect the Russian flank. Economic sanctions, imposed against Japan in July in agreement with the United States and Holland as a riposte for the Japanese occupation of French Indo-China, succeeded in upsetting the Japanese navy. In October 1941 General Tojo replaced the pacific Prince Konoye as Japanese Prime Minister and after some hesitations unleashed war in the Far East at the end of the year.

Meanwhile Churchill was anxious to impress the Russians and Americans by defeating the Germans in North Africa. He did not find the new commander-in-chief as co-operative as he had hoped. 'A serious divergence of views and values arose.' Auchinleck was summoned to London where his personality commended itself to the Prime Minister, though the general insisted that he could not mount a big new operation—which was to be known as

'Crusader'—before November. In his history Churchill records his conviction that 'the four and a half months' delay in engaging the enemy in the desert was alike a mistake and a misfortune.' He also disliked Auchinleck's refusal to appoint General Maitland Wilson, who had commanded the British forces in Greece and had much experience of desert warfare but was then sixty, to what was christened the Eighth Army. Again, Churchill vainly objected to Auchinleck's decision to send a freshly arrived British division to Cyprus instead of retaining it in Egypt. However, Auchinleck was under the impression that Cyprus was going to be attacked and that the holding of this detached post or 'forlorn hope' should be the duty of a British as distinct from a Commonwealth formation. Auchinleck also wrote to Sir John Dill, the Chief of the Imperial General Staff, on 21 July that he refused 'to hurl troops at the first possible moment, ill-equipped and under-trained into the torrent.'

'Crusader' was launched by the Eighth Army, commanded by General Sir Alan Cunningham, on 18 November 1941. The aim was to relieve Tobruk, reconquer Cyrenaica, and, if possible, push on into Tripolitania. General Rommel was surprised (he was in Rome when the offensive began) but he soon recovered his balance and the British armour was severely mauled, neither British tanks nor anti-tank guns proving a match for those of the Germans. Because of his tank losses Cunningham wanted to withdraw, but Auchinleck flew to the front on 23 November and ordered him to counter-attack the enemy. On Auchinleck's return to Cairo he replaced Cunningham by General Ritchie, the Deputy Chief of Staff. Then on 24 November Rommel himself collected most of his Afrika Korps and sweeping southward thrust across the border into Egypt, creating havoc behind the British lines. However the Air Force harried him, British detachments intervened, and he was finally compelled to retire. Churchill compares this episode to the romantic ride by 'Jeb' Stuart, the Confederate officer, round the Federal communications during the American Civil War in 1862. Meanwhile the Tobruk garrison had linked with the British relieving force and though Rommel restored the situation after returning from his daring raid into Egypt, he eventually decided to retire to the Gazala line, thus enabling the British to reoccupy Cyrenaica. In the action the Axis troops suffered larger casualties but the British lost more of their tanks. The official historian observes: 'Although "Crusader" achieved a large measure of success, and caused the enemy heavy losses, there were many disquieting features': the British tank crews were handicapped by being armed with only two-pounder guns; the latest cruiser tanks were far too prone to mechanical breakdowns; the German Me 109F fighter proved superior to any British fighter in the Middle East. Moreover British tactics were poor and there was a failure to concentrate strength at the decisive point. Churchill commends Auchinleck's conduct, but considers it a pity that he himself did not keep control of the battle instead of handing over its conduct to an untried subordinate. Other historians have accepted that criticism. However, Churchill wrote, at that point 'we reached a moment of relief, and indeed of rejoicing in the Desert war.' It was not to last for long.

During this autumn of 1941 the British had catastrophic losses at sea; Malta was faced with starvation; and substantial German air reinforcements were sent to Sicily and north Africa. Thus German and Italian supply ships could reach Tripoli in safety. With the aid of reinforcements General Rommel was able, at the end of January 1942, to capture Benghazi and reoccupy the greater part of Cyrenaica. Once again the German tanks proved better and more numerous. British soldiers fought hard, but the various commanders quarrelled with one another: one corps commander asked to be relieved of his post at the end of the battle. Churchill writes sourly that 'the British nation, in probing these matters,' should not 'be misled into thinking that the technical inferiority of our tanks was the only reason for this considerable and severe reverse.' According to Auchinleck's biographer the defeat was due to inferior armour and anti-tank guns, faulty tactical leadership, and lack of experience; also to a last-moment change in the command of the 1st Armoured

Division. 'Henceforward,' he adds, 'Churchill both as Prime Minister and as historian continued to regard Auchinleck as an old-fashioned orthodox soldier rigidly limited in his ideas and inflexibly opposed to his—Churchill's—dynamic and constructive projects. Nothing in fact could be further from the truth.'

Auchinleck was harried by Churchill to put matters right. But he refused to consider an offensive for another four months and shrank from going over to London for consultations. He also was unwilling to undertake the command himself (though assured that this was the most important theatre of operations) and would not withdraw the New Zealand division from Syria to reinforce his army in Cyrenaica. In the event Rommel struck again at the end of May 1942, and by 21 June Tobruk, which Churchill regarded as an impregnable fortress, had surrendered with 33,000 men. The Eighth Army was not handled at all effectively by its new commander, General Ritchie, and Rommel was able to push right on into Egypt itself. Eventually on 25 June Auchinleck did decide to take over the command himself and carried out a fighting withdrawal to what was called the El Alamein line. Here Rommel was repulsed in a series of capably directed counter-attacks and the position was finally stabilized. Writing of this part of the campaign in the desert, the official historian observes: 'The fighting during July had been costly and, except in the air, was in many respects disappointing, but it brought the Axis advance to a standstill and put a stop to the run of British disasters.' Rommel himself, looking back on the campaign, wrote: 'Although the British losses in this Alamein fighting had been higher than ours, yet the price to Auchinleck had not been excessive, for the one thing that had mattered to him was to halt our advance, and that, unfortunately, he had done.' And this was during the only few days 'during which we could have hoped to conquer Alamein and take the Suez Canal area.' In the Eighth Army itself it was felt that, whatever might have been wrong, the fabulous Rommel had been halted in his tracks and it became known that fresh troops and equipment were on their way. Thus

G

it seems unfair to suggest, as Churchill appears to do, that the morale of the soldiers had been undermined; but they were justly outspoken about the inferiority of their tanks, which was now at last to be put right.

In August Churchill himself visited Cairo and there took the decision to relieve Auchinleck of his command. General Alexander was put in his place and General Montgomery was eventually given the command of the Eighth Army. This army was now strengthened, as Churchill remarks, to an extent 'never before possible.' Two fresh divisions arrived in Egypt and seven armoured brigades became available, equipped with the far better American Sherman and Grant tanks. The British forces now had a numerical superiority of about 2 to 1 over those of the Axis. When on 25 October 1942 the second battle of El Alamein began, General Montgomery had a thousand guns, three armoured divisions, and seven infantry divisions at his disposal. This time the bad luck was on the other side. When the battle began Rommel was in a German hospital and his understudy suddenly died.

The story of this great British victory has often been told. The battle was far more similar to battles on the western front during the 1914 war (the casualty rate actually compared with that on the Somme) than to the bold manœuvres of Wavell or Rommel in the earlier and smaller desert contests. After an artillery barrage the infantry broke through in the centre, for there was no possibility of outflanking the enemy. Then the tanks followed up. Thirty thousand prisoners were taken and twelve enemy divisions virtually ceased to exist. But the Germans were not overwhelmed. Rommel carried out a masterly retreat with the remains of his army, for which the British Army laid the blame on the British Air Force. Churchill writes: 'Before Alamein we never had a victory. After Alamein we never had a defeat.'

If one looks back on the history of what is called the desert war in terms of the numerous examinations that have been made of it both by those who took part in it and by military historians since, one receives the impression that Churchill's account, though it

conveys admirably the feelings of the British people at the time—
particularly in London as reflected in the London newspapers
and in the House of Commons debates—it is not completely
balanced. He is as abashed by defeats—such as the surrender of
Tobruk, which he first heard about in Washington—as he is
elated by victories. That was how even the least informed felt:
rejoicing first in Wavell's unexpected victory over the Italians in
Cyrenaica in 1940, astonished by the setback when Rommel and
his Afrika Korps arrived, disappointed when Auchinleck was
driven back into Egypt, delighted when Montgomery won the
battle of El Alamein. Yet there is great conviction carried by the
view put forward in popular but persuasive form by Corelli
Barnett in his book *The Desert Generals* and to be disentangled
from the official histories and Rommel's own memoirs. This is
that, granted their infinitely inferior resources, Wavell and
Auchinleck served their country at least as successfully as did
Alexander and Montgomery. Personalities entered into the story.
Wavell upset Churchill by not telling him about his plans,
though thus he evaded the harassments to which Auchinleck was
subjected. Wavell's campaigns show a genuine mastery of the art
of war and Churchill was in fact to recognize his quality when he
made him successively Supreme Commander in the Far East,
commander-in-chief in India, when India appeared to be
threatened with invasion, and finally Viceroy of India at the end
of the war. Auchinleck was victorious whenever he took over the
direct command himself and it can be, and has been, argued that
the first battle of El Alamein when Auchinleck commanded was a
more notable victory, with still limited resources, than Montgomery's carefully prepared breakthrough in October when he
had been supplied with everything for which he had asked.
Auchinleck's weakness, it would seem in the light of history, was
in his bad choice of commanders; when generals squabble and
resign, confidence is bound to be undermined. But on his tactical
record Auchinleck must surely be regarded as one of the finest
fighting generals in British history.

Unlike Wavell and Auchinleck, Alexander and Montgomery

refused to begin a battle until they felt convinced that they were ready to fight it. Thus God showed himself to be on the side of the big battalions. By the time the second battle of El Alamein was fought the United States had entered the war and was sending more tanks for use in the desert. While Montgomery was preparing for his battle a large Anglo-American force was assembling to land in Algeria and Tunisia in Rommel's rear. Malta had been relieved and reinforced while Rommel was short of supplies because of the sinking of convoys in the Mediterranean. The British air force had established dominance over that of the Axis powers in the eastern Mediterranean. In the battle British casualties were relatively heavy and for one reason or another the pursuit of Rommel was unsuccessful. By abandoning Cyrenaica and most of Tripolitania he got away the remains of his army.

While these events were taking place in North Africa the Russians had, in the early part of 1942, carried out a counter-offensive against the Germans; but this was followed in the spring by a dual German assault in the south-east aiming to occupy the city of Stalingrad and reach the shores of the Caspian Sea. By the winter of 1942 a prolonged battle for Stalingrad had developed and in the end the German army there was trapped. Meanwhile the British Empire had sustained a series of defeats in the Far East at the hands of the Japanese.

At the same time that the Japanese destroyed much of the American fleet at Pearl Harbour they were sending out expeditions to capture Hong Kong and invade Malaya—both British colonial possessions. Hong Kong surrendered on Christmas Day 1941 and Singapore succumbed to the Japanese on 15 February 1942 after the British forces had been compelled to retreat from Malaya. The loss of Malaya and Singapore was followed by that of the Dutch colony of Java and by May the British were also driven out of Burma. Even India itself appeared threatened by the swiftness of the Japanese advance. But the main Japanese effort was to be concentrated upon the Southern Pacific. An attempt to land a Japanese contingent at Port Moresby in the south of New Guinea opposite Australia aroused alarm but was frustrated by an American naval victory in the battle of the Coral Sea in May 1942, and this in fact proved to be the turn of the tide in the Far Eastern war.

In describing the events in the Far East Churchill is writing to some extent as a historian recounting matters of which he had little first-hand knowledge. Both before the war and during the months preceding the Japanese assault at Pearl Harbour Churchill's attention had been concentrated on Europe and on Africa. As can be seen, for example, from Alan Brooke's memoirs, his overwhelming concern after the Battle of Britain was the Middle East. So I think it is not unfair to say that Churchill suffered from a number of misconceptions, if not delusions, about the Far East which affected his decisions as a statesman and his writing as a historian. In the first place, he tends to underestimate the fighting qualities of the Japanese and to overestimate the strength of the allied defences. The Japanese army was excellently trained for jungle warfare and was engrained with the belief that it was a disgrace ever to surrender. Thus it literally fought to the last man and the last round; and the Japanese illtreated their prisoners because they themselves were convinced that it was a betrayal of patriotism ever to be captured alive. In describing the campaign in Malaya, Churchill says that there were four or five Japanese divisions fighting there and that though the mainland was difficult to defend the 'island fortress' of Singapore itself had been expected to withstand a long siege. In fact no more than three divisions—one of which had horse transport—ever took part in the Malaya campaign and Singapore never was a fortress but only a naval base defended by shore batteries from assault from the sea. It was not overwhelming numbers but skilled fighting by highly trained infantrymen that brought about the loss both of Malaya and of Burma. When Singapore was attacked Churchill wrote a terrible telegram in which (after he had agreed to the decision to throw in the British 18th Division at the last moment to defend the island) he told General Wavell, now supreme commander in south-east Asia,

that 'commanders and officers should die with their troops.'
(What he wanted was that British soldiers should be shown to be
as capable of dying heroically as the Americans in the Philippines
or the Russians at Stalingrad.) Happily he changed his mind at
the very last moment and permitted the British commander in
Singapore to surrender to the Japanese with 60,000 men. However, to become a prisoner of the Japanese was a sufficiently cruel
fate.

Having uselessly thrust the 18th Division into Singapore,
Churchill now wanted to put an Australian division into Rangoon,
capital of Burma. He was angry with the Australian Prime
Minister for resisting his request and was equally angry with
Wavell for failing to accept a Chinese army to help defend
Burma against the Japanese and protect the Burma Road into
China. But Churchill was misled about the fighting value of the
Chinese troops—their 'army' was equivalent to a very poor
European division—and the importance of keeping open the
Burma Road was a major illusion. The Burma Road was merely a
source of embezzlement and corruption. Moreover Burma could
not possibly have been held in 1942 by inexperienced troops and
inadequate air protection. On the other hand, there was a serious
menace to Australia in view of the Japanese plans to occupy New
Guinea. Churchill was also worried about the Japanese threat to
Ceylon and India after the final loss of Burma in May 1942. Then
the Australian Government did generously allow two brigade
groups on their way home from the Middle East to stop and help
with the defence of Ceylon, but the Japanese had in fact no
serious intentions against India and it was Australia rather than
India that stood nearer to the main path of the Japanese advance.

When Churchill appointed Wavell as Supreme Commander
under pressure from the Americans, who were much enamoured
of tidy administrative solutions, he had been given a hopeless
task. A series of extremely unfortunate decisions—to send the
modern battleship Prince of Wales to frighten the Japanese off
Malaya, who promptly sank it; to reinforce the island of Singapore
with a division, which immediately had to surrender and might

more wisely have been employed elsewhere; to impose on Wavell the myths of the heroic Chinese army and the sovereign importance of the Burma Road—all reflected an ignorance of the facts about the Far East which, to some extent, vitiates Churchill's history. Admittedly the President of the United States and his political advisers were even more at fault because they were supposed to be experts. But ordinary British staff officers and diplomatists who had lived and worked in China and Japan were perfectly well aware of the realities. It is strange that their knowledge should not have percolated upwards until it was too late.

In fact it was left to the Americans to concentrate upon the Japanese. British troops were later to reconquer Burma, though India was never in great danger. Meanwhile the losses of territory in the Far East had to be accepted. Stalin, now desperately repelling the Germans, was demanding the opening of a second front against them in Europe and grumbling that the expulsion of the Germans and Italians from North Africa was taking so long. Churchill concludes his fourth volume by describing his meeting with President Roosevelt in January 1943 at Casablanca, where agreements were reached about the future strategy of the war. By May plans had been more or less concerted for the invasion of Sicily followed by an attack either on Sardinia or the Italian mainland. At Casablanca a resolution was taken to demand the 'unconditional surrender' of Germany and Japan. Churchill discusses the reason for this and the history of how such a questionable decision had been reached. But by the beginning of 1943 everything seemed possible to Great Britain and her new and powerful allies. The road to victory lay open. In February the Germans in Stalingrad capitulated; in May General Arnim, who had replaced Rommel, surrendered at Tunis and nearly 250,000 Italians and Germans were made prisoners. Thus Churchill was able to entitle the fourth volume of his absorbing story of the second world war *The Hinge of Fate*.

13

The Second World War—III

THE last two volumes of *The Second World War,* which he called *Closing the Ring* and *Triumph and Tragedy,* were completed by Churchill in 1951, the year when he again became British Prime Minister (though this time presiding over a peace-time Conservative Government). They might have provided him with the opportunity for a satisfyingly heroic story, for they recount the crushing defeats of Italy, Germany, and Japan and their satellites. They culminate in the shooting of Mussolini and his mistress by anti-Fascists in April 1945 and then, a week later, the suicide of Hitler and his mistress before their bodies were consumed in a funeral pyre beneath the Imperial Chancellery at Berlin. But the truth is that a note of constant frustration permeates both the volumes. After gearing itself for war in 1942 the Government of the United States of America, led by Franklin D. Roosevelt, became by 1943 the dominant partner in the west: American supreme commanders directed the invasions of Italy and of France, while American generals and admirals carried their soldiers and marines across the Pacific to the very threshold of Japan. Though meetings of 'the Big Three'—the United States, Russia and Great Britain—took place, first at Teheran in November 1943 and afterwards at Yalta and Potsdam in 1945, the wishes and advice of the British Prime Minister counted for less and less and in nearly every case he was obliged to yield his position under American pressure.

The book concludes with a vivid presentation of the British

point of view, as represented by Churchill, on world events, ranging from the preparation of a final offensive against the Germans to the treatment of Germany, Poland and the Balkans at the close of the war. As Churchill observes succinctly in his foreword to his fifth volume, he was not seeking to do more than make 'a contribution to history from the standpoint of the British Prime Minister and Minister of Defence': and that standpoint was, on the whole, one of disappointment.

In so far as Churchill attempts to examine the last years of the world war in the light of history, he does so from the standpoint of 1950 or 1951 when he was writing. Even academic historians, when examining contemporary history, inevitably have their thoughts coloured by the world in which they themselves have lived. (A striking example of this is Sir Llewellyn Woodward's recent *Great Britain and the War of 1914–1918*.) Thus any historian writing in 1968 cannot help reflecting on the humiliating way in which Roosevelt, reluctantly backed by Churchill, treated General de Gaulle, the leader of the 'Free French.' The refusal to forewarn him either of the invasion of French North Africa or of France itself (even if defensible for security reasons) explains much European political history and much French antagonism towards the United States and Great Britain since the war. Churchill was writing at a time when the war in Korea was in progress and when the French were involved in a prolonged conflict in Indo-China, both struggles sustained by Communist ardour and Communist support. Europe had become divided by an Iron Curtain (a phrase which Churchill had coined in a telegram he sent to President Truman in 1945) while the world had been split into two by the Cold War between the United States and Russia. Thus while dictating these volumes, Churchill remained incensed by the failure of the American Government to accept his advice in 1945 about the need to stand firm against Russian penetration of eastern Europe and was annoyed by the tendency both of Roosevelt and his successor Truman to 'gang up' with Stalin against the British Empire. But, again, writing in 1968, a historian of these events may feel less moved by concern

G*

over the British Empire, which has now ceased to exist, and be more exercised over the dangers to future peace presented by Communist China than by Communist Russia. So history very much depends on the point of view from which one happens to be looking at it.

In 1943 Anglo–American forces began to advance on all fronts. The American conquest of the island of Guadalcanal, north-east of Australia, finally brought to an end the forward surge of the Japanese. Fifteen thousand Japanese soldiers were killed by the Americans and Australians in the fight for New Guinea and any threat to Australia receded. On 10 July allied forces under the command of General Eisenhower invaded Sicily and Mussolini fell from power a fortnight later. Churchill pays a tribute to Mussolini. Like Neville Chamberlain, Churchill evidently felt that if Mussolini had only been on the British side the war might have been averted or at least been less catastrophic; but he could not forgive the 'stab in the back' of 1940. It was over Italy that Churchill's first difficulties with the Americans arose: he differed from Roosevelt both about the possible peace terms with the Italians and about the need to follow up the conquest of Sicily with a march on Rome. However, at a conference with the Americans in Quebec known as 'Quadrant' which was held in August, agreement was reached on planning an invasion of France from England in May 1944; the operation was to be known as 'Overlord.' Meanwhile Germany was to be softened up by heavy strategic bombing. No definite decisions were reached about the invasion of the Italian mainland (the Americans played with the idea of occupying Sardinia rather than Naples, but afterwards changed their mind) nor about the part to be taken by the British in the campaign against Japan in the Far East. Churchill had a scheme for an assault on the tip of Sumatra, but the Americans still wanted the British to clear Burma of the Japanese and thus open the road into China. Lord Mountbatten was appointed to be Supreme Commander in south-east Asia and to concentrate on the war against the Japanese, while Churchill proposed that a British naval force should be sent to help the Americans in the Pacific. Though the American navy was reluctant to accept the offer, ultimately Roosevelt did so.

Two points are perhaps worth making about this Quebec conference and its results from the historian's point of view. The first concerns Churchill's discussion in his book of the strategic bombing plan and its relationship to 'Overlord.' An American writer, Trumbull Higgins, in a book entitled *Winston Churchill and the Second Front* tries to prove that Churchill was never enthusiastic about the proposed landing in France and hoped that Germany might be beaten by bombing combined with economic pressure. This book has been commended by a British historian. The argument is that Churchill always had at the back of his mind the disaster of the Gallipoli landings in the 1914 war and the terrible casualties incurred in the fighting in France also during the Great War. Higgins asserts further that Churchill had a subconscious fear of an absolute decision in a general war and subordinated the war to considerations of domestic policy. His aim, it is claimed, was to avoid at all costs the heavy casualties of the first world war and therefore he sought by every means to avert the opening of a second front, fearing it would prove too costly, preferring to attack the 'soft under-belly of the Axis' in Italy and in the Balkans. There was evidently some contemporary feeling of this kind, mainly of Communist origin. For at the Teheran conference Stalin asked Churchill straight out if he really believed in the Second Front. I do not think that a careful reading of the documents printed by Churchill in these two volumes will leave any impartial reader in doubt that Churchill was in favour of the Second Front. The strategic bombing of Germany and the invasion of Italy were intended to contribute to the Anglo-American victory over the Germans but not to be a substitute for an assault upon France across the English Channel.

Equally I believe it is wrong to suggest that in this book Churchill overemphasizes the effects of British and American bombing of Germany. It would have been hard for him to admit, after all the effort that had been put into it and the many lives of gallant men which were sacrificed, that it had all been in vain.

Moreover Churchill was by nature aggressive. When for more than a year Great Britain was fighting alone against Germany and Italy the only way that the British could get to grips with the Germans was by fighting them in the air and upon the seas. The Italians were engaged and defeated in Africa. And again when the Americans entered the war the most that could be done was to invite them to establish air bases in our island and join us in a bombing assault on Germany. In 1942, Churchill confesses, the bombing of Germany resulted in no lowering either of war production or of civilian morale. In 1943, in accordance with an agreement reached at Casablanca, the so-called 'Pointblank' programme, aiming at the progressive destruction of German manufacturing output and the undermining of civilian morale, was put into effect by a mounting air offensive. The Americans attacked with their Flying Fortresses by day and the British by night. Sir Arthur Harris, in charge of the British Bomber Command, considered that saturation bombing of an area was more effective than precision bombing and, in fact, there is no evidence that the former caused more civilian casualties. But both methods proved expensive in airmen and aircraft and neither was notably successful. In an attack on 14 October 1943 by the United States 8th Air Force upon Schweinfurt, where ball-bearing plants, essential to the German aircraft industry, were situated, sixty American bombers out of 291 were destroyed and a further 138 were damaged. Equally the mass bombing of Berlin by British aircraft was, according to the official historians, 'more than a failure: it was a defeat.' A similar operation aimed at Nuremberg in March 1944 proved disastrous. German night fighters destroyed ninety-four British bombers and Bomber Command's tactics of massed and concentrated attacks on selected major targets was brought to a dead halt. Even the attacks on Hamburg, nearer to the British bases, though commended as successful by Churchill in his book, on the basis of post-war evidence from the former German Minister of Munitions, were far from decisive; for Hamburg recovered rapidly. In fact subsequent investigation by historians shows clearly that the damage inflicted on Germany by bombing was much exaggerated at the time. It is plain that the Germans could never have been defeated by bombing alone; nor, for that matter, could the British have been. On the other hand, Britain might have been defeated by submarine warfare; at one time the so-called Battle of the Atlantic was nearly lost and here, in the long run, the two air forces proved of immense value. Indeed, looking back as a historian, it would not be wrong to say that the greatest contribution of the air forces during the war was in attacking navies and armies rather than civilians.

Another point arising out of the Quebec conference, which Churchill tends to play down in his book relates to the war in Burma. Churchill was excited by the exploits and theories of a young army officer named Orde Wingate, who had been recommended by General Wavell, under whose command he had served in Abyssinia. Wingate advocated the use of long-range penetration groups moving forward without any traditional lines of communication and attacking the Japanese far in their rear by guerrilla tactics. So impressed was Churchill that he invited Wingate to accompany him to Quebec so that he might be introduced to the Americans as a pioneer of novel means for fighting the Japanese. According to Lord Moran, Churchill's doctor, who went with him to Quebec, Wingate was 'only a gifted eccentric . . . not another Lawrence' and 'when this became plain to the P.M. he lost interest in him.' Be that as it may, it was under Churchill's influence that long-range penetration groups were created in Burma. The first of them did arouse alarm among the Japanese, but a second larger effort cost many lives, including Wingate's own. Wavell, Mountbatten, and Churchill were all stimulated by Wingate—'a bright flame' Churchill called him—but the view of the official historian of the Far Eastern war is that the L.R.P. groups did not yield results commensurate with the resources devoted to them at the expense of the main British army in Burma, where an excellently trained division was broken up in order that Wingate might command six brigades. Indeed one-sixth of Mountbatten's infantry was locked up in this guerrilla warfare. Wingate became obsessed with the idea that he could capture an airfield at Indaw in the midst of Japanese-held territory and cast his brigades in the role of an assault force for which they were not intended. This special force wasted away through malaria, shortage of rations, and exposure to the monsoon rains and made a negligible contribution to the ultimate British victory in Burma. Churchill's support for Wingate again exemplified his aggressive intentions with limited resources. But in his book he lays little emphasis on the fact that a man whom he had thought to be a genius proved to be a military misfit.

One other thing may be said about Churchill's account of the campaign in Burma to which he was committed by the Americans at Quebec. He had, as we have seen, stated that he was opposed to war in the jungles of north Burma and preferred the idea of an amphibious operation against Rangoon or Sumatra, for which the resources were limited. Here, after the abortive attack by Wingate's long-range penetration groups or 'Chindits' at Indaw, the British 14th Army was faced in 1944 with an offensive by three Japanese divisions against the frontier of India at Imphal and Kohima. For a time the British troops there were hard pressed and Churchill writes as if India were in real peril. It has since become clear that the Japanese strategy in Burma was essentially defensive, but that they had realized the propaganda value of the threat to India. The attack on Imphal was a spoiling attack aimed at preventing a British offensive. And in fact it did help to delay the final assault upon Rangoon, the capital of Burma, until the spring of 1945.

The plan for the invasion of northern France, 'Overlord,' had been submitted for the approval—or at any rate the concurrence —of Marshal Stalin at the Teheran conference in November 1943; he had promised that a Russian offensive on the eastern front should be co-ordinated with it. Earlier at Quebec in August another operation with the code name 'Anvil' for a simultaneous landing in the South of France had been discussed. When President Roosevelt and Churchill returned from Teheran and met in Cairo it was agreed that 'Anvil' should have second

precedence to 'Overlord' and should be launched by the commander-in-chief in the Mediterranean, General Maitland Wilson,
who at this time succeeded Eisenhower on the latter's appointment as supreme commander for 'Overlord.' Both Eisenhower
and Montgomery, who was assigned to the command of the
cross-Channel invasion force, insisted that the initial assault on
Normandy must be on a five-division front and that 'Anvil,' the
landing in the French Riviera, should be on a two-division front.
Meanwhile although an Italian Government, formed under the
leadership of Marshal Badoglio after the fall of Mussolini, had
surrendered to the allies in September 1943, the Germans had
reinforced Italy, set up a puppet government under Mussolini in
the north, and were determined to fight in defence of Rome.
Churchill was deeply concerned to press on to the north of Italy
and, if possible, to get to Vienna before the Russians. He busied
himself in finding troops and landing craft for General Alexander
to enable his forces to occupy Rome. A landing at Anzio, forty
miles south of Rome, on 21 January 1944 had achieved surprise,
but the Germans resisted strongly both here and at Cassino
farther south. Churchill implicitly blames the American general
in charge of the Anzio landing for failure to follow it up quickly
enough and it was not in fact for nearly another six months, on the
eve of 'Overlord,' that Rome was to fall to the Anglo-American
armies. Nevertheless as a historian Churchill justifies the costly
landing at Anzio as a contribution to the success of 'Overlord' and
ultimately the liberation of Rome.

Churchill and the British Chiefs of Staff were now anxious to
continue the Italian campaign right up into central and northern
Italy. They therefore argued in favour of the abandonment of
'Anvil' which, if it were carried out, would deprive the command
in Italy of most of its resources: they maintained that when
'Anvil' was agreed to, it had not been realized that the Germans
would fight for Rome, that the operations there would pin down
twenty good German divisions, and that, in any case, the proposed
landing in the Riviera was too far distant from the main battle-
front in northern France to be of much assistance to it. All these

operations or plans for operations were hamstrung by the shortage of tank landing craft, a shortage which, according to Churchill, 'will never be understood by history.' The argument about 'Anvil' continued until D-day and beyond. In fact for one reason or another 'Anvil' (by then renamed 'Dragoon') was not launched until mid-August, while the 'Overlord' landing in Normandy, postponed from May, had taken place on 6 June 1944. The British Chiefs of Staff, supported by Churchill, had proposed early in August that instead of the landing in the French Riviera an amphibious assault should be made upon the Atlantic coast of France in order to capture one of the ports there, such as St Nazaire, so as to widen the lines of communication of the main Anglo-American armies who had so brilliantly opened the Second Front. The official historian, John Ehrman, takes the view that this suggestion was made too late and was therefore quite impractical. Churchill's own conclusion as a historian is that 'Dragoon' took place too late to help Eisenhower in northern France, while Alexander's offensive in Italy consequently failed through lack of resources. 'But for the deprivation of "Anvil",' he concludes, 'the campaign in Italy would have been over by Christmas, 1944.'

Apart from the question of 'Anvil' and the starving of the operations in Italy, Churchill's other concern about the preparations for the allied assault on France in 1944 related to the proposed preliminary bombing of the French railways. It had been decided by General Eisenhower that the whole weight of the air bombing of France in preparation for D-day should be concentrated on crippling the French railway system so as to hold up the arrival of German reinforcements in Normandy. For this purpose the strategic air forces were placed under his operational control. On 29 April, in a letter to Eisenhower, Churchill argued that the German army required only about ten per cent of the French trains: therefore ninety per cent of the railway system would have to be knocked out before valuable results could be obtained. Also he said that the experience in Italy had shown how difficult it was to stop the movement of traffic by bombing, while in the early stages of the war German bombing of marshalling yards in England had done little harm. Churchill was conscious that the bombing of the French railways might cost the lives of ten to fifteen thousand French civilians: hence his anxiety. (An earlier plan, which he had resisted, had been expected to inflict between eighty and a hundred and sixty thousand casualties among Frenchmen and Belgians.) Lord Moran remarks correctly that Churchill 'loved France like a woman.' The decision to destroy the French fleet at Oran in July 1940 had been agonizing to him and became more poignant in retrospect, since Admiral Darlan's order that the French fleet at Toulon should be scuttled when the Germans occupied the whole of France towards the end of 1942 had been loyally carried out. But little notice was taken either of Churchill's protests over 'Anvil' or about the bombing of the French railways. Such decisions were now made by the Americans. General Eisenhower was backed by the American Chiefs of Staff and the American Chiefs of Staff were sustained by Roosevelt. It was only to the judgment of history that Churchill could appeal as to who had been right.

On 6 June 1944—D-day—the landing of British and American forces in Normandy was carried out successfully at a relatively small cost in lives. Superiority in the air, the necessary condition for invasion, had been gained by the allies. The deception of the Germans had been complete, for at the time of the landings nineteen of their divisions in the west were still strung out between Calais and Belgium, while only ten were in Normandy. Field-Marshal Rommel, who was in command of the German army group in northern France, was actually with Hitler in Berchtesgaden when the invasion took place. Though the port of Cherbourg was captured on 28 June bitter fighting developed at Caen and it was not until 25 July that the Americans on the allied right broke out and cleared the whole of Brittany. On 24 August French troops entered Paris and by the end of the month the allies had crossed the Seine at many points. Meanwhile the first flying bombs—Germany's secret weapon—had fallen on

London and these were to be followed in September by long-range rockets fired from German bases in Holland. But these attacks on southern England did not interfere with the offensive in the west. The main limitation upon this was the inadequate supply ports available in France. Only Cherbourg and the artificial 'Mulberry' harbour set up at Arromanches (for which Churchill could claim much of the credit) were usable.

General Montgomery argued in August that in view of this limitation upon supplies the Supreme Commander, General Eisenhower, should order that all his resources be concentrated on a single powerful thrust striking northward and aiming to reach the Ruhr and then Berlin. The thrust could be made by forty divisions under one command (by implication that of Montgomery himself) while 'the rest of the front should be restrained for the benefit of the major thrust' which 'should be given all the resources and maintenance' needed. Eisenhower, however, rejected the plan as being too daring and stuck to an advance upon a broader front. All that Churchill has to remark is that 'strategists will long debate these issues.' What Churchill omits to say, or was unwilling to say as a historian, is that a clash of personalities and delicate Anglo-American relations entered into the debate. Montgomery was a forceful character and aroused antagonism when he gave orders, however tactfully, to American commanders. Chester Wilmot in his book *The Struggle for Europe* argues that if General Alexander had been appointed to the command of the 21st Army Group on D-day instead of Montgomery, these difficulties might never have arisen. As it was, Eisenhower himself took over the operational command on 1 September 1944, as he was entitled to do, and Montgomery was overruled.

In mid-December the Germans under General von Runstedt launched a surprisingly strong counter-offensive in the Ardennes, where they had originally broken through against the French over four years earlier. Montgomery was now put in command of the armies north of this break-through while General Omar Bradley commanded in the south. After a terrific battle the German advance was brought to a halt in January, the Americans doing most of the fighting and suffering most of the losses. Again Montgomery pressed for a single thrust across the Rhine in the direction of the Ruhr and he was now backed by Churchill and the British Chiefs of Staff. But once more Eisenhower opted for an advance on a broad front. Churchill was motivated to some extent by political considerations, as he wanted the Anglo-American armies to reach the heart of Germany at least as soon as the Russians. By now the Germans were everywhere weakening. The Ardennes offensive was their last burst of defiance on the western front. Hitler was about to order a final desperate stand against the Russians in southern Germany. Thus on purely military grounds Eisenhower's decision to cross the Rhine on a broad front was sound. Churchill himself watched, took part in, and later described the crossing of the Rhine. After that the Germans collapsed. At the end of April 1945 their armies in Italy surrendered and Hitler shot himself. On 8 May all hostilities in Europe ceased.

Churchill writes: 'As a war waged by a coalition draws to its end political aspects have a mounting importance.' During his last six months as war-time Prime Minister he was mainly absorbed in diplomatic questions. The specific problems over which he was most active concerned Greece and Poland. During a visit to Moscow in October 1944, Churchill had reached an agreement with Stalin that Greece should be considered as belonging to the British sphere of influence, Russia being allotted Rumania and Bulgaria, while Yugoslavia and Hungary were treated on a fifty-fifty basis. Though Communist risings broke out in Athens and British forces were used, on Churchill's instructions, to restore order there, Stalin remained true to his word and did not interfere. Thus Greece and Turkey, which had persisted in her neutrality in spite of Churchill's pressures, remained outside the Russian hegemony in the Balkans. Churchill himself flew to Athens on Christmas Day 1944 to arrange a political settlement, for which he was violently criticized in the British left-wing newspapers. Looking back in 1951, Churchill was proud of the part he had played in preserving Greece from Communism.

Churchill's efforts on behalf of the Poles received wider approval at home. It was generally felt that as Great Britain had originally entered the world war in order to protect Polish national independence from Hitler, it was her duty to see in the hour of victory that Poland regained her freedom. So at a meeting of the 'Big Three' at Yalta in the Crimea in February 1945 there were prolonged discussions about the future of the Poles, and Stalin agreed to the setting up of a Provisional Government of National Unity. The existing Russian puppet government was to be reorganized on 'broader democratic lines' and was to be pledged to hold a general election. All this proved in the long run to be so much window-dressing, as the Russians were understandably determined that the new Poland should be under their control and should be rewarded for yielding up parts of eastern Poland by being given large slices of conquered Germany, including East Prussia. Churchill, it may be observed, was less interested in the exact frontiers than in re-creating a free and independent Poland; but the Poles in London regarded the proposed new boundaries as constituting a 'fifth partition of their country.' The British people have no reason to be proud over the fate of the Poles. But Churchill did his best.

At this Yalta conference, where general discussions also took place about the dismembering and stripping of Germany and the setting up of a United Nations organization, Roosevelt was already a dying man and appears to have been bored by Churchill's long and eloquent speeches on behalf of the Poles. Earlier Churchill had hesitated over the American so-called Morgenthau plan for the pastoralization of Germany, which meant ruthlessly depriving the country of most of its industries, and then (I believe under the influence of Lord Cherwell) accepted it. The official historian says severely that 'the Prime Minister did not think it necessary to bring Mr Eden into the discussion or to ask for the views of the Foreign Office.' But in the end Churchill's magnanimous or practical instincts reasserted themselves and the plan was dropped by the Americans for realistic reasons. Also, ever loyal to the French, Churchill insisted that they should be allowed a share in the post-war administration of Germany; in consequence a French zone was carved out of the British and American zones in western Germany, which had been agreed upon with the Russians.

On the eve of the allies' victory over Germany—eighteen days before Hitler committed suicide in Berlin—President Franklin D. Roosevelt died, not unexpectedly, at Warm Springs in Georgia. Churchill pays tribute to 'our great friend' who was 'a shining personality.' It may be doubted, in the light of what we now know from the Harry Hopkins papers and other sources, whether Roosevelt had so deep a trust in Churchill as Churchill—on the surface, at least—had in him. Roosevelt, like his successor, Harry S. Truman, believed that Great Britain was still a thirsting 'imperialist power' while Stalin's Russia was not; and maybe Churchill helped to convey the former impression. Churchill felt Roosevelt's loss particularly deeply because he was now anxious to establish peace in Europe on a firm basis while sharing actively in the war against Japan. A first problem concerned Marshal Tito, the Yugoslav leader, who at this time had brought troops to Trieste with the apparent intention of staking out claims to parts of South Austria, Italy, and Hungary. On 12 May Churchill wrote to Truman saying, 'if the situation is handled firmly before our strength is dispersed Europe may be saved from another blood-bath.'

That may be said to be the theme of the remainder of Churchill's long book on the second world war. He was not worried about the coming general election in Great Britain 'where,' he wrote justly enough, though perhaps prophetically, 'party differences are now in practice mainly those of emphasis,' but he did fear that, as the American armies and air forces moved away from the west to take part in the Far Eastern war, most of Europe would be subjected to the rule of the Soviet Empire which was already regaining its Baltic littoral and establishing its influence throughout the Balkans. President Truman did not look at matters in that kind of way and sent over, as special ambassador to Churchill, Joseph Davies, a friend of the Russians: he reported back that Churchill's attitude to Europe was directed purely by British interests. When Truman said that he wanted to see Stalin before he met Churchill, the latter grew angry. He told Truman that he was 'profoundly concerned over the European situation' and that he could not accept the idea 'that the position of the United States is that Britain and Soviet Russia are just two foreign powers, six of one and half a dozen of the other, with whom the troubles of the late war have to be adjusted.' Soviet Russia was making 'imperialistic demands'; and 'except in so far as force is concerned, there is no equality between right and wrong.' Truman took all this in a kindly and even understanding spirit, according to Churchill, but when the new President, Churchill, and Stalin met together at the Potsdam conference in mid-July 1945, Churchill had to battle almost alone on behalf of the independence of Poland—and he lost (though the final surrender to the Russians took place after he had ceased to be Prime Minister). 'Frustration,' he writes, 'was the fate of this final conference of "The Three".' After he returned to England, he learned that he and the Conservative 'Caretaker Government,' which had been formed in May, had been overwhelmingly defeated in the general election and on 26 July he resigned office.

In his farewell message to the nation, which Churchill published that day, he said that he regretted he had 'not been permitted to finish the work against Japan.' But the war with Japan was soon over. Churchill had been intimately concerned with the arrangements that led to the manufacture of the atomic bomb and had given permission to British scientists to convey the information that they had accumulated about nuclear fission to the Americans so that the bombs could be made. In his book he approves of the dropping of the bombs on Hiroshima and Nagasaki as a means of saving millions of lives. It is not, however, easy for readers of Churchill's book to realize—so brief is his account of the dropping of the bombs and the subsequent unconditional surrender of the Japanese—that in fact the Japanese were already beaten and their Cabinet prepared to surrender before the bombs had been dropped, provided that a form of words recognizing the position of the Emperor had been framed and agreed. Whether the war in Europe was unnecessary or not, most historians would agree that the dropping of the bombs on Japan was unnecessary. It stemmed largely from the mystique of unconditional surrender. Churchill says that 'the historic fact remains and must be judged in the after-time that the decision whether or not to use the atomic bomb to compel the surrender of Japan was never in question.' One can only remark that it should have been.

Churchill's book is, as he says, a contribution to history which will remain an essential document as long as the twentieth century is a subject of historical study. It has to be remembered that Churchill was seventy-seven when he finished writing it and that throughout—except to some extent in the first volume—he was satisfied to link a valuable collection of letters and telegrams with a succinct, clear, and animated narrative. There was a lot he could not very well say at the time—he was writing when he knew he was likely to be appointed Prime Minister for a second time and to become responsible for British foreign policy in a much changed world. Roosevelt and Stalin were dead, but he had to negotiate with their successors. He was content to draw attention to the views that he had held, and was known to have held, during the war and to the warnings he had uttered about the coming domination of Europe by Communist Russia. It proved impossible for him, who had lived and laboured at the centre of events, to look at them in retrospect with the calm gaze of uncommitted historians. It may well be that when Churchill's official biography has been completed and all his letters have been published we shall know more about the way he later regarded what had happened and been decided during this war. Certainly the book contains reticences and there is in it a mingling of realistic and romantic outlooks that characterized so much of his writing and oratory—and often the oratory is in the writing.

One pictures Churchill (as one can through the reminiscences of Lord Moran) sitting in bed, a cigar in his mouth, dictating the linking narrative and reflecting on the documents collected together for him, recalling what he had done and what he had failed to do. But he can hardly have had either the time or the inclination to study maturely all that history had revealed—or was soon to reveal—about the waging of the war and the intricacy of the personal relationships which created those clashes of temperament that, more often than some historians are willing to acknowledge, determine the course of events. For that reason the book is not to everyone's taste. It is highly personal; and it lacks, I think, the excitement conveyed in some admirably written passages of *The World Crisis*. Still it is indispensable reading for any historian who would understand Churchill's part in this second world war. But the silences, one fancies, are often the most significant part of the story: and that, in any case, makes it incomplete history.

In 1959 an abridged one-volume edition of *The Second World War* was published, prepared by Denis Kelly, who had helped Churchill on some of the original volumes. The story was compressed into fewer than a thousand pages, largely by the omission of many of the documents. The abridgement is extraordinarily skilful and, to my mind, reads, on the whole, much more smoothly than the original. To it was added an epilogue, written by Churchill in 1957, covering the twelve years after the war in the field of foreign affairs. Even here Churchill is reticent, especially in discussing the policy of the United States and the conduct of the Korean war. He concludes by saying: 'I do not intend to suggest that all the efforts and sacrifices of Britain and her Allies recorded in the six volumes of my War Memoirs have come to nothing and led only to a state of affairs more dangerous and gloomy than at the beginning. On the contrary, I hold strongly to the belief that we have not tried in vain.' And he ends by expressing the hope that provided the free world held together, especially Britain and the United States, Russia would prefer the idea of peaceful progress to that of war. He does not analyse the threat to world peace from China. No doubt at the time he was writing Communist China still seemed to be merely one part of the Communist world and he still felt that the chief danger to peace lay in Russia and in Europe. Churchill remained at heart a European and hoped that the Americans would treasure, above all, their European heritage. This was to be the theme of his last book.

14

A History of the English-speaking Peoples

ALTHOUGH Churchill tells us that the arrangements for his book *A History of the English-speaking Peoples* were not completed until the mid-nineteen-thirties—his intention had been to start work on it as soon as he had finished *Marlborough*—in fact the idea of the book had certainly been in his mind long before then. I recall his speaking to me about it while I was helping him on the *Marlborough* around 1931. He then explained to me that his object was to lay stress upon the common heritage of the peoples of Great Britain and the United States of America as a means of enhancing their friendship. For he felt very strongly that the bonds between them should be cemented. As he told Congress during the war, he himself had an American mother and an English father, but if it had been the other way round, he might have got there under his own steam. The American blood that flowed in his veins helped shape his book and his aristocratic habits never dimmed his democratic sympathies, even if he attributed the achievements of the past to great men rather than to the masses. When he wrote his preface to the first volume after the war of 1939–1945 he said that 'language, law, and the processes by which we have come into being [that is to say, a common history] already afforded [before the war] a unique foundation for drawing together and portraying a concerted task.'

Churchill had in mind, I think, not only the concepts of equality before the law, trial by jury, and so on but the striking episodes about which he had been taught at school—the sealing of Magna Carta at Runnymede, the acceptance of the Petition of Right by King Charles I, the consummation of the Glorious Revolution in 1688 and similar dramatic events. He did not mention initially a common literature or philosophy of which the two nations have reason to be proud, ranging from Chaucer to T. S. Eliot or at any rate from Shakespeare to Locke, nor does he lay emphasis upon that Puritan form of Christianity that inspired the protagonists both in the English civil war and in the American war of independence. The Prince de Ligne said of Frederick the Great, King of Prussia, that 'his conversation was encyclopædic. The fine arts, medicine, literature, philosophy, morality and legislation passed, each in their turn, in review.' Though Churchill had a wide-ranging curiosity, I do not think that his admirers would claim for him the same breadth of vision as that attributed to Frederick the Great. For example, though Churchill himself was a painter, he was not much concerned over the work of other artists; his idea of music was chiefly the old Harrovian school songs. Thus when he says in his introduction to this book that he aims to give 'a personal view of the processes whereby the English-speaking peoples throughout the world have achieved their distinctive position and character' he means that he is concentrating on those aspects of history that appeal to him most—politics and war.

So it is that though in this book Churchill deals with such subjects as Magna Carta and the evolution of the British system of justice from the time of King Henry I onwards, he is, on the whole, concentrating more upon a narrative of events than on the evolution of ideas. It would obviously be impossible to carry out a precise statistical analysis, even with the aid of a computer, but I would estimate that well over half the book is devoted to war, politics, and rebellions. More than half of the first volume entitled *The Birth of Britain* consists of descriptions of fighting and insurrections from the first opposed landing of Julius Caesar on the shores of southern England to the defeat of King Richard III by the future Henry VII on the field of Bosworth.

Possibly one reason why Churchill does not linger long in studying constitutional signposts is that the investigations of them by modern historians have proved, only too often, that they are misleading. To this day experts are not in complete agreement about whether or not Magna Carta was a reactionary document or how and why the House of Commons came into being during the Middle Ages. Churchill as an author—and equally of course as a statesman—always took the best expert advice and generally, though not always, accepted it. Experts had to resign themselves to being grilled by him, and of all the history books that Churchill wrote this was the one in which he called upon the largest selection of experts for help. They partly succeeded in muffling his exuberance.

In fact a close reading of *A History of the English-speaking Peoples,* at any rate by one like myself who has tried his hand at writing British history, will, I think, inevitably yield the impression that this is a manufactured book. I am not suggesting that Churchill did not write it himself or that it does not embody his own views or personal approach to history. But one sometimes detects a dichotomy between what he felt and believed and what he was told to be true. The broad accuracy of the book as history —in so far as history can ever be said to be accurate—is not in doubt. One has only to study the list of distinguished historians who assisted him in his work to realize this: before the war there were F. W. Deakin, G. M. Young, and Keith Feiling, whom I have already mentioned and who was the author of a fine, if slightly Conservatively-orientated *History of England;* after the war Alan Hodge, now an editor of *History Today,* who worked for Churchill almost throughout, A. R. Myers, Joel Hurstfield, D. H. Pennington, now a Fellow of Balliol College, Oxford, A. L. Rowse, J. H. Plumb, Steven Watson, Asa Briggs, Maurice Shock, and Frank Freidel and M. A. Jones, the last two being pundits in American history. Here is a unique catalogue of names. After all, in view of his services to the English-speaking peoples, no historian would have grudged his advice, even if it were unpaid, to the great statesman.

Even this published list does not, I believe, exhaust all those who were consulted over the book. I have been told, for example, that one famous English medieval historian was invited to give advice, but his advice was then rejected. Another modern historian was extremely offended by the way in which he was treated. No doubt Churchill could be as ruthless to historians as he was to Civil Servants; and I don't suppose even those who helped him were always pleased about the way in which their material was handled. Churchill was capable of turning it to his own uses or putting together arguments which they did not regard as being consistent with one another. Still the fact remains that Churchill did not fall into any obvious traps and, on the whole, respected the counsels of his experts. Even if he insisted upon including the story of King Alfred and the burning of the cakes, which he had learned at his nurse's knees, he placed it in a respectable perspective.

Nevertheless in a book of this length some dubious statements are bound to be made and some events taken as facts which not all historians would regard as being facts. However good the advice is that one collects when writing a historical book, unless one has investigated a subject in depth oneself, one is tempted to follow the opinion of previous writers. If therefore I indicate a few points in Churchill's book where other interpretations are possible, it is not because I am impugning its general accuracy, but merely to indicate how much history is a matter not of conclusive fact but of individual opinion.

I find it hard to believe that King Henry VIII really sent 100,000 men under the Duke of Suffolk to suppress the rising known as the Pilgrimage of Grace in the days when 10,000 men constituted a sizable army (incidentally the Duke of Norfolk is described on a later page as having been the successful general). I do not regard the Puritans as having been necessarily democrats. John Calvin was certainly no democrat; nor, for that matter, was Oliver Cromwell. John Pym is described as the leader of the Puritan gentry, but it was not only the Puritans who were critical of the behaviour of King Charles I: Pym, I would have thought, constituted himself the leader of all those gentlemen who were upset by Charles I's policies, whether they were Puritans or not. Nor would I regard the Petition of Right as 'the main foundation of English freedom.' Whether Archbishop William Laud was Charles's 'evil genius' must be a question of personal judgment; my own view is that if Charles I had an evil genius, it was himself. Nor am I convinced that Charles I 'adhered unswervingly' to the Anglican prayer book and the episcopacy. At any rate he was ready to concede Presbyterian supremacy for three years as the price of regaining his throne. But Churchill himself of course was a consistent monarchist—in spite of his study of the behaviour of English monarchs—and he would obviously rather have fought alongside the Cavaliers than with the Roundheads, even if they did lay the foundations of English freedom. So, in his view, King Charles I's rule for eleven years without a parliament 'cannot be described as a tyranny' and the King died a heroic death on the scaffold.

If Churchill was attracted by the Martyr King, though recognizing that he had a few faults, he did not much care for Oliver Cromwell. The 'massacre' at Drogheda in Ireland, when a garrison of under 3,000 men was put to the sword for refusing to surrender after the walls of the town had been breached, shocked Churchill the historian. This 'wholesale slaughter of unarmed or disarmed men,' he wrote, 'marks with a mordant or eternal brand the memory of conquerors ... It is necessary to strip men capable of such deeds of all titles to honour.' We are informed in a footnote that Churchill wrote this passage in 1938–1939. Still, it is fair to recall that in Churchill's previous book *The Second World War* he had seen fit to defend the dropping of atomic bombs on Japanese civilians on the ground that by this means the lives of many American soldiers had been saved. It is true that warnings were given at Hiroshima and Nagasaki. At Drogheda, too, ample warning had been given by Cromwell; but the men who were killed there were soldiers and they knew that the rules of war in those days had made their lives forfeit. Cromwell justified the action because the example set had saved the lives of his soldiers when they had to besiege other Irish towns. This comparison may not be precise; but one has to remember that it was Churchill's own conviction that history is a judgment seat and that one cannot apply different standards of judgment in one age from those one applies in another.

At least that is a fair assumption from most of the judgments that Churchill applies as a historian. In the very next chapter of his book however he says that modern opinion is 'revolted by the spectacle of a King selling the foreign policy of his country for £100,000 a year.' (Some apologists for Charles II, about whom Churchill is here writing, have argued that the King's foreign policy was not in fact influenced by the small amounts he received from King Louis XIV of France.) Churchill's comment here is that '*if* present-day standards are to be applied' the religious intolerance of Parliament and the party violence of the Earl of Shaftesbury, the Whig leader in King Charles II's reign, 'must also be condemned.' A historian must make up his mind where he stands. Certainly if one is prepared to utter moral judgments, one cannot admit a double standard, one from the present, another from the past.

If I mention one or two other instances of controversial points from the second volume entitled *The New World*, it is only in order to illustrate the kind of mire into which one plunges when simplifying history or treating history as fact. Churchill writes that Mary, Queen of Scots, 'connived' at the murder of her husband, Lord Darnley. It is true that the best English historians believe this to have been so, but it has not generally been accepted north of the border. Immense books and lengthy articles have been written to establish that Queen Mary was as pure—or nearly as pure—as the driven snow. The Countess of Somerset is said by Churchill to have been 'undoubtedly guilty' of murdering her husband's former confidant, Sir Thomas Overbury, in the reign of King James I. It may be that she attempted to murder him, but the evidence comes from dubious sources, and it can plausibly be argued that Overbury was killed by his doctors, a fate which frequently befell the well-to-do in the seventeenth century. A third example of a murder plot (we have learned in our own times how difficult it can be to prove a murder) is that known as the Rye House murder plot, which Churchill accepts as a reality. But some historians would regard this as having belonged to the same world of fantasy as the Popish Plot during the same reign. Lastly Churchill says of King James II—whom he admired even less than Cromwell—that 'in letters which are still preserved the persecutions practised by the French monarch' on the Huguenots or French Protestants were 'approved' by the King. Churchill can hardly have read such letters, for they do not exist.

It is my own feeling that the latter two volumes of the four-volume *History of the English-speaking Peoples* make more attractive reading than the earlier two volumes. Churchill was not deeply interested in, nor did he know much about, medieval history. And the same applies to the history of the Elizabethan and Jacobean ages other than what he had derived from Shake-speare. Churchill appears to have preferred the Normans to the Anglo-Saxons—though the Normans were a French-speaking and not an English-speaking people—and the Royalists to the Parliamentarians, though it was Parliament and not the monarchy which formed part of the joint Anglo-American historical heritage. When in *The Age of Revolution* and *The Great Democracies* Churchill gives his narrative of events in the eighteenth and nineteenth centuries the story lights up, for Churchill is now describing persons and happenings that had always fascinated him, or even events in which he himself had taken part, at least vicariously. The first Duke of Marlborough, his ancestor, had flourished in the opening decade of the eighteenth century; Napoleon I, whose generalship Churchill had read about when he was a young man, dominated the closing years of the century. As to William Pitt the Elder, Earl of Chatham, the architect of the first British Empire in the middle of the century, it is difficult for any historian of modern England to resist comparing him with Churchill himself.

Churchill questions whether Chatham 'possessed the strategic eye.' 'Now, at all times,' Churchill writes, his policy was 'a projection on to a vast screen of his own aggressive dominating personality.' He 'called into life and action the depressed and languid spirit of England.' He was a magnificent orator, 'the first great figure of British imperialism.' It was war-weariness and dislike of continental entanglements that contributed to his fall. How many of these sayings may fairly be applied to Churchill himself; if Chatham was the first great figure of British imperialism, then surely Churchill himself was the last. But if Chatham had much to show by way of positive gains—the conquest of Canada and much of India, the demolition of the fortifications of Dunkirk, the town acquired by Cromwell from which the British army was to be evacuated in 1940—Churchill himself secured the independent survival of the British people and 'lifted the depressed spirit of England.'

Churchill's narrative of the American war of independence and, in his last volume, of the American civil war are excellent value for British readers of general history. American historical scholarship has of course meticulously examined these events and thousands of books and tens of thousands of articles have been written about them. But usually such books run to enormous length: the biographies of Washington and Jefferson alone, together with their letters, fill numerous volumes. For a succinct and reliable account Churchill's is hard to better.

There is some ambivalence about what Churchill writes on the origins and course of the war of independence. No doubt he felt romatically how agreeable it might have been if the British and American peoples could have remained politically united. At the back of his mind was the old feeling that King George III went mad and lost the American colonies. (Madness now seems to have been proved to be the wrong word for the monarch's affliction.) Churchill notes that the attitudes of some of the generals put in command of the British forces in America were contradictory: General Gage, for example, would have preferred to conciliate rather than to conquer. At the same time Churchill is reluctant to accept the Whig interpretation of history, having acquired a strong dislike for Macaulay as a historian when he

H

himself was writing about the first Duke of Marlborough. Speaking of India, he writes, for instance, of Warren Hastings that 'posterity has redeemed his name from the slurs of the Whigs.' He has a word of praise for Lord Shelburne, who negotiated the treaty that ended the war in America; and he clearly prefers Alexander Hamilton to Thomas Jefferson. He thinks the British commanders were not as black as they have sometimes been painted and believes that but for the French blockade the British war of attrition might have brought victory over the Americans—though wars of attrition were not usually to his taste. Yet one finds it hard to imagine that once the Americans had savoured the idea of independence, they would ever have yielded for long to an aristocratic government situated in London over three thousand miles away.

In his last volume *The Great Democracies* Churchill is writing about people and events that amused him and about matters of which he possessed some first-hand knowledge. As in the third volume he devotes two whole chapters to the French revolution and Napoleon, so in this last volume he finds room for a chapter on the rise of Germany. He writes with affection of India where he had served as a young man and of the United States where he had travelled extensively as a lecturer and afterwards as a famous visitor. He does justice to Queen Victoria, to Sir Robert Peel— 'it is true that he split his party but there are greater crimes than that'—to Gladstone, the Grand Old Man with whom his father had contended, to Benjamin Disraeli, the new-style imperialist of his day, to Abraham Lincoln, 'who saved the Union with steel and flame,' and to Robert E. Lee, 'one of the noblest Americans who ever lived.' His admiration for Lincoln is tempered, but he writes: 'It is sometimes necessary at the summit of authority to bear with the intrigues of disloyal colleagues, to remain calm when others panic, and to withstand misguided popular outcries.' Of the American civil war he observes that it 'must on the whole be considered the noblest and least avoidable of all the great mass conflicts of which till then there was record.'

Churchill understood as clearly as most men and certainly

more clearly than many historians how politics worked and particularly how they worked in the Victorian age. It is illuminating to read his comments on eighteenth-century politics. Sir Lewis Namier must be considered one of the ablest historians who wrote during Churchill's life time and he was, incidentally, an admirer of Churchill. Evidently one of Churchill's advisers drew his attention to Namier's writings on the eighteenth-century House of Commons which he investigated so comprehensively. Churchill has this to say: 'Modern scholars delving deeply into family history have sought to show there was no such thing as a two-party system in eighteenth-century Britain . . . not much of a conclusion to come to about a great age of parliamentary debate.'

This last volume concludes with a grand sweep of history comprising not merely the American civil war and its aftermath of reconstruction, ending in the abolition of slavery, but the rise of Canada and South Africa, Australia and New Zealand; the Victorian achievement of political and economic reforms; the evolution of the United States of America as a world power, the closing of the frontier, and the Spanish war; and finally a survey of the problems created by Irish demands for independence and the foundation of the Boer republics in South Africa. The book ends almost suddenly with the treaty of Vereeniging that brought the South African war to its close; only in epitome does Churchill speak of the two English-speaking peoples fighting side by side in the two world wars of the twentieth century.

Churchill reminds his readers of two facts that accord with his theme: the first is that the Constitution of the United States of America is 'a reaffirmation of faith in the principles painfully evolved over the centuries by the English-speaking peoples,' though in fact the Constitution was to create a form of political democracy rather different from that prevailing in England, the President becoming more powerful than the Prime Minister and the judiciary being able to declare invalid statutes incompatible with the original federal ideal. (It has been suggested to me that Churchill never entirely appreciated the implications of the

American constitution and that was why at times he and Roosevelt disagreed. Churchill's government, as Isaiah Berlin has written, 'was organized on clear principles,' Roosevelt believed in flexibility and improvisation and 'his bureaucracy was somewhat chaotic, perhaps deliberately so.') The second fact to which Churchill draws attention is that it was the British navy that 'for the best part of a century remained the stoutest guarantee of freedom for the Americas.' Without the Royal Navy the Monroe doctrine, enunciated in 1823, would have been hard to maintain, while it was a British statesman, George Canning, who 'called the New World into existence to redress the balance of the Old.' American historians do not always relish being reminded that the British navy provided the 'bulwark' or shield behind which the manifest destiny of their nation was worked out in the nineteenth century.

When the *History of the English-speaking Peoples* first appeared —Churchill was by now well over eighty—it was hailed by reviewers on both sides of the Atlantic as a magnificent book. J. H. Plumb, who assisted Churchill in writing the third volume, wrote of it in the *Daily Telegraph*:

> This history will endure; not only because Sir Winston has written it, but also because of its own inherent virtues—its narrative power, its fine judgment of war and politics, of soldiers and statesmen, and even more because it reflects a tradition of what Englishmen in the hey-day of their empire thought and felt about their country's past.

That is fair enough: in fact one cannot help but wish the book had included more of Churchill's own 'asides' such as those which I have quoted about Peel, Lincoln, and Namier. One would indeed gladly have sacrificed some of the carefulness of narration—the product of many hands on many proofs—for a few more of Churchill's own judgments on men and affairs. For whereas other leaders of their countries—such as Theodore Roosevelt and Woodrow Wilson—have written history books, few have done so, as Churchill did in this instance, after they have governed their nation both in war and peace.

One does not know whether to feel pleased or sorry that Churchill did not actually produce the book that he set out to write, a book that might conceivably have helped by its arguments to strengthen Anglo-American understanding. Undoubtedly Churchill was right in thinking that such a book was needed. Up to the time when the United States entered the first world war, the chief events in American foreign history had been the two wars fought against England: the war of independence and the war of 1812, which filled important pages in school text-books. Relations between the two countries have not been improved by accusations that the British were engaged in imperialist designs, and by their retorting with references to American behaviour in Mexico, Panama or Cuba. Suspicion of British imperial aims and motives ran deeply in the American mind and in the thoughts and attitudes of American Presidents from Thomas Jefferson to Franklin D. Roosevelt. This suspicion was not assuaged by the supercilious behaviour of Englishmen who visited the United States and often tended to be condescending about the American way of life. The novelist Anthony Trollope's mother, who travelled in the United States in the eighteen-thirties, criticized the uncouth and uncultured nature of the majority of the American people, while Charles Dickens in his *American Notes* and his *Martin Chuzzlewit* was also caustic about American habits and manners and methods of doing business. Nor had this frame of mind altogether disappeared by Churchill's day when two peers were sent to preside over the British Embassy in Washington where for a time Burgess and Maclean served on the staff. As late as 1944 I listened amazed to snide remarks made about Americans at Washington embassy cocktail parties.

Churchill, it has been said, was dominated by his sense of the historic past, while Roosevelt looked to the future. It is understandable, in the light of Anglo-American history, that doubts about British political motives were widely felt and that the kind of imperialism for which Churchill and his colleagues were still contending during the war was disliked by leaders of American opinion. We have seen in discussing Churchill's book on the

[221]

second world war how surprised he was when both President Roosevelt and President Truman failed to distinguish precisely between the aims of the Soviet Union, which had already gobbled up the Baltic States and was seeking hegemony over Poland, and the aims of the British, who were desperately attempting to defend India and reconquer Burma and Malaya from the Japanese. The difference, it may be said, has been proved by later events.

Another difficulty in trying to uncover a heritage in which both the English-speaking peoples might proudly share is that although Americans are English-speaking after their own fashion, many of the citizens of the United States, whose ancestors settled there during the immigration at the end of the nineteenth and the beginning of the twentieth centuries, came from eastern or southern Europe, from Asia or from an Ireland that hated the English. Nor has the Negro or Puerto Rican population of the United States much affinity with the historic English-speaking world. And it is understandable if Americans, thinking historically, are more inclined to look back to the French revolution than to the English as a source of inspiration. It may be argued that the American and French revolutions can be traced to common or cross-fertilizing sources and to the teaching of similar prophets from Montesquieu to Benjamin Franklin. It was the dying French Bourbon monarchy which aided the American people in their fight for independence, while the Marquis Marie de Lafayette, the personal friend of George Washington, was a hero in both revolutionary struggles.

It is sometimes said that the passion of Englishmen is liberty, that of the French equality. Whether this is true or not, it is surely fair to say that so far as white Americans are concerned egalitarianism is a first condition of their outlook; it is the atmosphere of equality which strikes the British visitor when he lands in New York for the first time. The use of the word 'sir,' still common in many parts of England, is equally surprising to American visitors who regard it as a lingering remnant of deeply embedded aristocratic traditions.

Thus in studying Anglo-American relations one is at least as conscious of differences as of a common heritage. Not that one would suggest that it does not exist at all, particularly in language, literature, and religion. In modern times teachers in British universities owe a debt to their colleagues in the United States for the rich contributions they are making to scholarship, especially in the fields of English history and literature. And one may hazard the view that pilgrimages to Stratford-on-Avon or Edinburgh or Oxford and Cambridge by Americans whose ancestors came from this island are at least as enthusiastic and meaningful as the pilgrimages to Eire by Irish Americans. If one questions whether the American people owe much to the Romanization or Normanization of England or even to that celebrated feudal document, Magna Carta, subjects which Churchill covers in his first volume, one may undoubtedly claim that many of the traditions, at any rate of New England and Virginia, can be traced back to the England of the sixteenth and seventeenth centuries. The pioneering spirit—the spirit of exploration, free enterprise, Jack-is-as-good-as-his-master, and possibly of matriarchy—was fashioned by the Puritans who left England in search of cheap land and religious toleration.

It is a pity, I think, that in writing this book Churchill did not tackle some of these questions more thoroughly than he did. It is valuable to have in one book the narrative histories of the British and American nations up to the end of the nineteenth century and to have them delineated by a man who was both a great British statesman and a real friend and admirer of the American people. But it is the memory of his own life and service to history rather than this book which in time to come will be recognized as an emblem of Anglo-American understanding.

15

Minor Works: Conclusion

ONE may reflect upon re-reading Churchill's sextet of volumes on the Great War of 1914–1918 and its aftermath that it is a pity that he does not include in them more elaborate biographical sketches of the characters concerned, who ranged from Asquith and the fantastic Lord Fisher to Lloyd George and the equally fantastic Lord Beaverbrook. In private life Churchill often used to indulge in reminiscent conversation-pieces about such famous men; but many of them, at the time he was writing, were his personal friends and colleagues. Moreover it was not his rule to pry into private lives or discourse about them. Psychological subtleties did not attract him. He measured men by what they did rather than by what they were. Not that he failed to derive amusement from the foibles of his fellow human beings, particularly those of politicians and soldiers, but the movement of events and the clash of steel were what he most enjoyed in the writing of history. Biography was a side line.

However, we are fortunate in possessing in his book *Great Contemporaries* a number of character sketches, mainly of statesmen and soldiers whom he knew and who had intrigued him. The biographical essays in this collection were originally written as articles. They vary in quality, the best being those of leading Victorian personalities whom Churchill had known and who had been the friends—or enemies—of his father. The sketches which he wrote about men he had not known (there are none about women) though often perceptive and entertaining are of smaller value. For example, what he has to say about Bernard Shaw, of whose moral and political opinions he disapproved, is hardly worth preserving and he met the Emperor Wilhelm II, 'the Kaiser,' Clemenceau, and Foch only once or twice. His views on Trotsky and Hindenburg are merely journalistic assessments.

But the group of eminent Victorians—the Earl of Rosebery, the Liberal Prime Minister of England whose horses twice won the Derby during his short term of office, Joseph Chamberlain, his father's friend and political opponent, Lord Morley, like Churchill a statesman and historian, Arthur Balfour, and Lord Curzon are admirably portrayed. Only two of Churchill's personal friends are included in the collection, Lord Birkenhead and T. E. Lawrence, both of whom died relatively young. Lloyd George and Beaverbrook were still active when Churchill published this book in 1937, though his opinions of Lloyd George may be found elsewhere. Both of them had reason to be grateful to him, though gratitude is not always a coin of the realm. But one may repeat two things about Churchill himself: the first is that he was a man with many friends to whom he was intensely loyal; if it was the eccentrics who amused him most—Lord Beaverbrook, T. E. Lawrence, Lord Cherwell, Lord Birkenhead, Brendan Bracken, Lord Montgomery—he was equally ready to extend his friendship to the young if he thought they had something in them. He writes that it is a gift of the able politician to be able to treat young men as his equals. As I have said, in my own limited experience he was certainly capable of doing so. Secondly, Churchill was a man of almost unqualified magnanimity. When it came to Trotsky or Hitler, well, he did not know them and he did not want to know them, but he had words of admiration for Hindenburg and the Kaiser—as he had for Mussolini. Asquith did not treat Churchill very generously, but he had nothing but praise for Asquith as Prime Minister, though Asquith does not lack his critics. Churchill includes in this volume of great contemporaries an appreciative sketch of Lord Snowden as Chancellor of the Exchequer. 'The British peoples,' he writes, 'should be proud of Philip Snowden.' Considering the virulence and even animosity with which Snowden used to attack Churchill from the Labour Opposition benches when Churchill himself was Chancellor of the Exchequer, one may say that this is characteristic of his generosity towards his contemporaries in historical writing.

I will quote briefly from one or two of these biographical sketches just to recall the character of the writing. The first sketch, that of Rosebery, is among the best. In some ways Rosebery was a typical Victorian figure, a kind of wealthy dilettante who found himself Foreign Secretary or Prime Minister, or an editor or author or racehorse-owner, almost, as it were, by accident. He was 'the aristocratic champion of the poor and depressed classes' who dreamed 'of a glorious and abiding British Empire' and first used the phrase Commonwealth of Nations. He 'flourished in an age of great men and little events.' He understood people's problems with a wide-ranging mind. 'But actually to handle them, to wrestle with them, to express their passion and win their confidence, that he could not do.' Moreover his knowledge of foreign affairs was profound. When the Anglo-French entente of 1904 was signed and welcomed throughout the two countries, Rosebery said it was far more likely to lead to war than to peace and in private he said 'straight to war.'

Sir John French, with whom for a time Churchill was on close terms of friendship, he describes as 'a natural soldier.' Although French 'had not the intellectual capacity of Haig nor perhaps his underlying endurance, he had a deeper insight. He was not equal to Haig in precision of detail; but he had more imagination, and would never have run the British Army into the same long-drawn-out slaughters.' Writing about Haig, Churchill speaks of the 'selfless, dispassionate equanimity' that 'ruled his spirit' and his utter determination upon victory.

Churchill's essay on Lord Morley is brief and mainly reminiscent, but he stresses his Victorian quality. Of Asquith he says that he was 'a man who knew where he stood on every question of life and affairs in an altogether unusual degree,' a man 'who drew a strict line between work and play,' 'one of the greatest peace-time Prime Ministers we have ever had.' He pays tribute to Joseph Chamberlain's warm heart and gift for friendship. Most moving of all are his observations on the men who were his own friends, such as Lawrence of Arabia—'one of those beings whose pace of life was faster and more intense than the ordinary'—and Birkenhead—'a sincere patriot; a wise, grave, sober-minded statesman; a truly great jurist; a scholar of high attainments; and a gay brilliant, loyal, lovable being.' But with men he did not much care for, like Curzon, he lacks insight. There is nothing to compare, for example, with Harold Nicolson's account of Curzon or, for that matter, with Roy Jenkins on Balfour or Asquith.

In the course of *Great Contemporaries* and *Thoughts and Adventures,* another collection of journalistic essays which Churchill published in the thirties, there are incidental remarks that throw a little light on his approach to political history. He observes, for instance, that 'the literary integrity of a work is capital.' He says of statesmen that 'they have at times inevitably to acquiesce in inferior solutions.' He remarks that it is a great pity to read a book too early in life. That is surely right. One is compelled to study a masterpiece like *War and Peace* when one is young, is bored by it, and fails to read it again.

In Churchill's descriptions of the introduction of the convoy system and the conflicts over the Dover submarine barrage in the Great War, based upon the official histories, which had appeared after he wrote *The World Crisis,* he draws attention to the conflicts between the Service experts and the civil power. It was, he says, the Cabinet that forced the Admiralty to agree to the convoy system, which materially reduced the losses in merchant shipping. He makes two points: the first is that in non-democratic countries it is much harder for the politicians to overrule their military advisers, whose skills are regarded as recondite, than it is in democratic societies where soldiers and sailors are not so highly respected as the guardians of technical secrets. That does not, however, appear to have applied to Hitler's Germany, while in time of war generals and admirals more often get their own way than lose it, even in democracies. Writing about Haig, Churchill expresses his strongly held view, which has been brought out again since his death by Lord Butler, that keeping diaries is a mistake. 'The reputation of the late Henry Wilson,' he observes, 'was grievously affected by his devoted widow's ill-considered publication of his night-thoughts.' He later disliked Alanbrooke's publication of his diaries; and what he would have thought of Lord Moran's lucubrations one shudders to imagine.

'The story of the human race is war,' wrote Churchill in 1925, repeating a similar phrase from one of his earlier books. The reading public to whom military history is anathema may find some of Churchill's writing distasteful, yet those of us who have lived through two wars cannot help but feel upon reflection that war has brought out some of the best qualities in human beings by way of courage, sacrifice and comradeship, even if it can also stimulate the worst. Broadcast appeals by political leaders to the public to tighten their belts are liable to fall on stony ground in peace-time.

Again, peace does not so easily lend itself to the romantic side of history. Churchill thought in terms of a brightly lit stage upon which a great story-teller performed before large audiences that could be charmed, persuaded, and led. Or he imagined, perhaps, sagas of Nordic heroes being related in a Scandinavian twilight: tales of heroes like Alfred the Great and the Black Prince, Pitt the Elder and Napoleon Bonaparte, Abraham Lincoln and Robert E. Lee, Gladstone, Lloyd George and their like. Too often in his own lifetime after the Victorian age had receded (when he ended his *History of the English-speaking Peoples*) all he had seen were pygmies. Though he never committed himself to the opinion in so many words, it is clear that he believed a man's capacities were tested at their highest in war and, with Thomas Carlyle, he thought it was great men who fashioned the course of history.

Churchill writes quite often, as we have seen, of the 'judgments' of history and of how men and decisions taken by men will ultimately be brought 'before the Bar of History' when the Great Judge or Jury will have moral precedents to aid them in reaching their verdicts. On the other hand, Churchill also describes history not as a judgment seat but as a 'calm flame' with which the past may be lit up. It is in a way odd that Churchill who regarded judgments on the events of the past as immutable, provided that a calm flame was cast upon them, was also no advocate of consistency in political behaviour. For example, in his writings he twice strongly defends the conduct of Sir Robert Peel, who, of all British political leaders, was one of the most inconsistent. Churchill does not think badly of Joseph Chamberlain for changing sides and indeed in Churchill's own long life he occasionally changed sides himself, though, as Isaiah Berlin has written, he 'remained inflexibly attached to first principles.' Nevertheless he recognized that circumstances alter cases and that when one appears before the judgment seat it is not enough to appeal only to principles but one must also present all the evidence. One may notice that Churchill rarely traduces men's motives; it is true that he sometimes regards their decisions as foolish or founded on inadequate information. But he never, except when writing of the wicked Adolf Hitler, fails to give men credit when they are brave. Nor does he try very hard to penetrate men's minds or examine if their conduct may have been guided by their emotions or sexual proclivities. Asquith and Lloyd George, among Churchill's contemporaries, were mighty lovers: for Churchill love was a thing apart and it scarcely entered into his historical firmament.

What Churchill thought of as the chief of virtues was courage: and to brave men most things could be forgiven. When one tries to gauge his historical judgments, therefore, one has to remember that they are often coloured by his own aggressive brand of courage. It is said that he was unfair to Admiral Jellicoe, with whom most modern professors seem to side. If that is so, it was because Jellicoe appeared to him to lack the true spirit of aggression needed in war. The German withdrawal at the battle of the Marne suggested to him that Moltke lacked this spirit. He felt the same of some of the generals and admirals who fought at the Dardanelles. Churchill practised what he preached; and one can read in his own story of the second world war how by sheer

[229]

will-power he persuaded his Service Chiefs into taking risks, sometimes unwisely, but not always.

Another virtue to which Churchill attached importance was 'honour.' When presented before the bar of history men will have to answer the question whether in a crisis they acted honourably. We have seen how Churchill condemned the way in which the Czechoslovak legionaries treated Admiral Koltchak as being dishonourable: they 'forsook the stage of History.' He felt the same about Pétain, but Darlan redeemed himself when the French fleet at Toulon was scuttled. It seems to me astonishing—and exemplifying a complete ignorance of Churchill's philosophy of history—for a German playwright and an English author to suggest that Churchill might have connived at the murder of the Polish General Sikorsky, who was an ally.

If history is indeed a science and historians should be realistic analysts, then it must be admitted that Churchill was wanting in that complete scientific application possible in the university cloisters, though his powers of concentration and ability to master detail were terrific. Yet at times he does take a rigidly scientific view of history. For example, he twice wrote that the historian's aim must be to describe 'what happened and why' and when he says that 'history' must resolve the reason for the short-age of tank landing craft in 1944 it is this kind of scientific investigation of the facts that he has in mind. But the fact is that Churchill wrote so many of his historical books so rapidly and often embarked upon them so readily that he can seldom have had the opportunity to study all the relevant information on what happened and why. A historian, after all, selects for himself from all the evidence that he has collected and even the celebrated 'amateur' historians like Voltaire or Gibbon or Grote soaked themselves in their subject before they started to write. The essence of historical writing is selection and though some of the preliminary sifting can be done for one, this is never entirely satisfactory. It is difficult to compress historical information on half a sheet of paper as one can the facts necessary for reaching a political decision. I have been told that when the late C. R. M. F.

Cruttwell, who was the Principal of Hertford College at Oxford and wrote an extremely able book about the Great War, once had an argument with Churchill at All Souls College it was not Cruttwell who got the worse of it. For though Churchill had the practical experience, Cruttwell had soaked himself in the sources and had the facts at his finger tips. Churchill could be obstinate, as those who helped him write his books were aware, and though he might yield to persuasion, he was hard to persuade.

That, I think it must be admitted, is Churchill's main weakness as a historical writer. Clio is a tough mistress and requires a lot of service. The writing of history was by no means a major part of Churchill's life: it had at first been a pleasant method of making money and in the end it was a means of self-justification. He never had either the time or inclination to absorb himself in it completely or to revise his work in detail in the light of later knowledge: he preferred to make history than to write it.

But there is no doubt whatever that Churchill possessed a powerful sense of history. It is to his credit that he valued the verdicts of history and that he was conscious in all he did and said as Prime Minister that historians would one day examine and judge him. Whether historians ought to act as judges at all, capable of lifting up the weak and beating down the proud, is another question. As Isaiah Berlin has written, Churchill's dominant category 'the single, central, organizing principle of his moral and intellectual universe,' was 'an historical imagination so strong, so comprehensive, as to encase the whole of the future in a framework of a rich and multi-coloured past.' This kind of historicism has been practised by many, from Roman Catholics, like Lord Acton, and Marxists to men of action. And if courage, honour, and magnanimity are the universal tests that Winston Churchill would have applied to others at the bar of history, they are certainly tests by which he is scarcely likely to be found wanting.

Appendix A

A list of Churchill's writings referred to in text

The first date of publication and date of revisions only are given.

The Story of the Malakand Field Force (1898)

The River War (two volumes 1899)

Savrola (1900)

Ian Hamilton's March (1900)

London to Ladysmith via Pretoria (1900)

Lord Randolph Churchill (two volumes 1906; one volume including previously unpublished material 1952)

The World Crisis (four volumes 1923–1927; abridged and revised edition 1931)

The Aftermath (1929)

My Early Life: A Roving Commission (1930)

Thoughts and Adventures (1931)

The Unknown War: The Eastern Front (1931)

Marlborough: His Life and Times (four volumes 1933–1938; volume I revised 1934; two-volume edition 1947)

Critical introduction to John Paget: *The New 'Examen'* (1934)

Great Contemporaries (1937)

The Second World War (six volumes 1948–1954; abridged with additional chapter 1962)

A History of the English-speaking Peoples (four volumes 1956–1958)

*   *   *

Winston Churchill: *Tributes broadcast by the BBC* (with an introduction by Maurice Ashley, 1965) includes observations on

Churchill as a historian by Alan Bullock, F. W. Deakin, Alan Hodge and J. H. Plumb. For Lord Moran's opinions on Churchill as a historian see *Churchill, the Struggle for Survival* (1966), pp. 779–780. For Isaiah Berlin on Churchill's view of history see *Mr Churchill in 1940* (undated, originally written in 1949). Randolph Churchill, *Winston S. Churchill*, volumes I and II (1966, 1967) contains information about his early writings. Violet Bonham Carter, *Winston Churchill As I Knew Him* (1965) has views about his writings: so has Robert Rhodes James in his books on Lord Randolph Churchill (1959) and Gallipoli (1965) and in a forthcoming book. *The World Crisis: A Criticism* (1927) contains essays by Lord Sydenham of Combe, Sir Charles Oman, Sir Frederick Maurice, and Sir Reginald Bacon. I was informed by Sir George Clark that the late Godfrey Davies once undertook an examination of Churchill's historical writings which was made available to Lord Moran and by Mr F. W. Deakin that he once gave a lecture on Churchill as a historian which has not yet been published. A bibliography of the Works of Sir Winston Churchill by Frederick Woods was published in London in 1963.

Appendix B

<hr>

Two of Churchill's letters about history

In 1932 when Churchill was engaged on writing his life of Marlborough, he visited the sites of the battlefields where his ancestor won his famous victories. He was accompanied by Lieutenant-Colonel Pakenham-Walsh. The following letter was written by him to Keith Feiling, later Professor Sir Keith Feiling, who assisted him with his advice on the writing of the biography:

    Sanatorium
Dr Gebhard Hromada   Salzburg 19th Sept. 1932

CONFIDENTIAL

My Dear Feiling,

Many thanks for your note. I am recovering fast and hope to return on Thursday.

The battlefields were wonderful. Packenham-Walsh [*sic*] presented them admirably and I am able to re-people them with ghostly but glittering armies. A surprise was their great size. Ramillies, Oudenarde, and Blenheim all seemed to me bigger than Austerlitz or Gettysburg, and far bigger than Waterloo.

The topography is practically unchanged—one could recognize all the well-known points and admire these masterly exhibitions of flexible moving action.

Oudenarde is particularly astonishing for its continuous improvisation. But just look what a team he had—Cadogan, Eugene, Argyll, and old Overkirk, all so experienced and comprehending; like sheep-dogs perfectly trained, rounding-up sheep under their unquestionably-obeyed shepherd.

The final stroke at Oudenarde, the launching of the Prince of Orange on the extreme left and the decisive results that followed were to carry forward to Malplaquet the seeds of disaster. The young Prince, already so fiery and valiant, thought he had learned by experience that war consisted only in headlong attack.

I was deeply moved by all these scenes and feel sure I can interpret them for *the first time*. We spent whole days on the fields picnicing [*sic*] there. A barn at Ramillies shows the artillery and bullet marks quite clearly. The trenches at the Schellenberg are recognisable—all very good. I am longing to get to work.

Yours very sincerely,
Winston S. Churchill

When Churchill became Prime Minister for the second time he was still engaged during leisure hours in working on his *History of the English-speaking Peoples* which he had begun before the war and was eventually to publish as his last book. F. W. Deakin, later Warden of St Anthony's College, Oxford, had helped him with the original draft of the book and had discussed it with him both during and after the war of 1939–1945. As related in the text, Churchill had been given Josephine Tey's *Daughter of Time* to read and this had convinced him that Richard III was not as black as he had been painted by Shakespeare and by modern historians and had not murdered the Princes in the Tower. He was, in fact, 'the victim of a monstrous falsification by Tudor hacks at Court.' Deakin had persuaded him to read James Gairdner's book on Richard III, which refutes this view, but at the time Churchill was not persuaded by it. Yet it seems that ultimately he must have been induced to change his mind or was not so convinced that he felt inclined to commit himself. For in the final version of the first volume of his *History* Churchill does not exonerate Richard III. The following letter at least represents his views in 1952:

10, Downing Street,
Whitehall.
July 12, 1952

My dear Bill,

I have read the pages in Gairdner. They are certainly not at all convincing or well argued and I do not think they sustain the case for the murder of the Princes. In fact the arguments in favour of Richard III seem very strong.

Yours sincerely,
Winston S. Churchill

I am obliged to the recipients for the text of the two above letters and to the Hon. Randolph Churchill for permission to publish them.

Index

INDEX

was Commander-in-Chief. Henry VIII planned to reconquer Bordeaux, lost sixty years before, while King Ferdinand invaded Navarre, an independent kingdom lying athwart the Pyrenees; and the Pope and Venice operated against the French armies in Italy.

The English expedition failed. Although Ferdinand took the whole of Navarre, and showed great readiness, according to Dr William Knight, the senior English ambassador in Spain, passing his cannon across the mountains and inviting the English to join him in operations against France, the English found that the style of warfare employed in the Wars of the Roses, with long bows and clumsy-armed mounted men, had become quite obsolete on the continent of Europe. Both Ferdinand and the French employed professional infantry, Swiss and Austrians, who advanced at a great pace in solid squares with eighteen-foot pikes bristling to every direction. The primitive firearms of the day known as arquebusses, were too heavy and slow-firing to inflict serious damage on these squares, owing to the rapidity with which pikemen advanced.

Ferdinand sent a great deal of advice to this effect for Henry, who could, Ferdinand suggested, use his great wealth to employ an overwhelming professional force himself. But Dorset's army decided on its own account to abandon a fruitless campaign and defying orders returned home.

After negotiations lasting throughout the winter of 1512–13, Ferdinand and the Venetians deserted Henry and the Pope, and made peace with France. The Holy League they concluded